GRAMMAR OF THE AMHARIC LANGUAGE

GRAMMAR
OF THE
AMHARIC LANGUAGE

BY THE

REV. CHARLES WILLIAM ISENBERG,

AUTHOR OF THE " AMHARIC DICTIONARY,"
AND MISSIONARY OF THE CHURCH MISSIONARY
SOCIETY IN EAST AFRICA

GYAN

Published by

GYAN

Gyan Publishing House
5, Ansari Road
Daryaganj, New Delhi-110002
Phone: 011-47034999, 9811692060
E-mail: books@gyanbooks.com

Distribution Network
gyanbooks.com
India, USA, Canada, UK, Australia, France

ISBN : 978-81-212-4385-8 (PB)
First Published, 1842

2nd Impression 2020

Printed at: Gyan Press, Delhi.

Grammar of the Amharic Language
Author: Rev. Charles William Isenberg

GRAMMAR

OF THE

AMHARIC LANGUAGE.

BY THE

Rev. CHARLES WILLIAM ISENBERG,

AUTHOR OF THE "AMHARIC DICTIONARY,"

AND MISSIONARY OF THE CHURCH MISSIONARY SOCIETY

IN EAST AFRICA.

LONDON:

PRINTED FOR THE CHURCH MISSIONARY SOCIETY.

1842.

PREFACE.

In presenting this work to the Public, the Author offers his humble thanks to God, for having enabled him to accomplish it. He was aware, when he first set his hand to it, not only of its importance with regard to Abyssinia—its character, religion, history, and destinies—but also of the difficulty of the task which he had undertaken. There was previously no Amharic Grammar extant, except Ludolf's*; which, however it attests the superior talents of its author, considering the circumstances under which it was compiled, is but a feeble aid in the grammatical exhibition of the language. Nor was there any other literary source, on which the Author of this Grammar could draw, except the Amharic Bible, and those Amharic works which he himself had prepared. Under these circumstances, he had very often to feel out his way, by a recollection of the living language, in which he conversed with the Abyssinian people while residing among them. This recollection, however, was kept alive by the Author's having been, without interruption, occupied with the Amharic press, from his arrival in this country from Abyssinia up to this day. The preparation and publication of the Lexicon, immediately preceding his commencement of this Grammar, was peculiarly suited to prepare him for this work; for whilst, on the one hand, it laid open to him the whole of the materials of which that language is composed, as far as they are at present known, it furnished him also with ample opportunities to investigate the grammatical rules by which it is regulated. Every one, who has

* See Preface to my Amharic Dictionary.

a judgment in these matters, will discover, when comparing the Dictionary with the Grammar, that the Author's own knowledge of the language has improved as he has advanced in his editorial labours. But although he is aware of the imperfections of his own works, he feels confident that a diligent study of this Grammar will, under the blessing of the Almighty, materially assist any Student in acquiring an accurate knowledge of the Amharic Language.

Although there is, as yet, no literature in the Amharic Language, its study is of considerable importance to Orientalists. Its Semitic origin cannot be questioned: it is evident in every feature. A little attention to what is said in this Grammar on the Nouns and Verbs, shows that it possesses a vigour and flexibility capable of expressing any idea; and that it may be very useful in throwing light on many subjects of difficulty in the cognate languages, especially the Hebrew, Syriac, and Coptic. Such a language, it is but reasonable to suppose, will be found rich in words. The Dictionary, which gives only those words which we at present possess, contains about 7000; and we may anticipate that a longer and more intimate acquaintance with the people of Abyssinia will furnish us with a great many more, and lead to important results, not only in reference to the Semitic, but also to the African Languages. With the latter the Amharic has much mutual interchange; as the Author has had opportunities to observe, in respect to the languages of the Danakil *, the Somal, the Gallas †, the Argobbans, the natives of Harrar (or Arargê), and those of Garaguê. But the advantages to be derived from the study of this language, which should be accompanied by that of its parent language, the Ethiopic, are not merely of a scientific

* See Dankali Vocabulary.

† See the Rev. J. L. Krapf's Galla Grammar, his Translation of St. Matthew's Gospel, and his Galla Vocabulary.

nature. When the covetous Abyssinian offers his hidden treasures to the speculating European—when he opens his barriers to the travelling naturalist, to explore his Ambas and his K'wallas—when that country, which stands single in the whole history of Eastern Nations, as a Christian State that was not overwhelmed by the sweeping floods of Islamism, attracts different and, in some measure, conflicting interests of religion, philanthropy and politics—the study of the living Abyssinian Languages, among which the Amharic stands foremost, will become indispensable; as is already experienced by those whom various motives induce to travel in Abyssinia.

With regard to the Church Missionary Society, the Author begs to repeat the same expressions of sincere gratitude, respect and solicitude, which he has uttered in the Preface to his Dictionary. Whatever the result of the present movements concerning Abyssinia and its future destinies may be; whether that nation is still to remain in its present uncivilized condition; whether it be doomed to fall a prey to that Spiritual Power which is assiduously endeavouring to regain the influence which it formerly possessed for a time, or whether it will open itself to the sound of the Gospel and its accompanying temporal and eternal blessings, and emerge into the light of truth and civilization; this Society has been the first instrument, in the hand of God, to offer the hand of Christian assistance and fellowship to them. If it pleases God to prosper their labours of love, they will be amply rewarded for all the difficulties and disappointments they have been subjected to, or which may be still awaiting them. May His blessing be upon them!

C. W. ISENBERG.

LONDON, *Jan* 4, 1842.

ERRATA.

Page	Line	from	Read	for
18	12	top,	First	Second.
28	11	. . .	ልቅሶ:	ልቅሳ:
31	12	. . .	ቆርቆር:	ቆርቆር:
38	4	bottom,	ኢይሁድ:	ኢይሁድ:
39	11	. . .	Form	From.
42	11	. . .	Twelfth	Eleventh.
48	17	top,	Suffixes	all Suffixes.
53	14	. . .	መጐት:	መጐት:
58	13	. . .	ተሺጠ:	ተሺሒ:
63	8	. . .	III.	3.
..	9	. . .	IV.	4.
64	14	. . .	ኣሉ:	ኦሉ:
65	23	. . .	Regular Triliteral	Triliteral.
81	4	. . .	conjugation	verb.
83	5	bottom,	መናገር:	መናገሯ:
88	8	. . .	ደሰግብራሉ:	ደስግብራሉ:
..	2	. . .	ደሰግብሯ:	ደስግብሯ:
90	7	top,	ያደራርግ:	ደደራርግ:
93	17	. . .	the peculiarities	and the peculiarities.
..	20	. . .	Radical	Conjugation.
119	10	. . .	ሼጣችሁ:	ሴጣችሁ:
129	4	. . .	አለመለመ:	አለምለም:
133	6	. . .	ደኰብለል:	ከኰብለል:
139	10	. . .	የሚያህል:	የሚያህ: ለ
145	5	bottom,	ደመግብዋት:	ደመግቡት:
146	11	. . .	thee	them.
147	10	. . .	መግብዋችኋል:	መግብዋዋችል:
...	1	. . .	chapters	chapter.
149	16	top,	ዝም:	ዘም:
...	26	. . .	ፈቀቅ:	ፊቀቅ:
150	9	. . .	"without"	"within."
152	6	. . .	ለምንድር:	ለመንድር:
158	20	. . .	ከ—:	ኳ—:
168	16	. . .	ሰደደ:	ለደደ:
174	15	. . .	show	to show.

CONTENTS.

CONTENTS.

CONTENTS.

AMHARIC GRAMMAR.

INTRODUCTION.

ON THE AMHARIC LANGUAGE IN GENERAL.

I. The *Amharic Language* (አማርኛ፡ ቋንቋ፡፡), a grammatical delineation of which the following pages propose to give, is that Abyssinian Dialect, which is spoken by the greater part of the population of Abyssinia: it prevails in all the provinces of Abyssinia lying between the Taccazê and the Abay or Abyssinian Nile, and in the kingdom of Shoa; and enters besides, extensively, into the languages of Argobba and Harrar. Its next cognate dialect is the *Tigrê Language* (ትግርኛ፡ ቋንቋ፡፡); which is spoken by the inhabitants of Tigrê or the N. E. part of Abyssinia, and has its modifications in the Dumhoeto Dialect at Massowa, and the coast N. of that island, and in the language of Gurāguê. Both the Amharic and the Tigrê Languages are modifications of the Ancient *Ethiopic* or *Gĕĕz* (ልሳን፡ ግዕዝ፡), to which they bear nearly the same relation as some of our Modern European Languages to the Latin; *viz.* that of origin and derivation. However, the present language of Tigrê has preserved a greater similarity to the Ethiopic, and received much less mixture from other languages than the Amharic; the Amhāra people being of a more changeable character, and having had intercourse with a greater variety of foreign nations than their Tigrê brethren.

II. The denomination "Amharic," which this language has received, is obviously attributable to the province called *Amhāra*, situate between Shoa, Godjam, Bagammeder, Lasta, and Angot. That province, which is now the seat of the Yedjows, Argobbans, and other Galla tribes—who partly speak the Argobba dialect, partly the Galla language—must have been considered the chief province of Abyssinia at the time the language obtained that name: for not only have all the countries in which the same language is spoken—excepting Shoa and Efat, *i.e.* all the N. W.

countries of Abyssinia to the W. of the Taccazê—been called Amhāra, but the natives also frequently apply it to their religion; so that the appellation *Amharic* is used synonymously with *Christian*, although at present the greater part of the population of that province are Mohammedans. But in what the superiority of that province consisted, and the time when it was so pre-eminent, remains still a matter of inquiry: for the reasons which Ludolf assigns, that Amhāra was in the neighbourhood of Shoa, from which the Royal Family of Solomon, which spoke this language, was restored, after the downfal of the Zagæan line; and that Amba Geshen (better *Gêshê*), where subsequently the Princes of that family were confined, was situate in Amhāra—seem rather unsatisfactory; nor have we at present to offer any thing better in lieu of them.

III. From the fact of the Amharic Language being a descendant of the Ethiopic—which will be evident, from a superficial knowledge of both—it claims the same *affinity to the Semitic family* as its parent; although it has adopted other forms and words from surrounding nations, which bear no relation to that family. A knowledge, therefore, of any of the Semitic Dialects, such as the Hebrew and the Arabic, facilitates, to a great extent, the study of the Amharic. We shall, in the course of this work, have frequent occasions to refer to the Arabic and the Hebrew; although it will be our endeavour also to suit the capacity of those who may have had no opportunity of learning any but European languages.

IV. According to the nature of a Grammar, this work will be arranged under the following heads: 1. *Phonology;* 2. *Etymology;* 3. *Syntax:*—treating, in the First Part, on the Sounds and Letters; in the Second, on the different Parts of Speech; and in the Third, on the Grammatical Construction of Words into Sentences. There is, as yet, no occasion to speak on Amharic Prosody; but instead of this, we shall annex a variety of Amharic expressions, and a few Exercises.

THE AMHARIC ALPHABET.

NUMERICAL ORDER of the LETTERS	ORDER of the VOWELS . .		I. ፩።	II. ፪።	III. ፫።	IV. ፬።	V. ፭።	VI. ፮።	VII. ፯።
	POWER of the VOWELS . .		*Short* ă, *or* ă, *as in* cat	oo, *or* ů, *as in* full, put	ĭ *as in* pin, finger	Long ā *as in* father	Bohemian ě, *or* iě, *as* German *jeder*	Vowelless *or* short ĕ, *as in* since, summer	o *usolly sharp, as in* so, *or like* wo
	ETHIOPIC NAMES of VOWELS		ግዕዝ፡ Gĕĕz (*original*)	ካዕብ፡ kăĕb (*altered, second*)	ሣልስ፡ săl̆is (*third*)	ራብዕ፡ răbĕ' (*fourth*)	ኃምስ፡ hămis (*fifth*)	ሳድስ፡ sădis (*sixth*)	ሳብዕ፡ săbĕ' (*seventh*)
	NAMES of Letters	POWER of Letters							
1. ፩።	Hoï	ה ء H	ሀ፡ hă	ሁ፡ hů, *or* hoo	ሂ፡ hĭ, *or* hee	ሃ፡ hā	ሄ፡ hě (*Boh.*)	ህ፡ hĕ, *or* h	ሆ፡ ho *or* hwo
2. ፪።	Lăwî	L	ለ፡ lă	ሉ፡ lů, .. loo	ሊ፡ lĭ, .. lee	ላ፡ lā	ሌ፡ lě ..	ል፡ lĕ .. l	ሎ፡ lo .. lŭo
3. ፫።	Hăŭt	ح H	ሐ፡ hă	ሑ፡ hů .. hoo	ሒ፡ hĭ, .. hee	ሓ፡ hā	ሔ፡ hě ..	ሕ፡ hĕ .. h	ሖ፡ ho .. hwo
4. ፬።	Măï	M	መ፡ mă	ሙ፡ mů .. moo	ሚ፡ mĭ .. mee	ማ፡ mā	ሜ፡ mě ..	ም፡ mĕ .. m	ሞ፡ mo .. mŭo
5. ፭።	Săŭt	ס ص S	ሠ፡ să	ሡ፡ sů .. soo	ሢ፡ sĭ .. see	ሣ፡ sā	ሤ፡ sě ..	ሥ፡ sĕ .. s	ሦ፡ so .. sŭo
6. ፮።	Rĕ-ĕs	R	ረ፡ ră	ሩ፡ rů .. roo	ሪ፡ rĭ .. ree	ራ፡ rā	ሬ፡ rě ..	ር፡ rĕ .. r	ሮ፡ ro .. rŭo
7. ፯።	Săt	ש س S	ሰ፡ să	ሱ፡ sů .. soo	ሲ፡ sĭ .. see	ሳ፡ sā	ሴ፡ sě ..	ስ፡ sĕ .. s	ሶ፡ so .. sŭo
8. ፰።	Shăt	ש ش SH	ሸ፡ shă	ሹ፡ shů .. shoo	ሺ፡ shĭ .. shee	ሻ፡ shā	ሼ፡ shě ..	ሽ፡ shĕ .. sh	ሾ፡ sho .. shŭo
9. ፱።	K'-ăf	K', ק ق } forced with a peculiar action of the palate and throat	ቀ፡ k'ă	ቁ፡ k'ů .. k'oo	ቂ፡ k'ĭ .. k'ee	ቃ፡ k'ā	ቄ፡ k'ě ..	ቅ፡ k'ĕ .. k'	ቆ፡ k'o .. k'ŭo
10. ፲።	Bĕt	B	በ፡ bă	ቡ፡ bů .. boo	ቢ፡ bĭ .. bee	ባ፡ bā	ቤ፡ bě ..	ብ፡ bĕ .. b	ቦ፡ bo .. bŭo
11. ፲፩።	Tăwĭ	ת ت T	ተ፡ tă	ቱ፡ tů .. too	ቲ፡ tĭ .. tee	ታ፡ tā	ቴ፡ tě ..	ት፡ tĕ .. t	ቶ፡ toe .. tŭo
12. ፲፪።	Tshăwĭ	Tsh *or* tšĕ	ቸ፡ tshă	ቹ፡ tshů .. tshoo	ቺ፡ tshĭ .. tshee	ቻ፡ tshā	ቼ፡ tshě ..	ች፡ tsh˘ .. tsh	ቾ፡ tsho .. tshŭo
13. ፲፫።	Harm	ח خ H	ኀ፡ hă	ኁ፡ hů .. hoo	ኂ፡ hĭ .. hee	ኃ፡ hā	ኄ፡ hě ..	ኅ፡ hĕ .. h	ኆ፡ ho .. hŭo
14. ፲፬።	Nâhâs	N	ነ፡ nă	ኑ፡ nů .. noo	ኒ፡ nĭ .. nee	ና፡ nā	ኔ፡ ně ..	ን፡ nĕ .. n	ኖ፡ no .. nŭo
15. ፲፭።	Gnâhâs	French GN	ኘ፡ gnă (*French*)	ኙ፡ gnů .. gnoo	ኚ፡ gnĭ .. gnee	ኛ፡ gnā	ኜ፡ gně ..	ኝ፡ gnĕ .. gn	ኞ፡ gno .. gnŭo
16. ፲፮።	Alf	א ا å *or* (') Spiritus Lenis	አ፡ å	ኡ፡ ů .. oo	ኢ፡ ĭ .. ee	ኣ፡ ā	ኤ፡ ě ..	እ፡ ĕ	ኦ፡ o .. ŭo
17. ፲፯።	Kâf	כ ك K	ከ፡ kă	ኩ፡ ků .. koo	ኪ፡ kĭ .. kee	ካ፡ kā	ኬ፡ kě ..	ክ፡ kĕ .. k	ኮ፡ ko .. kŭo
18. ፲፰።	Châf	כ German CH	ኸ፡ chă (*German*)	ኹ፡ chů .. choo	ኺ፡ chĭ .. chee	ኻ፡ chā	ኼ፡ chě ..	ኽ፡ chĕ .. ch	ኾ፡ cho .. chŭo
19. ፲፱።	Wăwĭ	ו و W	ወ፡ wă	ዉ፡ wů .. woo	ዊ፡ wĭ .. wee	ዋ፡ wā	ዌ፡ wě ..	ው፡ wĕ .. w, ŭ	ዎ፡ wo
20. ፳።	Ăïn	ע ع å (') Asth. Spiritus Lenis	ዐ፡ ă	ዑ፡ ů .. oo	ዒ፡ ĭ .. ee	ዓ፡ ā	ዔ፡ ě ..	ዕ፡ ĕ	ዖ፡ o .. ŭo
21. ፳፩።	Zăï	ז ز Z	ዘ፡ ză	ዙ፡ zů .. zoo	ዚ፡ zĭ .. zee	ዛ፡ zā	ዜ፡ zě ..	ዝ፡ zĕ .. z	ዞ፡ zo .. zŭo
22. ፳፪።	Zhăï	French J	ዠ፡ jă (*French*)	ዡ፡ jů .. joo	ዢ፡ jĭ .. jee	ዣ፡ jā	ዤ፡ jě ..	ዥ፡ jĕ .. j	ዦ፡ jo .. jŭo
23. ፳፫።	Yâmân	י ي German J	የ፡ jă (*German*)	ዩ፡ yů .. yoo	ዪ፡ yĭ .. yee	ያ፡ yā	ዬ፡ yě ..	ይ፡ yĕ .. y(cons.)	ዮ፡ yo .. yŭo
24. ፳፬።	Dent	D	ደ፡ dă	ዱ፡ dů .. doo	ዲ፡ dĭ .. dee	ዳ፡ dā	ዴ፡ dě ..	ድ፡ dĕ .. d	ዶ፡ do .. dŭo
25. ፳፭።	Jent	J	ጀ፡ jă	ጁ፡ jů .. joo	ጂ፡ jĭ .. jee	ጃ፡ jā	ጄ፡ jě ..	ጅ፡ jĕ .. j	ጆ፡ jo .. juo
26. ፳፮።	Geml	G (palatine)	ገ፡ gă	ጉ፡ gů .. goo	ጊ፡ gĭ .. gee	ጋ፡ gā	ጌ፡ gě ..	ግ፡ gĕ .. g	ጎ፡ go .. gŭo
27. ፳፯።	T'ăït	ט ط T' } forced with a peculiar action of the tongue in expelling the breath	ጠ፡ t'ă	ጡ፡ t'ů .. t'oo	ጢ፡ t'ĭ .. t'ee	ጣ፡ t'ā	ጤ፡ t'ě ..	ጥ፡ t'ĕ .. t'	ጦ፡ t'o .. t'ŭo
28. ፳፰።	Tsh'ăït	Tsh'	ጨ፡ tsh'ă	ጩ፡ tsh'ů .. tsh'oo	ጪ፡ tsh'ĭ .. tsh'ee	ጫ፡ tsh'ā	ጬ፡ tsh'ě ..	ጭ፡ tsh'ĕ .. tsh'	ጮ፡ tsh'o .. tsh'ŭo
29. ፳፱።	P'ăït	P', sudden expulsion of breath from between the lips.	ጰ፡ p'ă	ጱ፡ p'ů .. p'oo	ጲ፡ p'ĭ .. p'ee	ጳ፡ p'ā	ጴ፡ p'ě ..	ጵ፡ p'ĕ .. p'	ጶ፡ p'o .. p'ŭo
30. ፴።	Ts'ădăï	Ts', resembling t' and sh'	ጸ፡ ts'ă	ጹ፡ ts'ů .. ts'oo	ጺ፡ ts'ĭ .. ts'ee	ጻ፡ ts'ā	ጼ፡ ts'ě ..	ጽ፡ ts'ĕ .. ts'	ጾ፡ ts'o .. ts'ŭo
31. ፴፩።	Tsappa	צ Ts	ፀ፡ tsă	ፁ፡ tsů .. tsoo	ፂ፡ tsĭ .. tsee	ፃ፡ tsā	ፄ፡ tsě ..	ፅ፡ tsĕ .. ts	ፆ፡ tso .. tsŭo
32. ፴፪።	Aff	F	ፈ፡ fă	ፉ፡ fů .. foo	ፊ፡ fĭ .. fee	ፋ፡ fā	ፌ፡ fě ..	ፍ፡ fĕ .. f	ፎ፡ fo .. fŭo
33. ፴፫።	Pă	P	ፐ፡ pă	ፑ፡ pů .. poo	ፒ፡ pĭ .. pee	ፓ፡ pā	ፔ፡ pě ..	ፕ፡ pĕ .. p	ፖ፡ po .. pŭo
	DIPHTHONGS		ቈ፡ k'ŭă	. . . . . .	ቊ፡ k'ŭee	ቋ፡ k'ŭā	ቌ፡ k'ŭě	ቍ፡ k'ŭĕ	
			ኈ፡ hh'ŭă	. . . . . .	ኊ፡ hhŭee	ኋ፡ hhŭā	ኌ፡ hhŭě	ኍ፡ hhŭĕ	
			ኰ፡ kŭă	. . . . . .	ኲ፡ kŭee	ኳ፡ kŭā	ኴ፡ kŭě	ኵ፡ kŭĕ	
			ጐ፡ gŭă	. . . . . .	ጒ፡ gŭee	ጓ፡ gŭā	ጔ፡ gŭě	ጕ፡ gŭĕ	

Part I.—PHONOLOGY.

ON THE SOUNDS AND LETTERS OF THE AMHARIC LANGUAGE.

CHAP. I.

ON THE AMHARIC ALPHABET.

The Amharic Language is written with the same letters as the Ethiopic; each letter varying in seven different forms, in order to express different sounds; Vowels and Consonants not being separated. But besides the Twenty-six Ethiopic, the Amharic Language has seven peculiar Orders of Letters, which serve to express sounds not existing in the former: they are the following:

ሸ፡	ሹ፡	ሺ፡	ሻ፡	ሼ፡	ሽ፡	ሾ፡
ቸ፡	ቹ፡	ቺ፡	ቻ፡	ቼ፡	ች፡	ቾ፡
ኘ፡	ኙ፡	ኚ፡	ኛ፡	ኜ፡	ኝ፡	ኞ፡
ኸ፡	ኹ፡	ኺ፡	ኻ፡	ኼ፡	ኽ፡	ኾ፡
ዠ፡	ዡ፡	ዢ፡	ዣ፡	ዤ፡	ዥ፡	ዦ፡
ጀ፡	ጁ፡	ጂ፡	ጃ፡	ጄ፡	ጅ፡	ጆ፡
ጨ፡	ጩ፡	ጪ፡	ጫ፡	ጬ፡	ጭ፡	ጮ፡፡

These, added to the 26 Ethiopic orders, give to the Amharic Alphabet the number of 33 orders of letters; that is, each order consisting of 7 forms or characters, 231 different characters. Add to these the 4 times 5, *i.e.* 20 Diphthongs, you have 251; which, to commit to memory, call for the close application of the student. The Alphabetical Table opposite embodies them all; giving a correct exhibition of the numerical arrangement of the letters, with their names and value; and the phonical order, power, and Ethiopical designation of the seven different orders, with the pronunciation affixed in English to each character.

The Abyssinian Ciphers are as follow:

፩፡ 1. ፪፡ 2. ፫፡ 3. ፬፡ 4. ፭፡ 5. ፮፡ 6. ፯፡ 7. ፰፡ 8. ፱፡ 9. ፲፡ 10.
፲፩፡ 11. ፲፪፡ 12. ፲፫፡ 13. ፲፬፡ 14. ፲፭፡ 15. ፲፮፡ 16. ፲፯፡ 17. ፲፰፡ 18. ፲፱፡ 19. ፳፡ 20.
፴፡ 30. ፵፡ 40. ፶፡ 50. ፷፡ 60. ፸፡ 70. ፹፡ 80. ፺፡ 90. ፻፡ 100.
፪፻፡ 200. ፲፻፡ 1000. ፳፻፡ 2000. ፻፻፡ or ፻-፻፡ 10000. ፲፻-፻፡ 100000.

NOTE.—A greater number of Diphthongs might have been added; as the Abyssinians, not being accustomed to write the language they speak, like to contract several sounds together, and to express them by single characters. Ludolf has given, in his Amharic Grammar, several specimens, showing how they apply this to foreign languages. We observe, here, that we have seen several instances of the same mode of proceeding in their own language: especially do they like to combine the fourth with the sixth form; *e.g.* ቷ: twā, for ቱዋ:: ፏ: fwā, for ፉዋ:: ሟ: mwā, for ሙዋ: &c. But as those figures have not been generally adopted, and the number of characters is already large enough, and suited to express almost any sound, we have abstained from mentioning them in the Alphabet; noticing them here only, in order to put those on their guard who may happen, in their intercourse with Abyssinians, to meet such uncouth figures, that they may not be frightened.

CHAP. II.

NUMERICAL ORDER, AND NAMES OF THE LETTERS.

1. For the general Order, in which these letters follow each other, no reason can be assigned; as it has no analogy in other languages, nor any foundation in the natural developement of sound from the organs of speech, but seems to have been arbitrarily put together. Exceptions are, the succession of ሰ: and ሸ:: ተ: and ቸ:: ነ: and ኘ:: ከ: and ኸ:: ዘ: and ዠ:: ደ: and ጀ:: ጠ: and ጨ:: and ጰ: (for the resemblance of figure) ጸ: and ፀ::

2. The Names of the letters have been delivered to us from remote antiquity; and as most of them, if not all, are significant, we think it but proper to preserve them. They must have been formerly in general use among the Abyssinians, else it is not conceivable how they should have been transmitted to Europeans: but the natives of the present day know nothing about them, except from the schools of the Missionaries.*

3. The signification of most of the names of the letters is clear: they refer to the sound they express, adding the adjective termination *āwi*, contracted into *āi*, or mis-spelled *oi*, for the masculine, and *āwit*, *āūt*, *āit*, or *āt*, for the

* This, however, is no reason to omit them; because the Abyssinians do not at all dislike to have names put to their hitherto unnamed letters; many of which are the same as those which they know, from the Psalms, to belong to the sacred language of the Old Testament. Many of the most learned Abyssinians have applied to the Missionaries for the express purpose of learning the names of their own letters; and thought to have gained an invaluable treasure, when they had learned them.

feminine gender. A short analysis of these names, as far as it can be given, will establish this statement.

1. ሀ : Hoï, ሆይ : for ሃይ : or ሃዊ : the *h* letter.
2. ለ : Lāwï, ላዊ : the *l* letter.
3. ሐ : Hāüt, ሐውት : (f.) for ሓዊት : the *h* letter.
4. መ : Māï, ማይ : for ማዊ : the *m* letter.
5. ሠ : Sāüt, ሠውት : for ሣዊት : (fem.) the *s* letter.
7. ሰ : Sāt, ሳት : for ሳዊት : the *s* letter.
8. ሸ : Shāt, ሻት : for ሻዊት ::
11. ተ : Tāwï, ታዊ ::
12. ቸ : Tshāwï, ቻዊ ::
19. ወ : Wāwï, ዋዊ ::
21 ዘ : Zāï, ዛይ : for ዛዊ ::
22. ዠ : Zāï (French *j*), ዣይ : for ዣዊ ::
27. ጠ : T'āït, ጣይት : for ጣዊት ::
28. ጨ : Tsh'āït, ጫይት : for ጫዊት ::
29. ጰ : P'āït, ጳይት : for ጳዊት ::

The following names are derived from the cognate Semitic Dialects, probably from the Hebrew, since they have the names of the Hebrew letters in the Psalms:

6.	ረ:	Rĕ-ĕs,	ርዕስ:	Heb.	ר	Rēsh.
9.	ቀ:	Kāf,	ቃፍ:	..	ק	Kof.
10.	በ:	Bêt,	ቤት:	..	ב	Bēt.
16.	አ:	Alf,	አልፍ:	..	א	Alef.
17.	ከ:	Kāf,	ካፍ:	..	כ	Kāf.
20.	ዐ:	Āïn,	ዓይን:	..	ע	Āïn.
26.	ገ:	Geml,	ገምል:	..	ג	Gīmel.

With regard to their significations, the student is referred to the Hebrew Lexicon.

Concerning the rest, the signification of which is not so clear, we leave them for the amusement of such as will take the trouble of searching in the Ethiopic *and the cognate dialects.*

CHAP. III.

ON THE VIRTUE, ORGANICAL CLASSIFICATION, AND PRONUNCIATION OF THE LETTERS, CONSIDERING THEM AS SIMPLE CONSONANTS.

1. As to the VIRTUE of the letters, we must state, first of all, that Consonants and Vowels are combined in the same characters; and on this account, each letter is able to present a syllable by itself. But laying aside, for the present, the Vowel question, we proceed at once to CLASSIFY the letters according to the organs chiefly concerned in their pronunciation.

2. According to the *organs*, the letters are divided—

A. In *Gutturals:* ሀ: ሐ: ኀ: ኸ: አ: ዐ::

B. In *Palatals:* ቀ: ከ: የ: ገ::

C. In *Linguals* and *Dentals:* ለ: ሠ: ረ: ሰ: ሸ: ተ: ቸ: ነ: ዘ: ዠ: ደ: ጀ: ጠ: ጨ: ጸ: ፀ::

D. In *Labials:* መ: በ: ወ: ጰ: ፈ: ፐ::

E. *Nasal:* ኘ::

3. In speaking on the PRONUNCIATION of these letters, we must refer to the Ancient Ethiopic, the various dialects of Abyssinia, especially the Tigrê, and the cognate Semitic Languages.

A. The *Gutturals.*—In the present Amharic, ሀ: ሐ: and ኀ: are pronounced alike, like *h* in *horse*, and are often exchanged for አ:, thus entirely dropping the aspiration. The Tigrê language shows us, however, that each of these letters must have formerly expressed a distinct and different sound; for in it, ሀ: sounds like our *h* in *horse*, and answers the Arabic ه, and the Hebrew ה. ሐ: is pronounced with a pressure in the lower part of the throat, like the Arabic ح; ኀ: like the Swiss *ch*, the Arabic خ, and the Hebrew ח; and ኸ: like the Scotch and German *ch*, in *loch*, *nicht*, and answering the Hebrew כ without the Dagesh. This pronunciation of the ኸ: is equally in use in the Amharic language.

አ: and ዐ: are both pronounced alike, as the Greek Spiritus lenis ('); but in the Tigrê they are different among each other, አ: being like Spiritus lenis, ا, or א, and ዐ: like the Arabic ع and Hebrew ע, with the same pressure in the throat as the ح, but without the aspiration.

B. The *Palatals:*

ቀ: corresponds with ק in the Hebrew, and with ق in the Arabic Language. On account of its peculiar pronunciation, we may call it an *explosive* letter, such as ጠ: ጨ: and ጸ: in the third, and ጰ: in the fourth class: it is a sudden explosion of breath from the palate, after the latter has been spasmodically contracted. We have endeavoured to represent this pronunciation, after the example of Ludolf, by writing K', but it must be heard before it can be conceived. This pronunciation, however, is not uniform, although general. In Tigrê, it is besides often pronounced like the Arabic غ, often like ق; in Shoa generally, like a mere Spiritus lenis ('), similar to the ق as pronounced by common people in Egypt. Thus the word ተቀበለ: is pronounced in three or four different ways: in good language, Tăk'ab'bălă; in Tigrê, Tăghăb'bălă (تَغَبَّلَ) and Tăḳab'bălă (تَقَبَّلَ); and in Shoa, Tă-ăb'bălă.

ከ: sounds like our *k*, or *c* before consonants.

የ: is pronounced like *y* as consonant, or like the German *j* &c.

ገ: is pronounced like our *g* before *a*, *o*, *u*, and before consonants.

C. The *Linguals* and *Dentals:*

ለ: like our *l*.

ሠ: and ሰ: may originally (perhaps answering ص and س, ס and שׂ have sounded differently from each other: at present, they are pronounced alike, sounding like our *s*.

ረ: sounds like our *r*.

ሸ: formed in the Amharic by the accession of the *ï* sound to the ሰ: and ሠ:, is the same as ش, שׁ, and *sh*.

ተ: is pronounced like ت, ת, and *t*.

ቸ: formed by combining a soft sibilation with ተ, sounds like *tsh*, or rather like *t* with a German *j*.

ነ: is the same as our *n*.

ዘ: is like *z*.

ዠ: like the French *j*.

ደ: is the same with our *d*.

ጀ: sounds like the English *j*, or rather like the German *dj:* it is often used to express the Arabic ج.

ጠ: ጨ: and ጸ: are the same sort of letters in this class as the ቀ: in the Second, which we call Explosive; because they, as it were, explode from between the fore-part of the tongue and the roof of the mouth or the root of the teeth. We have in the Alphabet represented them by writing *t'*, *tsh'*, and *ts'*. But as some more or less hissing seems to accompany this explosion, ጠ: and ጸ: frequently interchange.

ፀ: is pronounced like *ts*, or the German *z*.

D. The *Labials:*

መ: is the same as our *m*.

በ: the same as our *b*. In Tigrê, it generally sounds like *v*, ב, or the Modern Greek β: and this pronunciation must have been formerly more general; for otherwise it seems unaccountable, how it could have been turned into a mere vowel *o*, as in **መዮር**:; whereas the soft *b*, our *v*, being a mere condensation of that Vowel, was more liable to that change.

ወ: is the same as *w*.

ጰ: the explosive letter of this class: the breath puffs off from between the lips, before the vowel is heard.

ፈ: is the same as פ, ف, and *f*.

ፐ: our *p*, merely used for foreign words.

E. The *Nasal* **ኘ**: is pronounced similar to the French and Italian *gn*, or rather like the Spanish *ñ*.

4. The letters are to be further divided, as in other Semitic Dialects, into *Radicals* and *Serviles*. Servile letters are those which are employed in the process of grammatical formation, derivation, and flexion: the radicals are never so employed. The serviles are often radical, though Radicals are never servile. The Servile Letters are,

ለ: መ: ሰ: በ: ተ: ነ: አ: ወ: ከ: የ::

CHAP. IV.

ON THE SEVEN VOCAL ORDERS OF THE ABYSSINIAN LETTERS.

1. As the Abyssinian Languages differ from the other Semitic Dialects (except the Coptic), in being written from the left to the right; so they are likewise different from them, as well as from most other languages, in the manner in which the Voices or Vowels are expressed.

2. This is done in the Abyssinian Languages, not, as in the other Semitic Dialects, by any smaller points or figures written above or below the line; nor, as in other languages, by a distinct sort of characters of equal value with the Vowelless Consonants; but by a system of changes which the original letter itself undergoes; each letter *expressing Consonant and Vowel in the same figure*, and *assuming seven different forms*, according to the Vowels which are attached to it; which forms (after Ludolf) we call *Orders of Letters*.

NOTE.—The terms "Consonant" and "Vowel" are not quite suitable to the Abyssinian Alphabet; as the Vowels themselves are but con-sonant, being inexpressible by themselves; and the Consonants being, as appears from the Sixth Order, in form more independent than the Vowels: but to be understood, we must use the expression.

3. The Seven different *Voices* or *Vowels* expressed by these Seven Orders are these:

A. Short ă, as in *fat, lad,* &c.; answering the Fat-ha (َ) in the Arabic, and the Patach (ַ) in the Hebrew. Like the former, it is modifiable, approaching the ĕ sound, or the short Hebrew Segol (ֶ).

B. ů, as in *full, put, lucid;* or ŏ, as in *move;* or oo, as in *fool,* &c.

C. ĭ, as in *pin, finger, hinder;* or ee, as in *bee, see;* or ea, as in *read, sea;* or e, as in *scene.*

D. ā, as in *far, father, rather.*

E. ë or ê; a sharp ê, with a slight ï sound before it, as in the Slavonian Dialects; as the German *je,* "ever," or the English *yea.*

F. ĕ or ў, as in *liv-er, ber-rў.* This order also is often mute or vowelless, as in the English and French Languages the mute ĕ. In fact, it completely resembles the Shwa simplex (ְ) of the Hebrew Language.

G. ó, generally sharp, as in *so;* or with *w* before it, as in *woe, wonder.*

4. In order to express these seven sounds by each letter, the Abyssinians have adopted the following plan:

A. The *Original Form* is used for the expression of the *First Vowel* (ă). It therefore is called, with its Ethiopic name, ግዕዝ፡ Gĕ-ĕz, which signifies "original"; and is therefore applied to the Ethiopic Language in general (ልሳን፡ ግዕዝ፡), in order to distinguish it from any translation. In reference to the letter forms, it means the original, simple, unaltered form, ሀ፡ ለ፡ ሐ፡ &c.

B. The *Second Vowel* (ů), which is called ካዕብ፡ Kā-ĕb, *i.e.* "altered," "second," is expressed by the affixion of a point (•) to the right-hand side of the letter, generally in the middle (ሁ፡ ቍ፡ ሙ፡ ኡ፡); in four instances at the bottom (ሩ፡ ዉ፡ ዩ፡ ጁ፡); and in one instance, under the letter (ፉ፡).

C. The *Third Vowel* (ĭ), which is called ሣልስ፡ Sālĕs, *i.e.* "third," is generally represented by a similar point annexed to the foot of the letter on the right side, and below the line, (ሊ፡ ቢ፡ ኢ፡ ኪ፡ ዪ፡). Where the original has no foot (*i.e.* line going downwards), a foot is formed; and in order thereby not to enlarge the general size of the letter, the rest is diminished where it has been thought necessary (ሂ: ሚ: ሢ: ዊ: ዒ:). Where the original has a point below, that is turned upwards (ሪ: ፊ:). An exception is, ዪ::

D. The *Fourth Vowel* (ā), called ራብዕ: Rābě' "the fourth," effects seven different changes:

(*a*) A foot line is made as in the preceding order, but without point: ሃ: ማ: ሣ: ዋ: ዓ: ፃ: ፋ::

(*b*) Foot lines on the right side are shortened: ላ: ሓ: ሳ: ሻ: ባ: ኣ: ካ: ኻ: ዛ: ዣ: ጣ: ጫ: ጳ: ጻ::

(*c*) A short horizontal line with point, is added, to the left at the bottom: ቃ: ታ: ቻ: ኃ: ያ: ጋ: ፓ::

(*d*) The same added to the right at the head: ና: doubled ኛ::

(*e*) Foot line broken: ራ::

(*f*) Foot point to the left shortened: ዳ: ጃ:

E. The change effected by the *Fifth Vowel* (ê), called ኃምስ: Hāměs "fifth," is simple: it consists in adding a small circular line or eye to the right side at the bottom, or in the middle: in instances where the letter has received a foot line in the two preceding forms, at the bottom of that line; *e.g.* ሄ: ሌ: ሜ: ዬ: ጬ: &c.

F. The greatest diversity is presented by the *Sixth Order* (ĕ or y̆) ሳድስ: *i.e.* "sixth." Instead of analyzing it, we recommend the scholar to examine that column himself in the Alphabet.

G. The *Seventh Vowel* (o) ሳብዕ: Sābě', *i.e.* "seventh," effects the following changes:

(*a*) A small circular line is formed at the top: ሆ: ሎ: ሮ: ቆ: ቶ: ቾ: ኆ: ኖ: ኞ: ፎ::

(*b*) Foot lines on the right side are shortened: ሖ: ሶ: ሾ: ቦ: ኦ: ኮ: ኾ: ዞ: ዦ: ዶ: ጆ: ጦ: ጮ: ጶ: ጾ::

(*c*) Foot lines on the left side or in the middle are formed: ሞ: ሦ: ዎ: ዖ: ፆ::

(*d*) Other forms are, ዮ: ጎ: ፖ::

5. As for the *quantity* of the vowels, it must be said, that those of the First and Sixth Order are constantly *short;* those of the Fourth and Fifth constantly *long;* and the rest are sometimes long, sometimes short.

NOTE.—Concerning the Diphthongs, as their pronunciation presents no difficulty, nothing remains to be said except what has been mentioned in Chap. I.

CHAP. V.

ON SYLLABIFICATION.

1. In the Abyssinian Languages, each letter, being Consonant and Vowel in the same figure, is able to constitute a *Syllable*; *e.g.* ነገረ: nă-gă-ră; ንፈቄ: nĕ-fă-k'ê. Such syllables, formed by single letters, we may call *simple* or *open syllables*.

2. But although this is the case, they *can* combine two or three letters (not more) together, to form one syllable; which will be called, if consisting of two letters, a *closed;* if of three, a *compound* syllable. Thus, *e.g.* ቃል: k'āl, "word," is closed; ሕዝብ: hĕzb, "people," is compound.

3. This is performed with the assistance of the Sixth Order; the vowel of which being short, and rather a semi-vowel, or the same thing as the Hebrew Shwā (ְ), is liable to become *mute*. Whenever this occurs, its letter must be added either to the preceding or to the following letter, in order to be pronouncible; *e.g.* ገር: gă-r, "meek." ብልሃት: bĕl-hā-t, "dexterity."

4. The question then is, *When is the letter of the Sixth Order mute* or *vowelless?* A few general rules, which will answer it, shall be laid down here.

A. Letters of the Sixth Order are MUTE *at the end of words* generally; *e.g.* ሀር: hăr, "silk"; ቃል: k'āl, "word"; ነገር: năgăr, "word," "thing"; ፀሓይ: tsa-hāy̆, "sun"; ዓለም: ā-lam, "world."

NOTE.—Seeming deviations, but no real ones, are those Ethiopic words which in the Amharic have been abbreviated: in such instances, the final letter of this form is not vowelless, reminding of the guttural letter, which is no longer written, but still pronounced:

ሰም: să-mĕ', "wax." Eth. ሰምዕ::
ብር: bĕ-rĕ, "pencil." Eth. ብርዕ::
እንጅ: en-djy̆, "but." Eth. እንጀዒ::

A real exception is this, which occurs in Feminine terminations of Pronouns or Verbs, in the Second Person Singular of the Feminine Gender, which are sometimes written in the third, sometimes in the sixth form, and may be pronounced or not; *e.g.* አንች: better አንቺ: an-tshy̆, "thou (female)!" ቀጅ: or ቀጂ: k'ă-dj, or k'ă-djy̆, "draw (thou female)!"

B. The same letters *remain* MUTE, when the words to which they belong, receive such additions at the end, by which their form is not changed: *e.g.* ቸር: tshăr, "kind." ቸርነት: tshăr-năt, "kindness." ባል: bā-l, "husband," "owner." ባልቴት: bāl-têt, "widow."

NOTE.—An exception is ቃለቻ: k'ā-lĕ-tshā, "sorcerer," "soothsayer."

C. When two letters of this order meet together at the end of a vowel, both are mute, unless want of organic affinity, or gemination, prevents their being so; but when such a word is augmented at the end, the last letter of this order is sounded:

(*a*) ደርቅ: dă-rk', "dry." ለምጽ: lă-mts', "leprosy."
መርዝ: mă-rz, "poison." ቀንድ: k'ă-nd, "horn."
ዓይን: ā-ўn, "eye."

(*b*) ልግም: lĕ-gĕm, "superficiality." ግብዝ: gĕ-bĕz, "hypocrite."
አቅም: ă-k'ĕm, "measure." አጭር: ă-tsh'yr, "short."

(*c*) ስምምም: sĕ-mĕm, "harmony." እልል: ĕ-lĕl, "huzzah!"
ክትት: kĕ-tĕt, "perfection," "fulness."

(*d*) ቅድስና: k'ĕd-sĕ-nā, "holiness." ዝምድና: zĕm-dĕ-nā, "relationship."

D. When a letter of the sixth form commences a word, its vowel is generally sounded:

ልደት: lĕ-dăt, "birth." ክፉ: kĕ-fŭ, "bad."
ስጠኝ: sĕ-t'ăng, "give me." ክረምት: kĕ-rămt.

E. In triliteral words, where all the three letters are of the sixth order, the first is generally sounded; the two following art not:

ሕዝብ: hĕ-zb, "people." ጽድቅ: ts'ĕ-dk', "righteousness."
ድንቅ: dĕ-nk', "wonder." እርም: ĕ-rm, "a thing prohibited."
ርስት: rĕ-st, "heritage." ምሽት: mĕ-sht, "wife."

F. In triliteral words, where the two first letters are of the sixth order, the first is sounded; the second is not:

ግርማ: gĕ-r-mā, "majesty." እንጃ: ĕ-n-djā, "I do not know."
ግምጃ: gĕ-m-dja, "muslin cloth."

But in many cases the second letter also is sounded:

ግሥላ: gĕ-sĕ-lā, "brown leopard." ቅምሻ: k'ĕ-mĕ-shā, "a bit."
እጅጌ: ĕ-djĕ-gê, "sleeve."

G. In quadriliteral words, beginning with two letters of the sixth order, and terminating in —ት: feminine, the first letter is sounded; the second is mute:

ፍልጠት: fĕ-l-t'ăt, "megrims." ፍርሃት: fĕ-r-hăt, "fear."
ንፍገት: nĕ-f-găt, "avarice." ንብረት: nĕ-b-rat, "state."

H. In quadriliteral feminine adjectives, whose letters are all of this order, the first and second letters are sounded, whilst the rest are mute:

ንጽሕት: nĕ-ts'ĕ-ht, "pure." ቅድስት: k'ĕ-dĕ-st, "holy."
ርክስት: rĕ-kĕ-st, "impure." ጽድቅት: ts'ĕ-dĕ-k't, "righteous."

I. In quadriliteral words, whose three first letters are of the sixth order, the first and second are generally sounded, whilst the third is mute, unless obviated by Lit. C.:

እልልታ: ĕ-lĕ-l-tā, "the shouting." ንጽሕና: nĕ-ts'ĕ-h-nā, "purity."

J. In pluriliterals, beginning with three letters of this order, these are generally formed into one syllable; either the first and third, or the second and third letters being mute:

ክርስቶስ: Krĕ-s-tos, "Christ." ፍረምቢያ: frĕ-m-bĭā, "breast-bone."

NOTE.—These rules will meet most cases: we refrain from adding more at this place, as it would swell this chapter to too large an extent; while in the further course of the Grammar, especially in those parts which treat on the Pronouns and the Verbs, the rest will be easily deduced.

CHAP. VI.

ON ACCENTUATION, AND POINTS OF DISTINCTION.

1. The Abyssinians have no marks for their accents. Some general Rules for Accentuation are as follow:—

A. In words consisting of long and short syllables (long and short either by the number of letters or by the quantity of vowels), the long syllable generally has the accent:

ጥሬ፡ : tĕrê, "raw," "genuine." ግራ፡ : gĕrā, "left." ብጎ፡ : băgò, "good."
ንጹ፡ : nĕtsŭ, "pure." ባ'ዶ: bādo, "empty." ዛ'ሬ: zārê, "*to-day.*"

In these two latter instances, the first syllable has the accent, because the long ā of the fourth order is the longest vowel:

ገዳ'ም: gădām, "convent." ንፋ'ቄ: nĕfāk'ê, "heresy."
ፈቃድ: fāk'ād, "will." ቅዱ'ስ: k'ĕdŭs, "holy."
መኖ'ር: mănòr, "the dwelling." ሆዳ'ም: hodām, "voracious."
መልካ ም: mălkām, "good," "beautiful." ዝም'ድና: zĕm'dĕnā, "affinity."

B. In Verbs, the radix without afformatives, as well as with light afformatives (*afformativa levia*), has the accent on the antepenultima (on the third syllable from the end):

ነበረ፡ năbără, "he was." ተቀ′መጠ፡ tăk'ă'măt'a, "he sat down."

ገ′ለጽሁ፡ gă'lats'hů, "I have revealed."

See, however, more under the Verbs.

C. Feminine Adjectives and Substantives of the form ንግሥት፡ have the accent on the last syllable; *e.g.* ርግም′ት፡ rĕgĕm't, "cursed."

D. Other Dissyllabic words with short vowels require the accent on penultima:

ል′ደት፡ lĕdăt, "birth." ወ′ምበር፡ wă'mbăr, "a seat," "chair."
ገ′ንዘብ፡ gă'nzăb, "property." ድ′ንግል፡ dĕngĕl, "virgin."

E. The heavier Suffixes (*suffixa gravia*) and Afformatives require the accent directly to precede them:

ቀ′ምበር፡ "the yoke." ቀምበራ′ችን፡ k'ămbărātshĕn, "our yoke."
መ′ለሰ፡ "he brought back." መለሳ′ችሁ፡ mălāsātshĕhů, "you brought back."

2. The *Interpunctuation* of the Abyssinians is very simple. A simple colon (:) serves to divide words from words; and a double colon (::) to separate sentences from sentences.

NOTE (*a*)—The colon, which is to prevent words running together, and thereby creating confusion, was formerly a perpendicular line (|), as is evident from inscriptions found at Axum; but that line has been divided into two points, as it was otherwise liable to have been mistaken for the numeral ፲ (10).

(*b*) The double colon (::) is, in Abyssinian manuscripts, generally reserved for the end of paragraphs; when five red points are inserted into it in the form of a cross, in this manner,

EXERCISE FOR READING.

(*From "the Church History,"* p. 223.)

Băhăwăr' yāt ză'măn băbêtă Crĕs tĭ yān ĕn dêhh yālătsh
በሐዋርያት፡ ዘመን፡ በቤተ፡ ክርስቲያን፡ እንዲህ፡ ያለች፡
In the Apostles' time in the Church such

ă'n dĕ năt nă'bărătshĕbāt, hůlātshăů ă'ndĕ sĕgā ăn' dit
አንድነት፡ ነበረችባት፡ ሁላቸው፡ አንድ፡ ሥጋ፡ አንዲት፡
a union was in her, all of them one body one

năfsem es ki ho'nů dĕ răs. Crĕs tĭyā nātem hů'lů ba Cres tòs
ነፍስም እስኪሆኑ፡ ድረስ። ክርስቲያናትም፡ ሁሉ፡ በክርስቶስ፡
soul and that they were the Christians and all in Christ

kă'to ăltă lă' yŭm. hŭlă'tshăŭ yă A'dăm lĕdjo'tsh ĕndă
ከቶ፡ አልተለዩም። ሁላቸው፡ የአደም፡ ልጆች፡ እንደ፡
never were separated. all of them of Adam children as

nă'băru bă sĕgă, hŭlătsh ă ŭm la răsă'tshăŭ
ነበሩ፡ በሥጋ፡ ሁላቸውም፡ ለራሳ ቸው፡
they were after the flesh, all of them and (as left) to themselves

yālă Crĕst os yăt'ă'fŭ hăt'e-'ān ĕn dă nă'bărŭ en dêh ŭm
ያለ፡ ክርስቶስ፡ የጠፉ፡ ኃጥአን፡ እንደ፡ ነበሩ፡ እንደሁም፡
without Christ lost sinners as they were, so also

băhă'imānot hŭlă'tshăŭ bānde Crĕ st'os dānŭ.
በሃይማኖት፡ ሁላቸው፡ ባንድ፡ ክርስቶስ፡ ዳኑ።
by faith all of them through one Christ were they saved.

hŭrlātsh ăŭm bān dĕ mats' rāt tăts'ă'rŭ. bān dĕ dă' mĕm
ሁላቸውም፡ ባንድ፡ መጽሬት፡ ተጸሩ። ባንድ፡ ደምም፡
they all and by one calling were called. by one blood and

ts'ădăk'ŭ bān dĕ măn'fă sĕm năts'ŭ tăk'ă'dăsŭm. P'êt'ros em
ጸደቁ፡ ባንድ፡ መንፈስም፡ ነጹ፡ ተቀደሱም። ጴጥሮስም፡
justified, by one Spirit and purified sanctified and. Peter also

lă mĭ yă mĕn hŭ lă ă lă: ĕ lān te yă mă'n gĕs tĕnā
ለሚያምን፡ ሁሉ፡ አለ። እላንተ፡ የ መንግሥትና፡
to believers all said: You of the kingdom (royalty) and

yăkĕhĕnāt wă'găn nātshĕhŭ, yătămă'răt'ătshĕm
የክህነት፡ ወገን፡ ናችሁ፡ የተመረጠችም፡
of the priesthood a people, are, which is elected and

yătăk'ă'dăsătshem tĕ ŭ' lid, tĕ g'ălt'ŭ zănd
የተቀደሰችም፡ ትውልድ። ትገልጡ፡ ዘንድ፡
and sanctified a generation, you should manifest that

kătsh'ă'lămā wădă mi yās dănĕk'ăŭ wădă bĕrhānŭ
ከጨለማ፡ ወደ፡ ሚያስደንቀው፡ ወደ፡ ብርሃኑ፡
from darkness unto marvellous unto his light

yăts'ără'tshĕhŭn sĕră.
የጸሬችሁን፡ ስራ።
of Him that hath called you the works.

IN ENGLISH CONSTRUCTION.

"In the time of the Apostles, there was such an union in the Church, that they (the Christians) were all one body and one soul. Christians were never (in no wise) separated in Christ. As all of them were Adam's children, after the flesh, and as in themselves and without Christ they were lost sinners, so also (now) by faith they were saved through one Christ. They were all called with one calling; justified by one blood; and purified and sanctified by one Spirit. Peter also said to all believers: Ye are a royal and priestly people, a chosen and a sanctified generation, that ye should shew forth the works of Him that hath called you out of darkness unto His marvellous light."

CHAP. VII.

VARIOUS CHANGES OF LETTERS.

In order the better to comprehend the various euphonical changes occurring in the constitution of words in the different parts of speech, it is necessary to point out the rules by which the changes in the letters are regulated.

1. *Addition of Letters.*

Speaking, in the first instance, of the ADDITION of letters to words, we regard them as they are joined either at the beginning, or in the middle, or at the end,—prosthesis, epenthesis, and paragoge.

A. When a word commences with a liquid letter, esp. ነ: or ረ:, the አ: is often preposed; *e.g.* አናርያ: for ናርያ: Nārĕā. The preformative, also, to the First Person Plural of Verbs, in the Present Tense Indicative and Subjunctive, has እን—: for the Ethiopic ን—:: እንመለሳለን: "we return"; not ንመለሳለን:: እራስ: for ራስ: "head." እርጥብ: for ርጥብ: "wet."

B. In the middle and at the end after long vowels, ው: is inserted or affixed; *e.g.* ጊዜው: for ጊዜ: "time." ስራውም: "and the work"; for ስራም::

NOTE.—This euphonical ው: must not be confounded with the suffixed pronoun ው:, which only by the context can be distinguished from it.

2. *Contraction of Letters.*

CONTRACTION occurs most frequently to the vocal letters አ: (ዐ:) ወ: and የ:, besides these to the gutturals ሀ: ሐ: and ኀ:: They answer the אהוי letters of the Hebrew Language, in their becoming quiescent. This is especially the case—

A. In verbs and words derived from them, which, originating in the Ethiopic, on their transition into the Amharic have dropped the gutturals, as not compatible with the character of the latter language. In compensation for this loss of the consonant, they have retained the vowel, and joined it to the preceding letter:

Amharic.		Ethiopic.	
ማረ:	*for*	ምሕረ:	"to pity," "have mercy."
ጻፈ:	..	ጸሐፈ:	"to write."
ተማረ:	..	ተመሀረ:	"to learn."
መላ:	..	መልአ:	"to be full," "to fill."
ገባ:	..	ገብአ:	"to enter."
ሰራ:	..	ሰርሐ:	"to work."
ሠራ:	..	ሠርዐ:	"to order," "to constitute."
አፈራ:	..	አፍረየ:	"to bring forth fruit."
ጽፈት:	..	ጽሕፈት:	"writing."

B. When a word beginning with አ: receives a preformative of the first, fourth, or sixth order, the አ—: consonant is dropped, and the vowel absorbed by the preceding letter. If አ—: stands in the first order, it changes the preceding short letter to one of the fourth order; if the fourth order precedes, no contraction takes place; if እ: is of the sixth order, it sometimes changes the preceding short into a long letter, sometimes it does not at all affect it:

አንገት: "the neck."	ባንገት: "on the neck."
እርያ: "a swine."	ለርያ: "to a swine."
አደረገው: "he did it."	ያደረገው: "he who did it."
አገኘ: "he found."	ታገኘለህ: "thou wilt find."

C. The same change, without loss of consonant, takes place with suffixes commencing with ā:

ስራችሁ: "your work," from ስራ: and ā ችሁ::

But when such suffixes are joined to letters ending in ū or *o*, these letters are changed into diphthongs:

ሰጠኋት: from ሰጠሁ: and āት: "I gave her."

When joined to letters of the fifth form, the suffix ā assumes the የ:, as similar to the fifth vowel; and rendering that in the fourth form, deprives the preceding letter of its vowel:

ምሳልያችን: from ምሳሌ: and āችን: "our likeness."
በርያቸው: and በሬያቸው: "their ox."

D. In those verbs which are called *geminant*, the two identical letters, *i.e.* second and third radicals, are, in several moods and tenses, contracted into one letter, which letter then is sounded as a double letter:

ቀለለ: "it was light." ይቀላል: for ይቀለላል: "it is light."
ሰደደ: "he sent." የሚሰድ: for የሚሰድድ: "he that sends."

NOTE.—The same change takes place in all languages. Cf. in the English: *refer, referring; compel, compelled; man, manned; stir, stirring; stab, stabbed;* &c. In the Hebrew, letters so contracted receive a compensative Dagesh (cf. סַבָּה, קַלּוֹ); in the Arabic, a Teshdid (حَسَّ, دَبَّ, غَنَّ). In the Abyssinian Languages they have no mark for this gemination; but in pronouncing the contracted syllable, the voice dwells on it for the same length of time as it would on the non-contracted two syllables.

E. The same change takes place in the conjugations of Verbs ending in ን: in the Second Person Plural, and in a few other instances; *e.g.*

ሆን: "We became," for ሆንን:: ምነው: ማነው: &c.

3. *Elision.*

A complete Elision, *i.e.* ejection without compensation, takes place—

A. At the end of certain words, with letters of the sixth order, which are not, or scarcely, pronounced; *e.g.* ሰም: for ሰምዕ: "wax." ብር: for ብርዕ: "pencil." እንጅ: "but," for the Eth. and Tig. እንደዒ::

B. With the የ: Relative Pronoun, and the የ: of the Genitive Case, when Prepositions are prefixed to or precede the word; *e.g.* ባየኹት: በወንድምህ: ቤት: "In the house of thy brother, which I have seen"; instead of በያየኹት: በየወንድምህ: ቤት:: እንደ: ታዘዝህ: instead of እንደ: የታዘዝህ: "As thou art commanded."

C. With the Preformatives አ: and ት: in Verbs and verbal derivations, beginning with አ: and ተ:: *e.g.*

አደርጋለሁ: "I do"; አሠራለሁ: "I bind"; አስጽፋለሁ: "I order to write"; instead of ኣደርጋለሁ: ኣሠራለሁ: and ኣስጽፋለሁ:: ትቀበላለህ: "thou receivest"; ትመታላችሁ: "you will be beaten"; instead of ትትቀበላለህ: and ትትመታላችሁ::

D. The Preformative ት:, with the negative አ:, is often suppressed before ተ: ቸ: ጠ: ጨ: ደ: ጀ: ሰ: ሸ: ጸ: and ፀ:: *e.g.*

አጽፍ: for አትጽፍ: "Do not write."
አጡብቅ: "Do not observe"; &c.

NOTE.—To this rule may be reckoned ድ: before ሰ: in one instance: ስሳ: instead of ስድሳ: "sixty."

4. *Changes produced and suffered by the letter* የ፡ *and its corresponding vowels* I *and* Ê.

Some of those changes have been noticed in the preceding. Here is to be added:

A. ይ፡ of the sixth order, as preformative to Verbs, resolves into the mere vowel *ï*, when any letter of the same order is prefixed; *e.g.*

	instead of		instead of
ሊሰሩ፡	ልይሰሩ።	ቢመጣ፡	ብይመጣ።
እንዲሆን፡	እንድይሆን።	ሲመለስ፡	ስይመለስ።
ኪናገር፡	ክይናገር።	የሚቆም፡	የምይቆም።
እስኪጨርሱ፡	እስክይጨርሱ።	&c.	&c.

B. Under the same circumstances, የ፡ not only remains, but, for the sake of assimilation, changes the preceding letter into one of the third order; *e.g.*

ሊያድርግ። ቢያልቅ። እንዲያወጣ። &c.

C. The Vowel I, when applied, changes the following letters:

ለ፡ into የ። ሠ፡ and ሰ፡ into ሸ። ተ፡ into ቸ። ነ፡ into ኘ።
ዘ፡ into ዠ። ደ፡ into ጀ። ጠ፡ ጸ፡ and ፀ፡ into ጨ።

	FOR
ሣይ፡ "painter"	ሣሊ።
ነጋሽ፡ "regent"	ነጋሢ።
ምላሽ፡ "answer"	ምላሲ።
ትመቻለሽ፡ "thou (*f.*) wilt be beaten,"	ትመቺአለሽ።
ትድኛለሽ፡ "thou (*f.*) wilt be saved,"	ትድኚአለሽ።
ጋዥ፡ "prince"	ጋዢ።
ወላጅ፡ "parent"	ወላዲ።
ሳጭ፡ "giver"	ሳጢ።
ቍራጭ፡ "piece"	ቍራጺ፡ or ቍራጢ።
ዐማጭ፡ "rebel"	ዐማፂ።

NOTE.—Under the same circumstances, የ፡ changes those letters into the fourth order.

D. When words ending in *i* and *ê* receive any of the heavy suffixes (*gravia*), or the auxiliary አለ፡ at the end, the third or fifth order is generally changed into the sixth, and የ፡ follows:

በሬ፡ "ox." በርያቸው፡ and በሬያቸው።
ጠባቂ፡ "guardian," "protector." ጠባቅያችን፡ "our protector."

ትጠብቂያለሽ: "thou (*fem.*) observest," for **ትጠብቂ: አለሽ**::

ጠብቄያለሁ: "I observe," for **ጠብቄ: አለሁ**::

E. When letters of the fifth order are shortened, they are changed into the third; when they are prolonged, they are changed into the fourth; and the original vowel *ê* or *i* is represented by **ይ**::

ሔደ: "he went." Imp. **ሒድ**: go!

ሼጠ: "he sold."

ተሻየጠ: "he bought and sold," "carried on commerce."

5. *Changes produced and suffered by the Letter* **ወ**: *and its corresponding Vowels* U *and* O.

The letter **ወ**: is often contracted into the vowel *o*, and still further into ů̊.

A. **ወ**: is contracted into *o*. This occurs,

(*a*) With the second radical in verbs:

ቆመ: for **ቀወመ**:: **ዞረ**: for **ዘወረ**:: **ጾመ**: for **ጸወመ**:

(*b*) In substantives:

ስጥወታ: "gift," is contracted into **ስጦታ**::

ችለወት: "power," into **ችሎት**::

ሕይወት: "life," into **ሕዮት**::

ጸለወት: "prayer," into **ጸሎት**::

B. **ወ**: and *o* are further contracted into ů̊.

(*a*) In the subjunctive, imperative, and constructive in verbs:

ይቁም: "let him stand." **ቁም**: "stand!" **ቁምዋል**: "he is standing."

(*b*) With the suffixed pronoun 3d person sing. masc., which, to nouns ending in a letter belonging to the sixth order, is attached as ů; but after a long vowel, and in verbs as **ው**:, except after an ů̊, where it is changed for **ት**::

ቤቱ: "his house." **ጌታው**: "his master."

ጠበቀው: "he observed it." **መቱት**: "they beat him."

C. *o* and ů̊, when an ā is joined to them, change the gutturals and palatals into diphthongs of the fourth order, and put other letters into the sixth order, adding **ዋ**::

ብሎ: "his saying." **ብልዋል**: "he is saying."

ሰጠሁ: "I gave." **ሰጧቸው**: "I gave them."

ሸንጎ: "senate." **ሸንጓቸው**: "their senate."

D. ወ: having been reduced to the vowel *o* in the radicals of verbs, is restored again when the first radical is amplified:

ተቃወመ: "he stood against," "resisted," from ቆመ: "he stood."

6. *Changes occurring with the Diphthongs.*

Diphthongs of the first order (ቈ: ኈ: ኰ: ጐ:) are, when lengthened, changed into the fourth (ቋ: ኋ: ኳ: ጓ:); when shortened, into the sixth (ቍ: ኍ: ኵ: ጕ:) order:

ቈጠረ: "he counted."

Lengthened	Shortened
ተቋጠረ: "he made accounts."	ይቍጠር: "let him count."

7. *Reduplication of Letters.*

Reduplication of letters takes place in the formation of nouns and verbs, generally with a design of giving intensity to the original meaning of the word, when the second or third radical is repeated:

ታናሽ: "small."	ታናናሽ: "very small."
ታላቅ: "great."	ታላላቅ: "very great."
መለሰ: "he brought back."	ተመላለሰ: "he walked," *i.e.* "went and returned," "went up and down."
	ተመለሰሰ: "he returned."
አደረገ: "he did," "performed."	አደራረግ: "a great work."

8. *Exchange of Letters.*

The following letters are frequently changed one for another, as belonging to the same organ, or at least being similar in sound.

A. *Gutturals.*—ሀ: for አ:: አ: for ሀ: ሐ: and ኀ:: ሀ: ሐ: and ኀ: for ኸ::
They write:

አረፈ: "he rested," for ዐረፈ::	አበሻ: "Abyssinia," for ሐበሻ::
አዘነ: "he regretted," for ሐዘነ::	አፈረ: "he was ashamed," for ኀፈረ::
ሆነ: "he became," for ኾነ::	ሔደ: "he went," for ኼደ::
ኋላ: "behind," for ዃለ::	

B. *Gutturals* and *Palatals.*—ሀ: ሐ: and ኸ: for ከ: *e.g.*

ኬድኩ: in vulgar language, for ሔድሁ: "I go."

ማኸል: and መኻከል: for መካከል: "the middle."

C. *Palatals* and *Dentals.*—ቀ: interchanges occasionally with ጠ: ጨ: and ጸ:: እንቄት: for እንጨት: "wood."

አስቄንቃቸዋለሁ: for አስጨንቃቸዋለሁ:: "I will harass them." Ps. xviii. 38.

D. *Palatals and Dentals.*—ገ: and ደ: and ጀ:: *e.g.*

ኣረጀ: "to be old," for ኣረገ::

ተንጓጓ: for ተንደዋደዋ: "to rustle."

E. *Linguals and Dentals.*—ለ: and ነ:: ሠ: and ሰ:: ተ: and ቸ:: (ዘ: and ዠ::) ዠ: and ጀ:: ጠ: and ጸ:: ጸ: and ፀ:: *e.g.*

ልጥር: "pound," for ንጥር:: ሠመረ: "to please," for ሰመረ::

ምናልባት: "perhaps," for ምናልበች:: ተበዠ: "to redeem," for ተበጀ::

ቈረጠ: "to cut," for ቈረጸ:: ጸብ: "quarrel," for ፀብ:

F. *Linguals* and *Labials.*—Where ነ: precedes በ: ጰ: and ፈ:, it is, as in the Greek and in other languages, exchanged for መ: a liquid of the same order.

እምቡልታ: "flute," for እንቡልታ::

ወምፊት: "a sieve," for ወንፊት::

ለንጴ: "a small tent," for the Greek λαμπήνη.

G. *Labials.*—መ: and በ:: መ: and ወ:: በ: and ወ::

ዝናም: "rain," for ዝናብ::

ወንበር: and ወምበር: "chair," for መንበር::

ኖረ: "to remain," (the ወ: resolved into the vowel *o*) from the Eth. ነበረ::

9. As for the liquids ለ: መ: ነ: ረ: and the changes to which they are liable, they having been embodied in the preceding remarks, nothing further remains to be said concerning them.

10. *Transposition, and further Contraction of Letters.*

Takes place merely in low language.

መርባት: "light," "candle," for መብራት::

ቅናቡግ: for ቅባኑግ: "nug-oil."

እዝጌር: for እግዜር: contracted from እግዚአብሔር: "God."

ክሮስ: "Christ." ክስያን: and ኩስታን: for ክርስቲያን: "Christian."

Part II.—ETYMOLOGY.

ON THE DIFFERENT PARTS OF SPEECH.

PRELIMINARY REMARKS.

In the Semitic Languages, it has been the custom (which also Ludolf has followed, in both his Grammars, of the Ethiopic and of the Amharic Languages) to class the different Parts of Speech under three heads; *viz.* Nouns, Verbs, and Particles; beginning the Etymological part of the Grammar with the Verb, as containing the roots of the whole language. But modern Grammarians have, for important reasons, adopted another course; following the practice of some ancient Arabic and Hebrew Scholars: and as that tripartition presents several inconveniences, especially to such as are unacquainted with the other Semitic Dialects, we divide the Amharic Language into Nouns, Pronouns, Verbs, Prepositions, Adverbs, Conjunctions, and Interjections. None of the Abyssinian Languages possess the Article.

2. It will, in a great measure, facilitate the study of the language, before we enter on each part of speech in particular, to premise a few general observations on the original forms of words; because it is in them, and in the manner in which from them the various formations have proceeded, that the peculiarity of every language consists. We must observe, however, that the Amharic not being an original but a derived language (see Introduction, I. III.), we must have frequent recourse to the Ethiopic; and it presents several formations which, in the present state of its knowledge, cannot yet be accounted for.

3. Now the principal elements—as it were the skeleton—of words in any language, consists in the *Consonants*, which are animated by the different Vowels, according to the purposes of formation, flexion, and dialect: and in speaking therefore of original forms, we must look, not to the Vowels, but to the consonants.* This, when applied to the Amharic, where Vowels are constantly attached to Consonants, signifies that the various orders of a letter do not come into consideration, but the letter itself.

4. One characteristic feature of the Semitic Languages is the prevalence

* This is more clear in the Hebrew, Arabic, and Syriac; in which the Vowels are represented by certain marks above and below the line, which are more frequently omitted than written.

of triliteral forms, which are partly derived from original biliterals, and partly amplified to quadri- and pluri-literals; but, for the greater part, are original, and form the majority. This peculiarity applies also to the Abyssinian Languages; although not to the Amharic with equal force, as to its parent, the Ethiopic.

5. We do not intend to enter into any inquiry about the logical priority of the Parts of Speech; although we believe, that, in the natural developement of the mind, the Noun has the precedence before the Verb; but in the grammatical formation of the Amharic Language, the Verb claims the priority, since all its roots are reducible to the first order, called Gĕĕz; *i.e.* "original." For the sake of convenience, however, we begin with the Noun, and follow the order stated under § 1.

CHAP. I.

ON THE NOUNS.

In speaking of the Nouns, we have to consider them according to their *Formation* (termination, species), *Gender*, *Number*, and *Declension*.

SECTION I.

Formation of Nouns.

1. As to the FORMATION of Nouns, they are either Simple, Augmented, or Compounds; either *Primitive* or *Derived*. Concerning their termination, they may end in any of the seven orders, except the first. We consider them, first, in respect to their *forms,* as simple, augmented, or compound; secondly, to their *formation,* as primitive or derivative.

2. *Simple* forms; consisting of two, three, or four letters.

A. *Biliterals.*

(*a*) Ending in the second order:

ክፉ: bad. ብዙ: much. ምሉ: full.
ንጹ: clean. ብሩ: clear. ጽሩ: pure.
ሥሡ: covetous, a miser. ሽቱ: spices.

NOTE.—Most of these forms are Ethiopic Verbal Adjectives, originating from, or rather representing, the Passive Participle.

(*b*) Ending in the third order, generally signifying an agent:

ሰሪ: workman, diligent. መሪ: guide. ሰፊ: wide, spacious.
ዘሪ: sower, seedsman. ፋቂ: tanner. ዘጲ: ebony.
ገቢ: the inside. ጋቢ: current in trade.

(*c*) Ending in the fourth order:

ሬሳ: a corpse.	ሞያ: rent, wages.	ሽታ: smell.
በዷ: emptiness.	ቤዛ: ransom.	በጋ: summer.
ካሳ: equivalent.	ዋዛ: mockery.	ዋጋ: price.
ገላ: body.	ሸማ: cloth.	ጫማ: sole of the foot.
ጫኛ: betrothed.	ውኃ: water.	ድዳ: dumb.
ሌባ: thief.	እቃ: vessel, utensil.	ምሳ: dinner.
ማታ: evening.	ሥጋ: flesh.	ሩጫ: course.
ስራ: work.	ቃራ: knife.	

(*d*) Ending in the fifth order:

ሎሌ: servant.	ሐፄ: the king's majesty.	ቅኔ: poetry.
መሴ: a certain measure.	ሰኔ: June.	ወሬ: news.
ቅቤ: butter, oil.	በሬ: ox.	ጦሌ: full-grown elephant.
ደዌ: disease.	ጊዜ: time.	ቋሬ: garment.
ጥሬ: genuine, original.	ፍሬ: fruit.	

(*e*) Ending in the sixth order. These are the most numerous.

ሀር: silk.	ቀን: day.	ቅን: equity.
ላም: cow.	ሆድ: belly.	ሉል: pearl.
ልክ: measure.	ልብ: heart.	ሕግ: law.
ሙቅ: warm.	ልጅ: child.	ማር: honey.
ማቅ: coarse woollen cloth.	ሙዝ: banana.	ሣር: grass.
ሩዝ: rice.	ሞት: death.	ስም: name.
ሰው: man.	ራብ: hunger.	ሹም: governor.
	ሴት: woman.	ቄስ: priest.

(*f*) Ending in the seventh order:

ሚሎ: a fillip.	ዳቦ: a sort of bread.	ርጎ: curds, cheese.
ዶሮ: hen.	ሢሶ: a third.	ጉዞ: a day's march.
ጎጆ: small thatched house.	ጆሮ: ear.	ኮሶ: cosso (a medicine).
	ቆሎ: fried grain.	

B. *Triliterals.*

(*a*) Ending in the second order are rare:

ግንኙ: meeting. ስሙሙ: harmonious.

(*b*) Ending in the third order, the second letter being generally of the fourth order. The latter, if their first radical is of the first order, are to be considered as Active Substantives or Adjectives; if of the sixth, as Passive.

ለጋሚ፡ groom.	ለቃሚ፡ gatherer.	መሓሪ፡ merciful.
ምካሪ፡ counsellor.	መጋቢ፡ steward.	ሰካሪ፡ drunkard.
በራሪ፡ flying.	ነደቂ፡ mason.	ነጋሪ፡ speaker.
ነጣቂ፡ rapacious.	ተማሪ፡ scholar.	ኣላፊ፡ passenger, passer-by.

To this class also belong those words whose third letter has been changed from the third to the sixth order. መላሽ፡ "the returner," "restorer"; ምላሽ፡ "answer," "return"; ቈራጭ፡ "cutter"; ቍራጭ፡ "a cut," "piece," &c., for መላሺ፡ ምላሺ፡ ቈራጪ፡ ቍራጪ።

(*c*) Ending in the fourth order:

ለማኝ፡ entreaty.	ልቡና፡ intellect.	መሓላ፡ oath.
መንታ፡ twins.	መራራ፡ bitter.	መከራ፡ affliction.
መጻጻ፡ sour, acid.	መኝታ፡ sleeping-place.	ሳምባ፡ the lungs.
ስፍራ፡ place.	ሸህላ፡ potter's earth.	ቅሬታ፡ remainder.
ባርያ፡ slave.	ተልባ፡ linseed.	ነቍጣ፡ a spot.
ኣለቃ፡ a chief.	ከፍታ፡ height.	ወርካ፡ sycamore-tree.

(*d*) Ending in the fifth order:

ህላዌ፡ substance, essence.	ፍጻሜ፡ perfection.	ምሳሌ፡ similitude.
	ልባቤ፡ intellect.	ቅዳሜ፡ Saturday.
ሥላሴ፡ trinity.	ስንዴ፡ wheat.	ከርቤ፡ myrrh.
ቡራኬ፡ blessing.	ነሐሴ፡ August (month).	ዕድሜ፡ age.
ወጠጤ፡ young he-goat.	ዝማሬ፡ song.	ጥያቄ፡ question.
ጀንዴ፡ cow's hide.	ጉማሬ፡ hippopotamus.	

NOTE.—It will be observed, that those Nouns, whose first radical is of the sixth, the second of the fourth, and the third of the fifth order, are generally Abstract Nouns of Quality.

(*e*) Ending in the sixth order:

α Nouns whose three letters are of the same order, generally denoting essence, quality, action, or concrete substances:

ልብስ፡ cloth.	ለውጥ፡ change.	ምንጭ፡ fountain.
ሕርም፡ prohibition.	ምርጭ፡ election.	ስልፍ፡ war.
ሥእል፡ image.	ርኵስ፡ impure.	ብርድ፡ coldness.
ሽልም፡ ornament.	ቅቅል፡ cookery.	እህል፡ corn.

ትርፍ: remainder. ንስር: eagle. ዝምብ: a fly.
ክምር: a heap. ዕፅፍ: a fold, time, turn. ጥልቅ: depth.
ድርቅ: dryness. ግምብ: tower. ዕንስ: pregnancy, fœtus.
ጭምር: addition. ጽምድ: a pair.
ፍርድ: judgment. ልጥር: a pound.

β Nouns whose first letter is the first, and the second and third of the sixth order, generally denoting qualities, concrete substantives, or adjectives:

ለምድ: hide. ለምጽ: leprosy. መልክ: form.
ረጅም: long. ቀንድ: horn. በርድ: cold.
በትር: a stick. ተክል: a plant. ነምር: leopard.
አትር: lentils. ከብት: property. ወንድ: a male.
ዐምድ: pillar. ዘውድ: coronet. ደርቅ: dry land.
ገብስ: barley. ጸጕር: hair. ፈትል: thread.

γ Nouns whose first and third letters are of the sixth, and second of the second order. They are of Ethiopic formation, being generally Verbal Adjectives and Substantives, the same as § 2. A. *a*.

ምውት: dead. ርብዕ: fourth. ቅብእ: anointed.
ቅዱስ: holy. ብሩር: silver. ትሑት: humble.
ንጉሥ: king. ንጹሕ: pure. ንፉግ: avaricious.
እኩል: half, equal. ውጉዝ: execrated. ርጉም: cursed.
ዕቡይ: proud. ዕዉር: blind. ግሩም: majestic.

δ Nouns whose second letter is of the third order. They are of Ethiopic origin, and generally Adjective.

መሪር: bitter. መጺጽ: sour. ረቂቅ: thin.
ቀሊል: light. ከቢድ: heavy. ዓዚዝ: mighty.
ጠቢብ: wise. ጸቢብ: narrow.

To the same class belong those Adjectives whose middle letter has been changed from the third into the sixth order:

ቀጭን: "thin"; አጭር: "short"; ረጅም: long"; instead of ቀጢን: አጺር: ረዚም::

Exceptions are:

ቃሊብ: "mould"; ቀሚስ: "shirt"; ነቢይ: "prophet"; ዘቢብ: "grape"; &c.

ε Nouns whose middle letter is of the fourth order. They are generally Substantives, though sometimes Adjectives.

ልማድ: custom. ልባብ: halter. ልጓም: reins, bridle.
ሕማም: disease. ሕከክ: itch. ሕፃን: infant.
መላስ: tongue. መካን: barren.

ζ Nouns whose middle letter is of the fifth order: ሰሌን: ሐሜት: መሬት ::

η Nouns whose middle letter is of the seventh order: አሞት ::

θ Nouns Verbal, ending in the feminine —ት :: They will be mentioned hereafter, when speaking of Derived Nouns.

(*f*) Nouns ending in the seventh order. They are all Substantives.

ልቅሶ: lamentation. ምርኮ: exile. ምንሾ: ague.
ምሰሶ: a pole. መስኖ: a canal. ሽሖቦ: wire.
ቀበሮ: jackal. ቆንጆ: girl, virgin. በረዶ: hail.
በቅሎ: mule. እርሾ: leaven. ከበሮ: drum.
ወስፌ: awl. ዓውሎ: tempest. ዘንዶ: poisonous serpent.
ድርጎ: a dĕrgo. ጎምቦ: water-jar. ጎሮሮ: throat.

C. *Quadriliterals:*

There are none ending in the second order.

(*a*) Single Nouns ending in the third order. Such as are derived from any derivation of Verbs are not included here.

ሰብሳቢ: gatherer. ሰን ጣቂ: a cleaver.
ስንጣቂ: a split. በርባሪ: a plunderer.

(*b*) Ending in the fourth order:

መንጋጋ: jaw. ሠረገላ: beam, carriage. ሽምብራ: a kind of pulse.
ሸንገላ: deceit.
ደብተራ: a learned man. አለንጋ: a whip. ኩብኩባ: grasshopper.
ጕልማሳ: a young man. አቆማዳ: leather bag

(*c*) Ending in the fifth order:

ልምላሜ: verdure. ሣንቲሌ: a rabbit. ርኅራኄ: clemency.
ሽማግሌ: an elder. በርበሬ: Cayenne pepper. ትርጓሜ: translation.
ዱብደቤ: bill of account.

(*d*) Ending in the sixth order:

ለምለም: green. መንደር: village. ምስኪን: poor.
ምንዝር: adultery. ሠልሰል: chain. ረግረግ: mud.

ስንዝር: a span.	ሰፍነግ: sponge.	ቀምበር: yoke.
ቅንድብ: eye-brow.	ትንኮል: shrewdness.	አሽከር: a youth.
አጠገብ: side.	ድምብር: frontier.	ድንግል: virgin.

(*e*) Ending in the seventh order:

መሰንቆ: a harp.	ቆርቆሮ: pewter.	አምልኮ: religion, godliness.
ወይዘር: prince, or princess.	ዝንጀሮ: monkey.	ደንቆሮ: stupid.

D. There are not many Simple Nouns of five and more letters: some of those which exist, we will mention here:

ሃረንጓይ: green.	ሐመልማል: vegetables.
ትንተራስ: supporter of the head.	ነበልባል: flame.
እንቍላል: egg.	እንቅልፍ: sleep.
አውራሪስ: rhinoceros.	ደንገጥር: chamber-maid.
ዝንጕርጕር: chequered.	

3. In speaking of *Augmented Nouns*, we do not refer to those casual additions they receive by inseparable Prepositions at the beginning, or Pronouns at the end; but we speak of those augmentations at the beginning, in the middle, and at the end, by which their original signification is modified. In order, however, not to fall into an unnecessary repetition, we postpone this subject till we come to speak of *Derived* Nouns. (See 5. c.)

4. *Compounds* are formed (*a*) from the Ethiopic *status constructus*; the *nomen regens* and the *nomen rectum* being combined into one word, as in our "house-door" for "house's door," only the reverse of our order. In the Ethiopic, as in the Hebrew, the word (nominative) which precedes, and which, according to our ideas, should have the nominative form, is changed; and the word (genitive) which follows, and which we should expect to be changed, is not changed at all. As this peculiarity does not affect the Amharic Language any further, we do not enter into it, but content ourselves with giving only a few instances.

Compounds.	Analysis.
ባለቤት: master of the house, self.	ባል: master, and ቤት: house.
ባልንጀራ: fellow, associate.	ባል: . . . . እንጀራ: bread.
ቤተሰብ: {domestic, one belonging to a house or family.}	ቤት: house . . {ሰብ: Eth. *i.q.* Amh. ሰው: man.
ቤተንጉሥ: state-room, parlour.	ቤት: house . . ንጉሥ: king.

Thus are many Ethiopic words compounded, especially their Christian names; *e.g.* ኃይለ: ማርያም: Haila Maryam, "the Power of Mary," commonly Hailu; ገብረ: እግዚአብሔር: or ገብረ: አምላክ: Gabra

Egziabeḥêr, or Gabra Amlāk, contr. Gabramlāk, commonly Gabru, or Zăĕgziabḥêr, or Zăămlāk, "Servant of God," &c.

(*b*) From Amharic words, combining either noun with noun, or the noun with any other part of speech:

Compounds.	Analysis.
ግራጅ፡ left-hand.	ግራ፡ and እጅ።
ግዛጅ፡ free-will, liberty.	ግዛ፡ (dominion?) & እጅ፡ hand.
ባዶጅ፡ empty-handed.	ባዶ፡ empty, & እጅ።
ኤኔታ፡ O my Lord!	የኔ፡ mine, & ጌታ፡ Lord, master.

5. *Primitive Nouns*, strictly speaking, are those whose origin cannot be traced to any other source but to themselves. Now there are a good number in the Amharic Language which are easily recognised as Primitive in this sense; but there are many others which can be called so only in a relative acceptation of the word, because in the Ethiopic, from whence they are taken, they are not Primitive; although either the original word is not current in the Amharic, or the mode of its derivation is not accordant with the idiom of that language. The first of these two latter clauses induces us to consider a number of Amharic Nouns as comparatively Primitive; whilst the second constrains us to leave to others the same derivative character which they have in the Ethiopic.

As the Primitive Nouns are found only among the *simple* forms, we refer to the above exhibition, N°. 2.

A. *Biliterals:*

Class (*a*) is entirely derivative.

Class (*b*) also.

Class (*c*) contains a number of Primitives; *e.g.* ሬሳ፡ በዳ፡ ቤዛ፡ በጋ፡ ካሳ፡ ዋጋ፡ ገላ፡ ሸማ፡ ጨማ፡ ውኃ፡ ድኃ፡ ሥጋ፡ ነጋ፡ ማታ፡ ድዳ፡ ሌባ፡ ቃሬ።

(*d*) *Primitives* of the *fourth* class: ሎሌ፡ ሐጼ፡ መሴ፡ ሰኔ፡ ጊዜ፡ ሞሌ፡ ቋሬ።

(*e*) In the fifth class, the majority are Primitives.

(*f*) In the sixth class, ሚሎ፡ ደሮ፡ ጀሮ፡ ጎጆ፡ ኮሶ፡ ደቦ።

B. *Triliteral Primitives:*

In class (*c*), መንታ፡ ሳምባ፡ ሸህላ፡ ባርያ፡ ተልባ፡ ዐግሸላ፡ ነቍጣ፡ ወርካ፡

In class (*d*), ስንዴ፡ ነሐሴ፡ ሐምሌ፡ ጀንዴ፡ ከርቤ፡ ወጠጤ፡ ዕድሜ፡ ጉማሬ፡

In class (*e*), almost the whole of the first (α); about half of the second (β);

TABLE OF PRIMITIVE FORMS OF NOUNS.

BILITERALS.

1. ultimâ ሂ::

ዲሪ: black horse.
ድሪ: neck-chain.
ዞጲ: ebony.

2. ult. ሃ::

ሸማ: cloth.
ዲባ: gourd.
ሚታ: grandmother.
ማታ: evening.
ሬሳ: corpse.
ውኃ: water.
ደማ: hatchet.
ቍሪ: raven.
ጓደ: alcove.

3. ult. ሄ::

ሙሴ: a massê.
ጊዜ: time.
ሻሜ: sort of pearl.
ዝዬ: duck.
ጦሌ: full-grown elephant.
ቋሬ: garment.

4. ult. ህ::

ሰው: man.
ሎል: pearl.
ሽል: fœtus.
ማቅ: sack-cloth.
ሴት: woman.
ብር: silver (dollar).
ሆድ: belly.

5. ult. ሆ::

በጎ: good.
ሚሎ: fillip.
ደቦ: sort of bread.
ፈቆ: gazelle.
ኮሶ: kosso (anthelmintic).

TRILITERALS.

1. ult. ሁ::

አሊሉ: orchitis.
ከንቱ: vanity.
ቁምሩ: little pigeon.

2. ult. ሂ::

ጠመኔ: chalk.
ተትጊ: urchin.
አምሊ: worthless.
ዕንቍ: gem, pearl.

3. ult. ሃ::

መከራ: affliction.
ጉበና: sort of lizard.
ማሸጋ: glue.
ጎዳና: path.
ዳጉሳ: dagussa.
ሽሉዳ: geminus muscle.
ጣቢታ: leavened bread-cake.
ትቢያ: chaff.
ናፋሳ: sheep's skin made up for dress.
ቋሊማ: sausage.
ቀናፋ: triangular piece of cloth in trowsers.
ቹፋዋ: silver bracelet.
ዲቃላ: bastard.
ፍላፃ: arrow.
ሞላላ: oblong.
ደጓሳ: strong, prominent.
አቴና: straw mat.
ባቄላ: lupine.
ወርካ: sycamore-tree.
ቡችላ: young dog.
ባርያ: slave.

ብዕዛ: bĕĕzā, an animal.
ነፋላ: tassel.
ቋንቋ: language.
ተኵላ: wolf.
ሰኰና: heel.
አሞራ: rapacious bird.

4. ult. ሄ::

ጠጠጤ: young he-goat.
ናሐሴ: August (month).
ብረሌ: glass bottle.
ጎፈሬ: curled hair.
አሞሌ: piece of salt.
ገባሬ: farmer.
ጉማሬ: hippopotamus.
ጎራዴ: sword.
አጬጌ: chief of all the convents.
ከርቤ: myrrh.
ስንዴ: wheat.
አሮጌ: old.

5. ult. ህ::

ሰፈር: camp.
ጉበት: liver.
ማገር: rafter.
ብረት: iron.
ኮከብ: star.
ከሙን: cumin.
ዋንፋ: sort of flute.
ብሩር: massy silver.
ቀሚስ: shirt.
ቅሊብ: mould.
ዋሪኝ: black pied horse.
መካን: barren.
ፈቃድ: will.

ዙፋን: throne.
ጳጳስ: prelate.
ሌማት: a lêmāt.
ልጓብ: halter.
ጎባን: sister-in-law.
ሰፌድ: flat straw plate.
ለምድ: hide.
ሙርት: genitals of quadrupeds.
ጊንጥ: scorpion.
ሣጥን: box, chest.
ልብስ: clothing, cloth.
ኮብሽ: swelling of feet.
ሰጎን: ostrich.
ሢኦል: hell.
ማሶብ: basket.
እቶን: furnace.

6. ult. ሆ::

ቀበሮ: jackal.
ማሰሮ: boiling vessel.
ምሰሶ: pole.
ፍየሎ: caprine animal.
በቅሎ: mule.
አታሞ: hand-drum.
ጋጋኖ: ibis.
ዮቋኦ: sort of bread.
ጼደና: a certain tree.
መስኖ: channel.
ጉርዶ: bran.
ዓውሎ: tempest.
ምንጮ: certain fever.
ቈንጆ: girl, virgin.
ምድጃ: fire-place.
ጉሮሮ: throat.

QUADRILITERALS.

1. ult. ሂ::

ወድምቢ: a certain quadruped.
ቍርንቢ: he-goat.
ግድግዲ: bird of prey.

2. ult. ሃ::

ሠረገላ: beam, carriage.
አንበሳ: lion.
ብርኩማ: small leather cushion.
ብርኩታ: sort of bread.
አሜካላ: sort of weeds.
አምባላ: certain bird.
አቆማዳ: leather bag.
ሽምብራ: sort of pulse.
ደምትራ: centipede.
አንኮላ: hollowed gourd.
ጎርጎማ: gap of a tooth.

3. ult. ሄ::

በርበሬ: red pepper.
ሽማግሌ: elder.
ጥንቸሌ: rabbit.
ቍንቍኔ: earwig.

4. ult. ህ::

ቸነፈር: plague.
ወታደር: soldier.
ሰፍነግ: sponge.
አሽከር: boy, girl.
ቀምበር: yoke.
ቋዝመን: strong knife.
ሠቅሠቅ: window-frame.
አርኩም: large blackbird.
ተካሪስ: necklace.

ብዕሪር: filix mas.
መሰላል: stairs, ladder.
አምላክ: God.
ዛምዛም: sort of gourds.
ችንካር: nail.
ቍልቋል: k'welqu'āl.
አጎበር: bedstead.
አስኳል: yolk of an egg.
አጋዜን: capricorn.
ቀለንጀ: small elephants' tusk.
ብሪንዶ: unfermented wine.
ሃውልት: obelisk.
ምንዝር: adultery.
ምርምር: inquiry.
ህምህም: yellow pigeon.
ትንኮል: shrewdness, craftiness.
ቍንቍን: moth.
ስንዝር: span.
ሰርክሽ: back-door.
እንኮይ: acrimonious fruit.

5. ult. ሆ::

ከርከሮ: a certain quadruped.
ኮርኮሮ: flat basket.
አሬዛዞ: sort of beads.
ትምባኾ: tobacco.
ብሩንዶ: raw flesh.
መሰንቆ: harp, lyre.
ምጺምጮ: an anthelmintic.
ብርጭቆ: glass.
አሽቆቆ: kind of marmots.
ቆርቆሮ: pewter.

PLURILITERALS.

1. ult. ሃ::

አርግሬሳ: a parasitic plant.
እንቆቅላ: kind of lizards.
ፍርምቢያ: breast-bone.
ሙጭልጭላ: weasel.

2. ult. ሄ::

ሀረንጓዴ: green.
ጉሬማዴሌ: a certain bird.

3. ult. ህ::

አምፃዘሉብ: saddle's crupper.
እንከሊስ: measles.
ቍንጥሬት: a small handful.
ቍርጭምጭሚት: ankle-bone.
እንድርማሚት: lap-wing.
ሆልስዋል: glutton.
ነበልባል: flame.
አምበላይ: white horse.
እንቍላል: egg.
እንክርዳድ: a weed.
መንከሴን: chin.
መቅለምት: large knife.
ሰንጠረጅ: game of chess.
እንቅልፍ: sleep.
ልክስክስ: light-minded.
መንኰራኵር: carriage.
ቍንጥርጥር: curled hair.
አምቢያጉስም: martingal.

4. ult. ሆ::

አብርጣሞ: sort of plaited hair.
እንጉብሮ: sort of bread.

To face page 30.

none of the third (γ); few of the fourth (δ), ቋሊብ: ቷሪክ: ቀሚስ: አሪዝ: ነቢይ: ዘቢብ:, and fifth (ε), ልባብ: ልጓም:; but none of the sixth (ζ) division.

In class (*f*), the greater part are Primitives.

C. *Quadriliteral Primitives:*

(*a*) None.

(*b*) መንጋጋ: ሠረገላ: ሸምብራ: አለንጋ: ኩብኩባ: ድብተራ: አቆማዳ::

(*c*) Few; *e.g.* መንትሌ: በርበሬ::

(*d*) The majority.

(*e*) መሰንቆ: ቆርቆሮ: ወይዘሮ: ዝንጅሮ: ደንቆሮ::

D. Those mentioned as simple *pluriliterals* are all Primitive.

6. *Derived Forms* take their origin either from Nouns, Verbs, or Particles; and are formed in various ways, either by *contraction* (elision), or by *change*, or by *augmentation* of their letters.

A. By *Contraction* (see Part I. Ch. VII. 2.), and *Elision* (ibid. 3.), they are changed more seldom within the limits of the Amharic than in their transition from the Ethiopic Language into the Amharic. It takes place most frequently in Biliterals:

Amh.	Eth.	Amh.	Eth.
ንጹ: pure,	from ንጹሕ::	ምሳ: dinner,	from ምሳሕ::
በሬ: ox,	.. ብዕራይ::	ላም: cow,	.. ላህም::
ማር: honey,	.. መዓር::	ሣር: grass,	.. ሣዕር: sometimes Amharic.
ቅቤ: butter, oil,	.. ቅብእ::		

Sometimes in Triliterals, derived from the Ethiopic Quadriliterals:

Amh.	Eth.	Amh.	Eth.
ብርቱ: strong,	from ብርትዕ::	ስሙሙ: harmonious,	from ስሙዕሙዕ::
ባሕሪ: essence,	.. ባሕርይ::		

B. By *change* of one, two, or of all the primitive letters, according to the rules laid down in Part I. Ch. VII. 4, 5, 7. A few instances will suffice for illustration:

Derivative.	Primitive.
ቀዳም: that which is before, ቀዳሚ: saddle's pommel, ቅዳሜ: Saturday,	from ቅድም: the former time.
ቅዱስ: holy, ቅዳሴ: consecration, ቀዳሽ: sanctifier,	from ቀደሰ: to sanctify.

Derivative.	Primitive.
መላሽ: a restorer, ምላሽ: return, answer,	from መለሰ: to return, bring back.
ምሳሌ: likeness, ምሳይ: kind, resemblance,	from መሰለ: to resemble.
ንጉሥ: king, ነጋሽ: regent,	from ነገሠ: to be king.
አደኝ: hunter, አደን: game,	from አደነ: to hunt.

C. *Augmentation* of letters in the derivation of Nouns takes place either *in the beginning* (preformation), or *in the middle* (reduplication), or *at the end* (afformation).* The letters used for this purpose are መ: ሰ: ተ: ነ: ኘ: ኧ: ወ: ያ:: Of these, መ: ሰ: ተ: ነ: ኧ: ወ: ኧሰ: and ኧሰተ: are *prefixed;* and መ: ተ: ነ: ኘ: ወ: and ያ: are *affixed.* *Reduplication* takes place by repeating any of the radical letters.

(a) *Preformation:*

መ: is used for Infinitives, and retained in Nouns derived therefrom:

መጠበቅ: the watching.

መጠበቂያ: watch-house, from ጠበቀ: to watch.

ተ: ተን: ኧ: ኧሰ: ኧሰተ: and ኧን: are retained in Nouns derived from those derivations of Verbs which have these characteristic Preformatives:

Noun.	Verbal derivation.	Radix.
ተናጋሪ: speaker.	ተናገረ: to speak.	ነገረ: to say, tell.
ተንቀጥቃጭ: trembler.	ተንቀጠቀጠ: to tremble.	ቀጠቀጠ: to bruise.
አፍራሽ: breaker.	አፈረሰ: to break.	ፈረሰ: to burst.
አስታማሚ: nurse for sick persons.	አስታመመ: to nurse sick persons.	አመመ::
አንሻታች: cheater.	አንሻተተ: to cheat.	ሻተተ: (*non occ.*)

ኧ: is prefixed to Verbs, and one of the radical letters doubled; *e.g.*

አገባብ: አቀማመጥ: አደራረግ::

ት: and ቲ: are prefixed to Verbs to form Nouns of action; *e.g.*

ትዕግሥት: ትምሕርት::

Sometimes the ኧ: or ተ: is cut off, and ነ: retained in these Preformatives:

---

* This is analogous to the Hebrew הֶאֱמַנְתִּי and the Arabic يَتَسَمَّنَا Nouns.

Noun.	Verbal Derivation.	Radix.
ነጐድጓድ: thunder.	አንጐደጐደ: to thunder.	ጐደጐደ: Eth. to beat.
ነጠብጣብ: a drop.	ተንጠበጠበ: to drop.	ጠበጠበ: to trot.

ወ: occasionally interchanges with the መ: of the Infinitive, the Noun being considered no longer as an Infinitive: *e.g.*

ወምበር: (or ወንበር:) chair. መንበር: the sitting, (Eth.) ነበረ: to sit.

ወምፌት: (for መምፌት:) or ወንፌት: "sieve"; from ነፋ: to blow, to fan, to make wind.

(*b*) *Reduplication;* repetition of any of the radical letters:

Derivative.	Primitive.
ታናናሽ: very small.	ታናሽ: small.
ታላላቅ: very great.	ታላቅ: great.
መልካካም: very beautiful.	መልካም: fine, beautiful.

In Verbal Nouns, which take it from the Verb, Reduplication is retained:

Nouns.	Verbal Derivation.	Radix.
ተመላላሽ: walker.	ተመላለሰ: to walk.	መለሰ: to return.

Reduplication with transposition:

ጥርጣሬ: doubt.	ተጠራጠረ: to doubt.	ጠረረ::

(*c*) *Afformation* of the letters መ: ተ: ነ: ኛ: ዊ: and ያ::

α The Afformation of āም: to Substantives, forms Adjectives and Substantives of Fulness, Intenseness, &c., similar to the Latin *osus*, and English *ous* and *ful;* *e.g.*

Form in *ām*.	Origin.
መልካም: beautiful (formosus).	መልክ: form.
ሆዳም: glutton (man of a large stomach).	ሆድ: belly.
ፍርያም: fertile.	ፍሬ: fruit.
ወፍራም: thick.	ወፍር: thickness.

β Afformative ማ: forms Substantives:

አይጥማ: mouse-coloured mule.	አይጥ: mouse.
ውሽማ: fornicator.	ውሻ: dog.

γ The Afformative ት: ăt, et, it, ĭtu, āt, lā, produces feminine forms:

Form in ት::	Origin.
ልደት: birth.	ወለደ: to bring forth.
ትምህርት: doctrine.	ተማረ: to learn.
ንጽሕት: (*fem.*) pure.	ንጹሕ: (*masc.*) pure.
ልጂቱ: daughter.	ልጅ: son.
ፍርሃት: fear.	ፈራ: (Eth. ፈርሀ:) to be afraid.
ቀሬታ: remainder.	ቀረ: to remain, to be left.
ዝቅታ: lowness.	ዝቅ: low.

δ The Afformative ን: āን: forms Substantives of Quality, from Verbs which in Latin frequently answer those ending in *tas*, in English in *ty*:

Forms in *ān*.	Verbs.
ሥልጣን: authority.	ሠለጠ: & ሠለጠነ: to have authority.
ብርሃን: light, clarity.	በራ: Eth. በርሃ: to be light or clear.
ኪዳን: covenant.	ከየደ: ተካየደ::
ቅልጣን: delicacy, vanity.	ቀለጠ: to melt.
ቍርባን: offering, eucharist.	ቈረበ: to take the sacrament.

Exceptions are, ጕንዳን: "ant"; and ጉምፋን: "cough."

ε ና: and ነት: are affixed to Adjectives, Substantives, and Particles, in order to form Abstract Substantives; generally answering our *ence*, *ance*, *ness*, *cy*, *ty*, *hood*, and *ship*.

Forms in ና: and ነት::	Radices.
ልቡና: intelligence, sagacity.	ልብ: heart, mind.
ልዕልና: highness.	ልዕል: (Eth.) high.
ልዩነት: difference, variety.	ልዩ: different, various.
ልጅነት: childhood, sonship.	ልጅ: child, son.
ሕፃንነት: infancy.	ሕፃን: infant.
መልካምነት: beauty, goodness.	መልካም: beautiful, good.
መምህርነት: teachership.	መምህር: teacher.
ቅድስና: holiness.	ቅዱስ: holy.
እውነተኛነት: veracity.	እውነተኛ: true.
አስማተኛነት: witchcraft.	አስማተኛ: sorcerer.

ζ The Afformative ኛ: is affixed to Nouns, to form Adjectives and Substantives of Office, Habit, or Quality.

Forms in ኛ:	Radices.
ሀኬተኛ: lazy, an idler.	ሀኬት: idleness.
መርከበኛ: sailor.	መርከብ: ship.

They often assume a ተ: before the ኛ:

ሰራተኛ: labourer.	ሰራ: work, labour.
እምቢተኛ: refractory.	እምቢ: I will not.

η The Ethiopic Afformative āዊ: is affixed to Nouns Substantive with the same effect as those formed by the Afformative ኛ:: They, besides, form Gentile Nouns.

Form in āዊ::	Radix.
ወንጌላዊ: evangelist.	ወንጌል: gospel.

θ The letter ያ: is affixed,

א To *Infinitives*, to form Nouns of Agency, Instrumentality, Locality, Object, &c.; whereby it must be observed, that when the letter to which it is

TABLE OF DERIVATIVE NOUNS.

I. SIMPLE FORMS.

1. *Verbal Adjectives and Substantives, with Ult. or Penultima* ሁ::

ክፉ: bad, evil.
ሙት: dead.
ሹም: officer, governor.
ስሙሙ: harmonious.
ብርቱ: strong.
ፍጹም: perfect.
ጉንደል: castrated.

2. *Nouns, with* ሂ: *Ultima or Penultima.*
(See Part I. Ch. VII. 4. c.)

A. *Ultima.*

(a) *Active.*

ሰሪ: labourer, artist.
ፋቂ: tanner.
ጋቢ: full measure.
ገዢ: a ruler.
ሰጪ: a giver.
ሸሺ: a fugitive.
ሰጋሚ: an ostler.
ተማሪ: a scholar.
አድራጊ: a performer.
አሳላፊ: butler.
አስተማሪ: teacher.
አስተማሚ: nurse for sick persons.
ሰንጣቂ: one who splits.

(b) *Passive.*

ገቢ: the inside.
ቍራሽ: a morsel.
ጥማቂ: that which is dipped.
ስንጣቂ: a splinter.

B. *Penultima.*

መሪር: bitter.
ጠቢብ: wise.
እንግሊዝ: English.

3. *Ult. and Penult.* ሃ::

A. *Defectives.*

(a) *Ultima:*

ስራ: work.
እቃ: instrument, utensil.
ሳምባ: lungs.
አርባ: forty.

(b) *Penultima.*

ላም: cow.
ማር: honey.
ሣር: grass.
መላስ: tongue.

B. *Nouns of Essence, State, Action, Quality, derived chiefly from Verbs.*

ልመና: petition.
ተራራ: mountain.
መራራ: bitter.
ስፍራ: place.
ጥንቈላ: soothsaying.
ሽንገላ: fraud.

4. *Verbals in* ሄ: *form* ሀሃሄ: *and* ሁሃሄ::

ሀላዌ: the being, existence, essence.
ቡራኬ: blessing, benediction.
ልምላሜ: verdure.
ትርጓሜ: interpretation.

5. *Ultima* ሀ::

(a) *Passive Penultima* ሁ: Vid. 1.

(b) *Penult.* ሂ: Vid. 2.

(c) *Form* ሀሃሀ::

ልማድ: custom, habit.
ልጓም: reins.
ንፋስ: wind.

(d) *Form* ሀሂሀ: and ሀሄሀ:: *are generally Feminine.*

ግሌጥ: interior margin of a written page.
መሬት: dust.

(e) *Form* ሀሀሀ::

ለምጽ: leprosy.
ረጅም: long, high.

6. *Ethiopic Infinitives in* ሆ::

ልቅሶ: lamentation.
ምርኮ: exile.
ሽቦ: wire.
አምልኮ: Divine Service, Religion, godliness.

7. *Contracted Preformatives.*

ነጠብጣብ: a drop.
ነጐድጓድ: thunder.

8. *Further Contractions.*

ክርስ: Christ.
ክሳን: Christian.
እግዜር: God.
ደጃጅ: provincial governor, &c. &c.

II. AUGMENTED FORMS.

1. *Augmented by Preformatives.*

(a) *Infinitives with* መ::

መጠበቅ: the keeping.
መዓርግ: step, degree. } (Eth.
ምሥዋዕት: sacrifice. } forms.)

(b) *With* አ: *before* ረ: *and* ነ::

አራስ: (*for* ራስ:) head, chief, Rās.
እናርያ: Enārea, n. pr.

(c) *Intensive forms with* አ: *and reduplication.*

አቀማመጥ: trestle, seat.
አተዳደግ: education.

(d) *Feminines &c. with* ተ::

ተግሣጽ: reproof, discipline.
ትእግሥት: patience.
ትምሀርት: doctrine.
ትምላስ: threshold.

(e) *With* ወ: *instead of* መ:

ወምበር: seat, bench, &c.

2. *Augmented by restoring original* ወ: *and* የ::

ቀቀሚ: standing slave, *i.e.* wood-cutter.
ሸያጭ: seller.

3. *By reduplication.*

ታናናሽ: very little, very small.
መልካካም: very handsome, very good.

4. *By Afformatives.*

(a) ām *to Substantives and Adjectives, denoting fulness.*

መልካም: beautiful.
ፍርያም: fruitful.
ሆዳም: gluttonous.

(b) ·ማ: *to Simple Roots, forming Substantives.*

ስጥማ: a certain fever.
ኮርማ: stallion.
ውሽማ: fornicator.
አይጥማ: ash-coloured (*lit.* mouse-coloured) mule.

(c) ት: AT, ET, IT, UT, ቶ: and ታ: *Feminine Forms.*

ልደት: birth, nativity.
ችሎት: (ችልወት:) power.
ትምክሕት: boasting, glorying.
ልጅቶ: (ልጅቶ:) daughter.
ግርማት: majesty.
ፍርሃት: fear.
ዝሙት: fornication.
ቅሬታ: the rest, remainder.
ዝቅታ: lowness.
ስጥወታ: gift.

(d) ān *to Simple Roots, forms Substantives of Essence (Concrete Substantives), Power, Quality.*

ሥልጣን: authority, privilege.
ብርሃን: light, clarity.
ኪዳን: covenant, treaty.
ሕፃን: infant.
ቅልጣን: delicacy.
ቍርባን: offering, eucharist.
ጉንዳን: ant.
ግምፋን: coughing, a cold.

(e) ና: *and* ነት: *to Substantives, Adjectives, and Particles, form Abstract Substantives of Quality, State, &c.*

ልቡና: intelligence, prudence.
ልዕልና: highness, elevation.
ዝምድና: relationship.
ልዩነት: difference, variety.
ልጅነት: sonship.
መልካምነት: goodness, beauty.
እውነተኝነት: verity.
አምላካዊነት: divine nature.

f. ኛ: *to Nouns and Particles, forms Adjectives and Substantives of Office, Habit, and Quality.*

ሀኬተኛ: idler.
መርከበኛ: navigator, sailor.
Often assumes ተ::
አዘንተኛ: mournful.
ስራተኛ: workman, labourer.
እምቢተኛ: unwilling.

(g) āwi, *with the same effect as the preceding.*

ወንጌላዊ: evangelist.
ፈሪሳዊ: Pharisee.
ፍረንሳዊ: French.

(h) ያ: *expressed or implied, forms Nouns of Instrumentality, Agency, Locality, Object, Individuality.*

α *To Infinitives.*

ማሠርያ: a tie.
መለኪያ: measuring instrument.
መላገጂ: object of scorn.

β *To Simple Roots.*

ቅምያ: spoil, booty.
ቅምሻ: bit, morsel, taste.
ጽርጊያ: rubbish, sweepings.

To face page 34.

to be joined, is one of those changeable Linguals or Dentals mentioned in Part I. Ch. VII. 4 c., both ያ: and the letter to which it was to be joined, are dropped, and exchanged for such a cognate Lingual or Dental as combines the joint sounds. (See the above-mentioned paragraph.)

Forms with ያ:, the ያ: being either expressed or implied.	Infinitives.
መለኪያ: measure.	መለኪ: the measuring.
መላገጃ: object, means of scorn.	መላገጥ: the scorning.
ማለፊያ: passage, excellent.	ማለፍ: the passing.
መኅተሚያ: printing-office.	መኅተም: the printing.
መመለሻ: place, or means of returning.	መመለስ: the returning.
ማሠሪያ: a tie, band, bond.	ማሠር: the binding.

ב To Simple Roots, with the same object and in the same manner as to Infinitives:

Forms with ያ::	Roots.
ቀምያ: booty.	ቀማ: to plunder.
ቅምሻ: a bit, taste.	ቅምስ: the tasting.
ጉተቻ: trail, train.	ጉተት: the dragging.
ጽርጊያ: rubbish.	ጽርግ: sweeping.

Section II.

On the Species of Nouns.

1. Nouns are to be considered, either as *Substantives*, names of things, or as *Adjectives*, names of properties. In the Amharic, as in the other Semitic Languages, they both belong together; and they have been jointly treated in the preceding Section as to their Formation. It remains now to say a few words concerning the Adjectives.

2. As to their Formation, but few of them, as the preceding Tables show, are *original:* such are,

በጎ: good.	ደህና: well.	አሙሌ: bad.
ሞላላ: oblong.	ደጊሳ: prominent.	አሮጌ: old.

Even these are but primarily Adjectives; and when isolated, may be, and are, used as Substantives. Most Adjectives are of derivative forms, being derived either from Verbs (see Table II.) or from Substantives; *e.g.*

ግሩም: አዋቂ: መሪር: መልከኛ: መልካም: አሳዊ::

Participial Adjectives, የማይናገር: የታመነ::

3. As for Comparison, the Amharic Language, like the Hebrew, has no

Adjective form to express the Comparative or Superlative: we therefore must defer this subject to the Syntax.

4. The Numeral Nouns will be treated in a separate chapter.

We now proceed to the consideration of the *Gender* of the Nouns.

Section III.

On the Gender of the Nouns.

1. The Amharic Nouns have but two *Genders*, Masculine and Feminine. We shall endeavour to point out a few general rules, showing what Nouns belong to either of the two genders, and by which forms they are to be recognised. We have to complain, however, that there is yet much confusion; both masculine and feminine forms being alternately applied to words where the sex is not palpably distinguished.

A. Masculine are:

(*a*) The names of God, angels, and men; also the names of nations, and of all male animals:

እግዚአብሔር: God, the Lord. ሰይጣን: Satan. ዓረብ: an Arab.
ገብርኤል: Gabriel. ሀበሺ: an Abyssinian.
አምላክ: God. ሰው: man. ፈረንሲስ: a Frenchman.
የሱስ: Jesus. ዮሐንስ: John. አንበሳ: a lion.
መልአክ: angel.

(*b*) The names of the sun and the stars, of ranks and offices of men:

ፀሐይ: sun. ሹም: governor. ጠባቂ: guardian.
ኮከብ: star. ገዢ: ruler. ሎሌ: servant.

B. Feminine are:

The names of women and female animals; the names of the moon, the earth, countries, towns, &c.; plants; the names of female ranks and offices; collective names; and the names of several abstracts:

ማርያም: Mary. ከተማ: city, camp. ወይዘሮ: princess, lady.
ዶሮ: hen. መንደር: village. እመቤት: mistress.
ጨረቃ: moon. ጎንደር: Gondar. ገረድ: female servant.
ምድር: earth, country. ዛፍ: tree. ጉባኤ: assembly, society.
ሐበሻ: Abyssinia. አበባ: a flower.

And see 2.

C. Common, are several conditions of life; as, "child," "slave," and others, where the termination of the word does not distinguish the sex.

2. The two Genders are distinguished,

(*a*) By the addition of distinct words denoting the Male and the Female. These are: ወንድ: and ተባት: for Males, and ሴት: and አንስት: for Females: besides this, አውራ: for several male animals, who are without this distinction considered as females; as, goats, fowl, &c.: *e.g.*

ወንድ: ልጅ: a son, boy. ሴት: ልጅ: a daughter, girl.
የንስሳ: ተባት: male of animals. የንስሳ: አንስት: female of animals.
አውራ: ፍየል: he-goat. አውራ: ዶሮ: cock (he-fowl).

In Shoa, they carry this distinction further; calling "clayish earth" ወንድ: or ተባት: ምድር: (male earth), and "loose earth" አንስት: or ሴት: ምድር: (female earth). They call wood which splits perpendicularly, ወንድ: እንጨት: "male wood"; and wood which splits transversely, ሴት: እንጨት: "female wood." Maria-Theresa dollars, which have the requisite coinage, አንስት: ብር: "female dollars"; and those which are any way deficient, being M. T. dollars, ተባት: ብር: "male dollars." The latter distinction obtains in all Abyssinia.

(*b*) The Female is distinguished by the termination ት: ታ: and ቱ:: (See the Table of Derivatives, II. 4. c.)

(*c*) The same by ያ: and ኒት: (See Derivatives, II. 4. c.)

(*d*). The Primitives are mostly *Masculines.*

(*e*) As to the Derivative forms, the following rule obtains:

Classes I. 1. 2. 3. 6. and II. 4. *f. g.* are predominantly Masculine; and Classes I. 4. and II. 4. c. *d. e.* predominantly Feminine. The rest are of Mixed Gender.

3. The remaining Nouns are undetermined as to the sex; the Adjective and Verb being promiscuously applied to them in the Masculine and in the Feminine Gender.

4. Several Adjectives and Substantives, whose form is Masculine, are changed into a Feminine form:

Masculine.	Feminine.
ንጹ:	ንጽሕት: pure.
ብሩ:	ብርህት: clear.
ግሩም:	ግርምት: wonderful.
ጠባቂ:	ጠባቂቱ: guardian.
አሮጌ:	አሮጊት: old.
ወራሽ: heir.	ወራሺቱ: heiress.
ሀኬተኛ:	ሀኬተኛዪቱ: lazy.
አረማዊ: heathen man.	አረማዊት: heathen woman.

Section IV.

On the Number of the Nouns.

1. The *number* is but twofold; viz. *Singular* and *Plural.* We might add the *Collective;* but that being considered either as a body, when it is Singular, or as an aggregate of individuals, when it is plural, it constitutes no particular form; and we therefore proceed to consider these two, the Singular and the Plural; there being no Dual in this language.

2. As the Singular is that form in which each Noun, before it is changed, presents itself, we need not say any thing about it, but direct our attention at once to the formation of the *Plural* Number.

3. The truly Amharic Plural is very simple; it has but one form, and that is the termination *otsh* (Tigrê *ot*); in which we recognise the Hebrew וֹת, the Arabic اتٌ, and the Ethiopic *āt*; *e.g.*

Singular.		Plural.	
ቤት፡	house.	ቤቶች፡	houses.
ውሻ፡	dog.	ውሾች፡	dogs.
ልጅ፡	child.	ልጆች፡	children.
አባት፡	father.	አባቶች፡	fathers.
ጠባቂ፡	guardian.	ጠባቆች፡	guardians.
በጎ፡	good.	በጎች፡	good.

Note.—The Plural termination of several Nouns ending in the fifth order is divided into two Consonants; the original letter being put into the sixth order, and a ዮ፡ being added, to which the Plural ች፡ is affixed; *e.g.*

ምሳልዮች፡ similitudes, from ምሳሌ።

4. But besides this Amharic, we have the following Ethiopic Plural forms; which sometimes are applied, although the true Amh. Plural always may be put.

(*a*) Termination *ān.*

For the Derivates, I. 1. II. 4. *g.* and some other forms; *e.g.*

Singular.		Plural.		Singular.		Plural.
ቅዱስ፡	holy.	ቅዱሳን፡ saints.		ፈሪሳዊ፡	Pharisee.	ፈሪሳውያን፡
ጠቢባ፡	wise.	ጠቢባን።		ኃጥእ፡	sinner.	ኃጥኣን፡
ሕያው፡	living.	ሕያዋን።		ነዳይ፡	poor.	ነዳያን።
ሙት፡	dead.	ሙታን።		መምህር፡	teacher.	መምህራን።

Note.—Irregular: አይሁዳዊ፡ "Jew." አይሁድ፡ "Jews."

(*b*) Termination *āt.*

The Feminines of the Plural Adjectives in *ān.*

ቅዱሳት፡ ነዳያት፡ ቡሩካት፡ ሕያዋት።

The Derivative forms terminating in *ān*.

ሥልጣን፡ authority. ሥልጣናት። ብርሃን፡ light. ብርሃናት፡ lights.
ሕፃን፡ infant. ሕፃናት፡ infants.

Besides these:

Singular.	Plural.
ሰማይ፡ heaven.	ሰማያት፡ heavens.
ደመና፡ cloud.	ደመናት፡ clouds.
ፊደል፡ letter.	ፊደላት፡ letters.
ቃል፡ word.	ቃላት፡ words.
ምሥጢር፡ secret.	ምሥጢራት፡ secrets.

Some forms ending in the fifth order:

ምሳሌ፡ likeness.	ምሳልያት፡ likenesses.
ጊዜ፡ time.	ጊዜያት፡ times.

Words ending in the servile ት።

ዓመት፡ year.	ዓምታት፡ years.
ሰማዕት፡ martyr.	ሰማዕታት፡ martyrs.

Other forms:

ሐዋርያ፡ apostle.	ሐዋርያት፡ apostles.
ነፋስ፡ wind.	ነፋሳት፡ winds.
ሕግ፡ law.	ሕጋጋት፡ laws.
ቤት፡ house.	አብያት፡ houses.*
ካህን፡ priest.	ካህናት፡ priests.
ጳጳስ፡ metropolitan.	ጳጳሳት፡ metropolitans.
ኤጲስቆጶስ፡ bishop.	ኤጲስቆጶሳት፡ bishops.
ዲያቆን፡ deacon.	ዲያቆናት፡ deacons.

(*c*) Form አግቡር።

አገር፡ village.	አህጉር፡ villages.

(*d*) From አግባር።

ወትር፡ string.	አውታር፡ strings.
ሕዝብ፡ people.	አሕዛብ፡ people.
ዖፍ፡ bird.	አዕዋፍ፡ birds.
ዐምድ፡ pillar.	አእማድ፡ pillars.

(*e*) ገባሪት።

Singular.	Plural.
አርዌ፡ wild.	አራዊት፡ wild beasts.
ሠርዌ፡ beam.	ሠራዊት፡ army.

---

* Used only in አብያት፡ ክርስቲያናት፡ "Churches," from ቤት፡ ክርስቲያን፡ "a Church."

(ƒ) አጋብርት።

ቄስ: priest.	ቀሳውስት: priests.
መንፈስ: spirit.	መናፍስት: spirits.
አንበሳ: lion.	አናብስት: lions.
መኰንን: judge.	መኳንንት: judges.
ከንፈር: lip.	ከናፍር: lips.
ኮከብ: star.	ከዋክብት: stars.
አምላክ: God.	አማልክት: gods.
ነምር: leopard.	አናምርት: leopards.
መልአክ: angel.	መላእክት: angels.
መስኮት: window.	መሳኩት: windows.
ሊቅ: chief.	ሊቃውንት: chiefs.
በቅሎ: mule.	በቅሎች: and አባቅልቶች: mules.
ጋኔን: demon.	አጋንንት: demons.

Rare forms:

ንጉሥ: king.	ነገሥት: and ነገሥታት: kings.
መነኰሴ: monk.	መናክሶች: መናኩስት: & መነኳኩስት: monks.

5. It is well to attend to these various forms, as they frequently occur in the Amharic Bible as well as in conversation: but it must be borne in mind, that they are all of Ethiopic origin, and superseded by the simple Amharic form *otsh;* and a beginner will never be mistaken in using the latter, until he is sufficiently acquainted with the language to know where he has to apply any of the other forms.

SECTION V.

On the Declension of the Nouns.

The Declension of Nouns is very simple and uniform. Nouns are inflected through four Cases, equally in the Singular and the Plural, *i.e.* the Nominative, the Genitive, Dative, and Accusative. One example may suffice to show the whole mode of proceeding:

	Singular.	Plural.
Nom.	ቤት: a house.	ቤቶች: houses.
Gen.	የቤት: of a house, a house's.	የቤቶች: of houses.
Dat.	ለቤት: to a house.	ለቤቶች: to houses.
Acc.	ቤትን: a house.	ቤቶችን: houses.

OBSERVATIONS:

(*a*) The Genitive answers the Eth. ዘ:, and is not to be confounded with the Pronouns Relative or Distributive.

The Accusative Case must not be confounded with the Interrogative Adverb ን፡, nor with the termination ን፡ of Nouns. On the Construction, and on the various uses of the Accusative, see Syntax.

2. It occasionally happens, that they make use of the Ethiopic Genitive or *status constructus*, i.e. that mode of construction which prevails in the Hebrew, and which has been noticed in the First Section of this Chapter, § 4. The two nouns, which stand in a genitive relation to each other, one of which is the *regens* (Nominative), and the other the *rectum* (Genitive), are so closely connected as to appear as one word. The Genitive follows the Nominative, and receives the tone or accent; in doing which, the preceding Noun, the Nominative, is modified: in the Hebrew it is shortened: in our case, the last letter, if it is of the sixth order, is changed into the first, and the two words are considered as one compound, separated merely by the (:) colon; but even this, in the Amharic, is often dropped, especially when the Genitive begins with a vowel consonant, or when it is a short word:

ባለ፡ ቤት፡ and ባለቤት፡ "master of the house."

ባለዕዳ፡ for ባለ፡ ዕዳ፡ "owner of debts," *i.e.* "creditor" or "debtor."

Another change is produced by the affixion of Pronouns to Nouns, of which we shall speak under the head of Inseparable Pronouns.

CHAP. II.

ON THE NUMERALS.

1. The Numerals are of two kinds, *Cardinals* and *Ordinals*. The Cardinals specify the number of things which are the subject of speech: the Ordinals exhibit the order in which they occur.

2. The *Cardinal Numbers* in the Amharic are as follow:

Cipher.		Amharic.	English.	Cipher.		Amharic.	English.
፩፡	1.	አንድ፡ / *f.* አንዲት፡	One, a, an.	፴፡	30.	ሠላሳ፡	Thirty.
፪፡	2.	ሁለት፡	Two.	፵፡	40.	አርባ፡ or አርብዓ፡	Forty.
፫፡	3.	ሦስት፡	Three.	፶፡	50.	አምሳ፡	Fifty.
፬፡	4.	አራት፡	Four.	፷፡	60.	ስድሳ፡ or ስሳ፡	Sixty.
፭፡	5.	አምስት፡	Five.	፸፡	70.	ሰባ፡ or ሰብዓ፡	Seventy.
፮፡	6.	ስድስት፡	Six.	፹፡	80.	ስማንያ፡	Eighty.
፯፡	7.	ሰባት፡	Seven.	፺፡	90.	ዘጠና፡	Ninety.
፰፡	8.	ስምንት፡	Eight.	፻፡	100.	መቶ፡	Hundred.
፱፡	9.	ዘጠኝ፡	Nine.	፲፻፡	1000.	ሺህ፡	Thousand.
፲፡	10.	አሥር፡	Ten.	፻-፻፡	10000.	እልፍ፡	Ten Thousand.
፳፡	20.	ሀያ፡	Twenty.				

Compound Cardinals.

፲፩፡ 11. አሥራ፡ አንድ፡	Eleven.	፲፮፡ 16. አሥራ፡ ስድስት፡	Sixteen.
፲፪፡ 12. አሥራ፡ ሁለት፡	Twelve.	፲፯፡ 17. አሥራ፡ ሰባት፡	Seventeen.
፲፫፡ 13. አሥራ፡ ሦስት፡	Thirteen.	፲፰፡ 18. አሥራ፡ ስምንት፡	Eighteen.
፲፬፡ 14. አሥራ፡ አራት፡	Fourteen.	፲፱፡ 19. አሥራ፡ ዘጠኝ፡	Nineteen.
፲፭፡ 15. አሥራ፡ አምስት፡	Fifteen.		

The same order is observed with all the Tenths, to a Hundred; *e.g.*

ሀያ፡ አንድ፡፡ ሠላሳ፡ ሁለት፡፡ አርባ፡ ሦስት፡ &c.

The numbers upward of a Hundred are joined to the Hundreds by ከ፡ or ተ፡; *e.g.*

፻፮፡ 106. መቶ፡ ከስድስት፡፡ . . . . One hundred and six.
፻፷፡ 160. መቶ፡ ተስሳ፡ or መቶ፡ ከስሳ፡ One hundred and sixty.
፻፺፱፡ 199. መቶ፡ ከዘጠና፡ ዘጠኝ፡፡ . . One hundred & ninety-nine.
፪፻፡ 200. ሁለት፡ መቶ፡ . . . . . . Two hundred.
፲፰፻፵፩፡ 1841. ሺሀ፡ ተስምንት፡ መቶ፡ ካርባ፡ አንድ፡ or አሥራ፡ ስምንት፡ መቶ፡ ካርባ፡ አንድ፡ One Thousand Eight Hundred and Forty-one.

3. The *Ordinal* Numbers are formed by the termination ኛ፡ affixed to the *Cardinals.*

አንደኛ፡፡ መጀመርያ፡ or ፊተኛ፡፡ } the First.	ስድስተኛ፡ the Sixth.
ሁለተኛ፡ the Second.	ሰባተኛ፡ the Seventh.
ሦስተኛ፡ the Third.	ስምንተኛ፡ the Eighth.
አራተኛ፡ the Fourth.	ዘጠኘኛ፡ and ዘጠነኛ፡ the Ninth.
አምስተኛ፡ the Fifth.	አሥረኛ፡ the Tenth.
	አሥራ፡ ሁለተኛ፡ the Eleventh.

&c. &c.

The Simple Numbers, Twenty, Thirty, and upwards, scarcely admit of the termination ኛ፡, but are generally given to the Cardinal form. In compounds, the last number receives the termination ኛ፡; as,

ሀያ፡ አንደኛ፡ ምዕራፍ፡ the Twenty-first chapter.

4. They have no particular form for the Distributive Numbers; but they express them, either by reiteration, as,

አንድ፡ አንድ፡ (contr. አንደንድ፡) one-by-one, some, several, one or other, singly, severally.

ሁለት፡ ሁለት፡ two-and-two;

Or by እየ: or ኢየ: as,

ኢያንዳንዱ: each, every. ኢየሁለት: by twos, by pairs, two-and-two, every two, every couple, &c. &c.

በየሦስት: ቀን: every three days.

CHAP. III.

ON THE PRONOUNS.

1. The Amharic *Pronouns* are, as to their *logical* character, divided, as in other languages, into, 1. Personal; 2. Possessive; 3. Demonstrative; 4. Relative; 5. Interrogative; 6. Reflective; and 7. Distributive Pronouns. As to their *forms*, they are classed, as in other Semitic Languages, into Separable and Inseparable Pronouns. We begin with the *Separable Pronouns*. They are Personal, Possessive, Demonstrative, Interrogative, and Reflective.

Section I.

Separable Personal Pronouns.

They are Three for the Singular, and Three for the Plural. The Singular has some peculiarities. The First Person has not the Gender expressed: the Second and Third have distinct forms for the Masculine and for the Feminine Gender: the Second Person has, besides, three distinctions of honour, as the following Paradigm shows:

	SINGULAR.			PLURAL.
	Masc.	Com.	Fem.	Com.
1 Pers.		እኔ: I.		እኛ: we.
2 Pers.	አንተ:		አንቺ: / አንቺ: } thou.	እላንተ: you.
		አንቱ: / እርስዎ: } you.		
3 Pers.	እርሱ: he, it.		እርስዋ: she, it.	እርሳቸው: they.

Note. (*a*) On the application of the three different forms for the Second Person: አንተ: and አንቺ: are applied to inferiors, to God, to intimate friends; and in universal address, where you need not pay any regard to rank, &c. አንቱ: is used for a *lesser;* እርስዎ: for a *higher* degree of honour. These two forms resemble the German *Ihr* (in Switzerland *Er*), and *Sie*, and the Italian *Voi* and *Lei*, for the Second Person Singular.

(*b*) In speaking of a *distinguished* person, the form of the Third Person Plural is used, as a mark of honour.

2. The *Declension* is the same as with the Nouns.

SINGULAR.

	1st Pers. Com.	2d Pers. Masc. Fem.	2d Pers. Com.	3d Pers. Masc.	3d Pers. Fem.
N.	እኔ: I.	አንተ:: አንቺ: thou.	አንቱ:: እርስዎ: you.	እርሱ: he, it.	እርስዋ: she, it.
G.	የኔ: of me, my, mine.	ያንተ:: ያንቺ: of thee, thy, thine.	ያንቱ:: የርስዎ: of you, your, yours.	የርሱ: of him, it, his, its.	የርስዋ: of her, her, hers, its.
D.	ለኔ: to me, me.	ላንተ:: ላንቺ: to thee, thee.	ላንቱ:: ለርስዎ: to you, you.	ለርሱ: to him, him, it.	ለርስዋ: to her, her, it.
A.	እኔን: me.	አንተን:: አንችን: thee.	አንቱን:: እርስዎን: you.	እርሱን: him, it.	እርስዋን: her, it.

PLURAL.

	1 Pers.	2 Pers.	3 Pers.
Nom.	እኛ: we.	እላንተ: ye, you.	እርሳቸው:: they.
Gen.	የኛ:: of us, our, ours.	የላንተ:: of you, your, yours.	የርሳቸው:: of them, their, theirs.
Dat.	ለኛ: to us.	ለላንተ:: to you.	ለርሳቸው:: to them.
Acc.	እኛን: us.	እላንተን: you.	እርሳቸውን:: them.

Thus far the Separable Personal Pronouns. The Inseparable Personal Pronouns are those Verbal Suffixes which will be mentioned in their proper place.

SECTION II.

Separable Possessive Pronouns.

They are formed by the Genitive of the Personal Pronouns; and are as follows:

Singular.	Plural.
የኔ: my, mine.	የኛ: our, ours.
ያንተ: *m.* ያንቺ: *f.* thy, thine.	የላንቱ: your, yours.
ያንቱ:: የርሰዎ: your, yours.	
የርሱ: *m.* his. የርሷ: *f.* her, hers.	የርሳቸው: their, theirs.

SECTION III.

Demonstrative Pronouns.

They are two in number; one for near, and one for remote objects.

1. *Demonstrative for Near Objects.*

ይህ: *masc.* ይህች: or ይች: *fem.* "This."
Shoa Dialect: እዜህ: *masc.* እዜህች: *fem.*

DECLENSION.

COMMON FORM, IRREGULAR.

SINGULAR.

	Masc.	Fem.			
Nom.	ይህ::	ይህች:	contr.	ይች:	this.
Gen.	የዚህ::	የዚህች:	. .	የዚች:	of this.
Dat.	ለዚህ::	ለዚህች:	. .	ለዚች:	to this.
Acc.	ይህን: & ይህነን::	ይህችን:	. .	ይችን:	this.

PLURAL.
Common Gender.

Nom.	እለዚህ:	or	እነዚህ:	contr.	እሌህ:	these.
Gen.	የለዚህ:	. .	የነዚህ:	. .	የሌህ:	of these.
Dat.	ለለዚህ:	. .	ለነዚህ:	. .	ለሌህ:	to these.
Acc.	እለዚህን:	. .	እነዚህን:	. .	እሌህን:	these.

SHOA FORM, REGULAR.

	SINGULAR. Masc.	Fem.	PLURAL. Common.
N.	እዜህ:	እዜህች: this.	እለዜህ: or እነዜህ:
G.	የዜህ:	የዜህች: of this.	contr. እሌህ: &c. the same as above,
D.	ለዜህ:	ለዜህች: to this.	but the ዜ: prevailing throughout.
A	እዜህን:	እዜህችን: this.	

ANOTHER REGULAR FORM, OCCASIONALLY USED IN SHOA.

	SINGULAR. Masc.	Fem.			PLURAL. Com.		
N.	ይህ:	ይህች:	contr.	ይች::	እለየህ:	contr.	የሌህ:
G.	የይህ:	የይህች:	. .	የይች::	የለየህ:	. .	የሌህ:
D.	ለይህ:	ለይህች:	. .	ለይች::	ለለየህ:	. .	ለሌህ:
A.	ይህን: ይህነን::	ይህችን:	. .	ይችን:	እለየህን:	. .	እሌህን::

2. *For Remote Objects.*

	SINGULAR. Masc.	Fem.	PLURAL. Common.		
N.	ያ:	ያች: that.	እለዚያ: & እነዚያ:	contr.	እሊያ: those.
G.	የዚያ:	የዚያች: of that.	የለዚያ: & የነዚያ:	. .	የሊያ: of those.
D.	ለዚያ:	ለዚያች: to that.	ለለዚያ: & ለነዚያ:	. .	ለሊያ: to those.
A.	ያነን:	ያችን: that.	እለዚያን: & እነዚያን:	. .	እሊያን: those.

FORM OCCASIONALLY OCCURRING IN SHOA.

	SINGULAR. Masc.	Fem.	PLURAL.
N.	እዛ:	እዛች: that.	Like the above, only contracting ዚያ: to ዛ::
G.	የዛ:	የዛች: of that.	
D.	ለዛ:	ለዛች: to that.	
A.	እዛን:	እዛችን: that.	

NOTE.—The Demonstrative Pronouns form Adverbs; which see, under the head of Adverbs.

SECTION IV.

Interrogative Pronouns.

There are four: One Personal, ማን: *pl.* እለማን: "who?" "which?" "what sort of?" One Impersonal, ምን: "which?" "what?" One Common, የት: "what?" "which?" One Universal, ምንድር: "what?"

The Personal is ማን: "who?" "which?" *e.g.*

ማን: አደረገ: ይህነን: *Who* did this?

ይህ: ማን: ነው: (or ማነው:) *Who* is this?

ከሁለቱ: ማን: *Which* of both?

The Impersonal is ምን: "which?" "what?" *e.g.*

ምን: አደረግህ: *What* hast thou done?

ምን: ቤት: *Which* house?

The Universal Interrogative Pronoun is ምንድር፡ "what?" *e.g.*

ይህ፡ ምንድር፡ ነው፡ *What* is this?

ማን፡ and ምን፡ are declinable, thus:

SINGULAR.

	Pers.	Impers.
Nom.	ማን፡ who? which?	ምን፡ what? which?
Gen.	የማን፡ of whom? whose? of which?	የምን፡ of what? of which? whose?
Dat.	ለማን፡ to (for) whom? to (for) which?	ለምን፡ to (for) what? to (for) which? wherefore?
Acc.	ማንን፡ whom? which?	ምንን፡ what? which?

PLURAL.

Nom.	እለማን፡ who? which?	እለምን፡ which?
Gen.	የለማን፡ whose? of which?	የለምን፡ of which? whose?
Dat.	ለለማን፡ to whom? to which?	ለለምን፡ to which?
Acc.	እለማንን፡ whom? which?	እለምንን፡ which?

ምንድር፡ has no Plural; and is defective in the Singular, having no Accusative Case.

Besides the preceding, they have the Interrogative Pronoun የት፡ or Euphonic የቱ፡ "what?" "who?" "which?" It is indeclinable, and used chiefly in forming Adverbs, by joining with Prepositions; as, እንዴት፡ ወዴት፡ &c.

SECTION V.

Reflective Pronouns.

They are three, ባለቤት፡፡ ራስ፡ and ነፍስ፡ with the signification of *self.* They assume the Suffixes of the Possessive Pronoun, as in the English *myself, thyself,* &c. So is in all Abyssinia ራስ፡ with Suffixes ራሴ፡ ራስህ፡ ራስሽ፡ ራሰው፡ ራሷ፡ ራስዋ፡ ራሳችን፡ ራሳችሁ፡ ራሳቸው፡ "myself," "thyself," &c. ባለቤት፡, with Suffixes, is not used in Shoa; but in N.W. Abyssinia, it is common. ነፍስ፡ with Suffixes is used in all Abyssinia, though not so often as ራስ፡፡ But the reflective mode of speaking is more frequently used in Verbs, without these Pronouns, as will be shown afterwards.

SECTION VI.

Distributive Separable Pronoun.

This is እያንዳንድ፡ "each," "every," with Suffixes. As it is composed of a double አንድ፡ and the distributive እያ፡, it has been numbered already among the Distributive Numerals.

Section VII.

Indefinite Pronouns.

These are the following:

መንም: any, each, every one, whoever, whosoever.

ማናቸው: *m.* ማናቸይቱ: *fem.* whosoever.

ሁሉ: all, each, every, any.

ሌላ: other.

አንዳች: some, something.

1. መንም: ማናቸው: and ማናቸዪቱ: are used only in the Singular, nor receive they any Suffix. When used with the Verb in the negative, they adopt the reverse to their natural signification, "none," "none whatever."

2. ሁሉ: is rather the Substantive ሁሌ: "totality," with Suffixes. It assumes all Suffixes, and is declinable; but has no Plural.

3. ሌላ: is used in both the Plural and the Singular Numbers, and is declinable.

4. አንዳች: is declinable, and used only in the Singular.

5. አያሌ: "some," "several," is declinable, and has but one number. Besides this, the words, "some" and "such," are circumscribed by Verbs; *e.g.* "Some men like it," የሚወዷት: አሉ: *lit.* "There are men who like it." "Such:" እንዲህ: ያለ: or *pl.* እንዲህ: ያሉ:: "who is," or "who are so."

Section VIII.

Inseparable Pronouns.

They are, with regard to their character, Personal, Possessive, Relative, and Distributive; and with regard to their position, they are either Prefixes or Suffixes.

1. *Personal Suffixes to Verbs.**

They consist partly in modifications of the Personal Pronoun; and are annexed to any part of the Verb except the Infinitive; for that Mood, being considered in this respect as a Noun, assumes Nominal Suffixes.

---

* We do not speak of those personal designations the Verbs receive at their beginning or end; because they are so intimately connected with the Verb, that we cannot consider them separately.

The following Table contains them all:

	SINGULAR. Masc.	Fem.	Com.	PLURAL. Com.
3.	ăው፡ ት፡ him.	āት፡ her.		āቸው፡ them.
2.	ህ፡ thee.	ሽ፡ thee.		
.. honorif. 1.	. . . . . .		āችሁ፡ you.	āችሁ፡ you.
. . . . . . 2.	. . . . . .		ăዎ፡ you.	
1.	. . . .		ኝ፡ me.	ን፡ perfect. ን፡ pres. &c., us.

	SINGULAR.		PLURAL.
Suff. 1.	ጠበቀኝ፡ he protected *me*.	1.	ጠበቀን፡ he protected *us*.
			ጠብቁን፡ (*imp.*) protect *us!*
.. 2.	ጠበቀህ፡ } he protected		
. . . .	ጠበቀሽ፡ } *thee*.	2.	ጠበቃችሁ፡ he protected *you*.
. . . . hon.	ጠበቃችሁ፡ } he protect-		
	ጠበቀዎ፡ } ed *you*.		
.. 3.	ጠበቀው፡ { he protected *him*.	3.	ጠበቃቸው፡ he protected *them*.
	ጠበቃት፡ he protected *her*.		

NOTE.—Suffix 3d pers. sing. masc. to Prepositions has ት፡; *e.g.*

በት፡ in him. ለት፡ to, or for him.

---

2. *Possessive Suffixes to Nouns.*

They are, to a certain degree, similar to the preceding.

	SINGULAR. Masc.	Fem.	Com.	PLURAL. Com.
3.	ů (3), or ăው፡ his.	ዋ፡ her.		3. āቸው፡ their.
.. hon.	. . . .		āቸው፡ his, her.	
2. com.	ህ፡ thy.	ሽ፡ thy.		2. āችሁ፡ your.
.. hon. 1.	. . . . . .		āችሁ፡ your.	
.. .. 2.	. . . .		ăዎ፡ your.	
1.	. . . .		ê፡ my.	1. āችን፡ our.

Ex.—ቤት፡ "House," with Suffixes.

	SINGULAR. Masc.	Fem.	Com.	PLURAL. Com.
3.	ቤቱ፡ his house.	ቤትዋ፡ her house.		ቤታቸው፡ their h.
.. hon.	. . . .		ቤታቸው፡ his (her) h.	
2.	ቤትህ፡	ቤትሽ፡ thy house.		ቤታችሁ፡ your h.
.. hon. 1.	. . . .		ቤታችሁ፡ your h.	
.. .. 2.	. . . .		ቤትዎ፡ your house.	
1.	. . . .		ቤቴ፡ my house.	ቤታችን፡ our h.

3. *Prefixed Relative Pronouns.*

There are two; *i.e.* የ: for the Preterite, and የም: for the rest; *e.g.* የመጣ: ሰው: "the man who came." የሚመጣ: ቀን: "The day which comes"; *i.e.* "the coming," "following day." See more under the Verbs.

4. *Prefixed Distributive Pronoun.*

There is but one, which has been mentioned already, under the Numerals: it is, እየ: or ኢየ:: ኢየሦስት: ቀን: "Every three days." Prepositions have the power of absorbing the first letter; when care must be taken not to confound the remaining የ— with the Relative Pronoun; bearing in mind, that the Relative itself would be absorbed by the Preposition: nor stands it, except before Verbs.

CHAP. IV.

ON THE VERBS.

The Verb being, next to the Noun, the most essential part of speech, we are to give it our fullest consideration. In entering upon it, we treat, 1. On its Formation and Quality; 2. On the Derivations, or different Forms or Voices of Verbs; 3. On their Flexion; 4. On their Conjugation; 5. On the Affixion of Pronouns to Verbs.

SECTION I.

Formation and Quality of Verbs.

1. The Verb, in general, seems to represent the chief developement of those roots of the language which are contained in the Noun. The original idea of the Noun is exhibited as a thing of time, found in a certain condition, and undergoing or producing various actions and changes. This consideration implies, that the Verb, in general, originates in the Noun. In the Hebrew, we can trace its course from the Primitive Nominal Form, through the Participle (in Kal), to the 3d pers. masc. preterite; the latter being, in all the Semitic Languages, the grammatical root of the Verb. In the Amharic, the Constructive Mood, of which we shall speak afterwards, seems to be the medium of transition from the Primitive Noun to the 3d pers. masc. preterite of the Verb.

2. Now the latter, the 3d masc. pers. sing. of the preterite in the Simple Forms of Verbs, constitutes, as has been just now alluded to, the origin of all the other Verbal Forms; the same as, in our languages, the Infinitive; or in the Greek, the Latin, the Italian, and others, the 1st pers. sing. of the present tense: on this account it is put forward, for grammatical and

lexical purposes, as the radix, or rather (because the true radices of the Verbs are contained in the Noun) as the stem, from which all the other forms branch off. In the Amharic, it presents various formations, as well as the Noun—bilitera, trilitera, quadrilitera, and plurilitera: but in it, as well as in the Noun, the majority consists of triliteral forms; which majority is still augmented, whenever the present contracted biliteral forms, and many pluriliterals evidently amplified, are restored to their original fulness or simplicity.

3. In reference to *Quality*, then, the Verbs present two grand divisions; *i.e. Perfect* and *Imperfect* Verbs, which again may be sub-divided in other classes. *Perfect* Verbs are those which are flexible in, at least, several Derivations, and throughout all the Moods, Tenses, and Persons in Conjugation, without losing any of their Radicals. *Imperfect* Verbs are either Defective, Augmented, or Irregular.

NOTE.—(*a*) Perfect Verbs may be divided into Primitives, *i.e.* whose origin cannot be traced to any further root; and Derivatives, which have for their origin either a Noun (Denominatives), or another Verb (Verbals). We subjoin here a few specimens of each.

PRIMITIVES.

ቀበረ: he buried.	ቀሠፈ: he chastised.
መለሰ: he turned, returned.	ሸፈነ: he covered.
ሰገደ: he worshipped.	

DENOMINATIVES.

	Original Noun.
ከበረ: he was honoured.	ክብር: honour.
ገለጸ: he revealed.	ግልጽ: the public.
መሰከረ: he testified.	ምስክር: witness.
ሰነበተ: he remained.	ሰንበት: Sabbath.
በረከተ: was flatulent.	በረከት: blessing.
አመሰቀለ: crucified.	መስቀል: cross, crucifix.

VERBS DERIVED FROM VERBS.

	Original Verb.
መሰገነ: he was glorious.	ገነ: it flourished, he was glorious.
መሠረተ: he laid a foundation.	ሠራ: he built.

(*b*) Under Defective Verbs, we mean, (1) Those which occasionally lose some of the Radicals; and (2) Such as have not all the Moods or Tenses, or Persons in conjugation. They will be mentioned in their proper places.

(c) Irregular Verbs are of various kinds:

A. Such in which the Afformatives are irregular.

B. Such as have either the first or second, or second and third Radical Letters contracted.

C. Geminants.

D. Reduplicated and Transposed forms.

All these will be exhibited, with their respective Conjugations, after the Regular or Perfect Verb.

Section II.

Various Derivations, or different Forms or Voices of Verbs.

1. In every language, the original idea of a Verb must be determinable by the relation of the subject to the object; and those various relations must be in some way or other expressible by the form of the Verb. The state of any subject of speech, or its action, is either confined to itself, or it exerts an influence on an object, or is itself the object of extraneous influence. This circumstance renders, in every language, three classes of Verbs, or three conditions of the same verb, necessary; *i.e.* neutrality (immanence), action upon other objects, and suffering. In the English Grammars, these qualities are called *Voices*; in the Semitic languages, *Conjugations*, or better, *Derivations*.

2. The ways to express these Voices are different in different languages, according to the pliability and vigour the latter possess.

The more original and vigorous a language is, we conceive, the more will it be able to derive all it requires, for the purpose of expressing the various relations of the verb, from the original verb itself, without the assistance of auxiliaries, and without circumscription: and this seems to show the superiority of the Semitic over the European Languages; because the former fully possess that power, while the latter are deficient in it.

In the English, the Passive Voice is not expressible, but by the Auxiliary *To be*. The Greek language has the power of expressing it by a change of the Active in the termination, converting ω in *ομαι*, &c. The Transitive is, in a few instances, formed by a change of the vowel, as "to fell" (*i.e.* make fall), from "to fall"; sometimes by Prepositions, as "to *en*force," "to *be*labour," &c.; but, on the whole, European languages are deficient in this respect.

3. In the Semitic languages, the form of the original verb is altered, either by the mere change of vowels in the same radical consonants, or by an addition of servile letters with a suitable change of vowels, in order to express the various determinations and modifications, *i. e.* Voices or Conjugations, of which the verb is susceptible. Of these derivations, the

Hebrew Verb has seven; the Arabic, thirteen; the Ethiopic, ten different forms. For the Amharic, Ludolf has assigned but four Conjugations; but an attention to the following will show that there are many more.

4. As the Triliterals are the most numerous and the most perfect words, we present the reader, first, with a list of all the Forms of Conjugation, to which the perfect Triliteral Verb is liable. And since all these forms do not proceed from any single stem, we take several stems together. The Verbs which will serve us for this purpose are the following:

መለሰ፡ *act.* he returned. ሰበረ፡ he burst.
ከበረ፡ he was glorious, respectable. (ደረገ፡ non occ.)
ሰደበ፡ he reviled. አደረገ፡ he did.
ነገረ፡ he said. ደነዘ፡ was blunt.
መጐተ፡ he contradicted. ፈተለ፡ spun.
መሰለ፡ he resembled. በረቀ፡ he fulminated.*
ወረደ፡ he descended.

LIST OF CONJUGATIONS OF THE REGULAR AND PERFECT TRILITERAL VERB.

I. መለሰ፡ *act.* "he returned," "repeated." ከበረ፡ *neut.* "he was respectable."

II. ሳደበ፡ *intens.* "he scolded exceedingly."

III. አከበረ፡ *trs.* "he honoured."

IV. ተመለሰ፡ *pass.* "was returned." *refl.* "returned."

V. አናገረ፡ *trs.* & *caus.* "he made speak," "caused to speak."

VI. ተናገረ፡ *contin.* "he spoke." *intens.* ተሳደበ፡ "reviled," "blasphemed;" *i.q.* ሳደበ። ተማከረ፡ *recipr.* "he counselled," "gave and took advice."

VII. ተሞዋገተ፡ *recipr.* "he disputed."

VIII. አስመለሰ፡ *caus.* "he caused to return."

---

* These are the known forms of each of these Verbs: መለሰ፡ ተመለሰ፡ አስመለሰ፡ ተመላለሰ፡ ተመለሰሰ። ከበረ፡ አከበረ፡ አስከበረ። ሰደበ፡ ሳደበ፡ አሰደበ፡ ተሰደበ፡ አሳደበ፡ ተሳደበ። ነገረ፡ አናገረ፡ ተናገረ፡ ተናጋገረ፡ ደነገረ፡ አደነገራ፡ አወሸነገረ። መጐተ፡ ተመጐተ፡ ተሞዋገተ። መሰለ፡ ተመሰለ፡ አስመሰለ፡ አስመሳለ። ወረደ፡ አወረደ፡ አዋረደ፡ ተዋረደ፡ ተዋዋረደ፡ ወራረደ። ሰበረ፡ አሰበረ፡ ተሰበረ፡ ሰባበረ፡ ተሰባበረ። (ደረገ፡) አደረገ፡ ተደረገ፡ አስደረገ፡ አደራረገ። ደነዘ፡ አደነዘ፡ ደነዘዘ፡ አደነዘዘ። ፈተለ፡ ተፈተለ፡ አስፈተለ፡ ፈተለተለ፡ ተፈተለተለ። በረቀ፡ አንጸበረቀ።

IX. አስመሰለ: *caus.* & *intens.* "he caused to resemble," "dissimulated," "flattered."

X. አስተነገረ: *caus.* "he made speak." አስተሰረየ: "procured forgiveness." አስተነፈሰ: *reiter.* "he inhaled and exhaled," "he respired," "breathed."

XI. ተዋዋረደ: *intens., pass.,* & *refl.,* "he was completely humbled," "humbled himself completely."

XII. ሰባበረ: *intens.* "broke into pieces."

XIII. አደራረገ: *intens.* "he performed great things."

XIV. ተመላለሰ: *reiter.* "he returned repeatedly;" *i. e.* "walked." ተመካከረ: *recipr.* "he consulted with others," "took and gave advice."

XV. ተናጋገረ: *reiter.* & *recipr.* "conversed with another," "spoke frequently."

XVI. ደነዘዘ: *intens.* & *intrans.* "to be blunt," "stiff," "obdurate."

XVII. አደነዘዘ: *trs.* "to blunt," "stiffen," "obdurate."

XVIII. ተመለሰሰ: *refl.* & *pass.* "he returned," "was returned."

XIX. ተሸማጠጠ: "he reviled."

XX. አደናገረ: *intens.* "he talked one out of any thing," "dissuaded."

XXI. አወሸናገረ: "he folded his hands."

XXI. ፈተለተለ: "he rubbed thin between his fingers."

XXII. ተፈተለተለ: *pass.* "it was rubbed thin between the fingers."

XXIII. አንጸበረቀ: *diminut.* "it shone," "glittered," "sparkled," "resplended."

These Forms are not of equally frequent occurrence. Those occurring most frequently, are, Nos. I. III. IV. V. VI. VIII. X. XIV. and XV. The rest are more rare.*

5. Observations on this List:—Most of the forms it contains are analogous to the forms of derivation in the Hebrew, the Arabic, and more especially in the Ethiopic Verb; which will be evident from the following remarks:

I. መለሰ: comprises the Ethiopic and Arabic I. and II. forms, and the Hebrew *Kal* and *Piēl.*

---

* We beg to observe here, that, on account of the haste in which the Dictionary was prepared for press, the Forms XVI. to XXIII. were not arranged in it under their roots; as the Author was not then aware, that they were simple derivations from the Triliteral Verb. To this conviction he arrived when drawing up this Grammar.

II. ሳደበ፡, of rare occurrence, answers the Ethiopic and Arabic III. form, ጋበረ፡ and فَاعَلَ.

III. አከበረ፡ answers to the Ethiopic IV. and V., and to the Arabic IV.

IV. ተመለሰ፡ corresponds with the Eth. VI. and VII., and with the Arabic V.

V. አናገረ፡ "he made speak," answers the Arabic XI.

VI. ተናገረ፡ "he spoke," answers the Eth. VII. ተጋበረ፡ and Arabic VI. تَفَاعَلَ.

VII. ተጐቀገተ፡ seldom occurs, and has no correspondent in the other languages.

VIII. IX. and X. answer the Ethiopic and Arabic X. አስተገበረ፡፡ إِسْتَفْعَلَ.

The rest are peculiar to the Amharic; although modifications of the same forms occur, especially in the Arabic.

6. Before we proceed, we notice the Conjugations of the other classes of Verbs:

I. TRILITERALS WHOSE FIRST RADICAL IS A GUTTURAL.

They are affected by the rules laid down in Part I. Ch. VII. 2. B. 3. C.

The following list contains their several conjugations:

Radices, አመነ፡ "he believed"; and አለፈ፡ "he passed."

I. አመነ፡ "he believed."

II. ታመነ፡ "he was believed," "creditable," "trustworthy"; "he entrusted."

III. አሳመነ፡ "he persuaded," "he made believe."

IV. አስታመነ፡ "he entrusted," "accredited," "attested."

V. ተላለፈ፡ "he trespassed," "varied."

VI. አስተላለፈ፡ *recipr.* & *trs.* "he made pass in different ways."*

* Other Verbs of this class: አረመ፡ አረሰ፡ አረቀ፡ አረዘ፡ አረደ፡ አረገ፡ አረጠ፡ ዐረፈ፡ አቀፈ፡ አበረ፡ አበደ፡ አበጠ፡ አተመ፡ አነሰ፡ አነቀ፡ አነጸ፡ አከለ፡ አወቀ፡ አወከ፡ አዘለ፡ አዘነ፡ አደላ፡ አደመ፡ አደረ፡ አደሰ፡ አደነ፡ አደገ፡ አደፈ፡ አገመ፡ አገዘ፡ አጠረ፡ አጸረ፡ አጠነ፡ አጨደ፡ አጸፈ፡ አጸበ፡ አፈረ፡ ዐበየ፡ ዐረቀ፡፡ The Dictionary shows, that the original Forms of these Verbs are not all of prima አ፡; but in the Amharic, they may be all comprised in this form.

II. GEMINANT TRILITERALS.

They are originally Biliterals, whose second radical letter has been doubled. See Part I. Ch. VII. 2. D.

List of Triliteral Geminants.

I. **ለቀቀ፡** *intrs.* & *act.* "went away," "dismissed."

II. **አረቀቀ፡** *trs.* "he thinned," "rarefied."

III. **ተለቀቀ፡** *pass.* "he was dismissed"; *refl.* "he abandoned himself."

IV. **አላቀቀ፡** *intens.* "he yawned." **አሳደደ፡** "he persecuted."

V. **ተሳደደ፡** *pass. int.* "he was persecuted."

VI. **አስመረረ፡** *caus.* "he embittered," "exasperated."

VII. **አንሻተተ፡** "he glided down" on his posteriors; "he cheated."

VIII. **ተንሻተተ፡** *pass.* "he was pushed down," "was cheated."

ተንጋለለ፡ "he fornicated."

IX. **አንጠራራ፡**
X. **ተንጠራራ፡** } "stretched himself." *

III. GEMINANTS WHOSE FIRST RADICAL IS A GUTTURAL. †

I. **አመመ፡** *intrs.* "was painful"; *trs.* "gave pain."

II. **ታመመ፡** *pass.* "felt pain."

III. **አሳመመ፡** *caus.* "gave pain," "made sick."

IV. **አስታመመ፡** *sympathetic,* "nursed sick persons."

IV. PERFECT BILITERALS. ‡

I. **ገነ፡** "was beautiful." **ደገ፡** "was great."

II. **አገነ፡** "beautified," "praised." **አደገ፡** "he grew."

III. **ተሰጠ፡** "was given."

---

* These Verbs are very numerous. Cf. in the Dictionary ለቀቀ፡ ለከከ፡ ለጠጠ፡ መረረ፡ መነነ፡ መዘዘ፡ መጸጸ፡ ረቀቀ፡ ዘለለ፡ ሰለለ፡ ሰረረ፡ ሰቀቀ፡ ሰደደ፡ ሰፈፈ፡ ሸለለ፡ ሸረረ፡ ሸተተ፡ ቀለለ፡ ቀደደ፡ በረረ፡ ባነነ፡ ታለለ፡ ነበበ፡ ናዘዘ፡ ነደደ፡ ነጠጠ፡ ከረረ፡ ከሰሰ፡ ከበበ፡ ከተተ፡ ኰነነ፡ ወረረ፡ ወደደ፡ ዘፈፈ፡ ደሰሰ፡ ደቀቀ፡ ገለለ፡ ጐለለ፡ ገረረ፡ ጎተተ፡ ገደደ፡ ጐደደ፡ ገፈፈ፡ ጠመመ፡ ጠራራ፡ ጸበበ፡ ጠበበ፡ ጸለለ፡ ጸገገ፡ ፈዘዘ፡

† አመመ፡ አለለ፡ አበበ፡ አከከ፡ አዘዘ።

‡ ገነ፡ ደገ፡ መሸ፡ ሸሸ፡ ረጨ፡ ሰጠ፡ ሸረ፡ ሸኘ፡ ቀረ፡ ቀኘ፡ በጀ፡ በጠ፡ ተኘ፡ ነጨ፡ ጠጠ።

IV. አስገነ፡ "he beautified," "glorified."

V. አሳደገ፡ "made grow," "trained," "educated."

VI. ገነነ፡ "flourished."

VII. አገነነ፡ "made to flourish."

VIII. ተሰጣጠ፡ "to betray each other."

V. IMPERFECT BILITERALS. Prima አ፡፡

I. አየ፡ "he saw."

II. ታየ፡ *pass.* "was seen," "appeared."

III. አሳየ፡ *trs.* "made to see," "showed."

IV. አስታየ፡ *trs.* "made to be seen," "brought into sight."

V. ታያየ፡ *recipr.* "looked at each other," "was over against each other." "made look at each other."

VI. DEFECTIVE VERBS; *i.e. Verbs which have dropped one or two Radical Letters, either in the middle or at the end.*

1. *Verbs with Absorbed Guttural at the end.*

I. ገባ፡ *intrs.* "he entered." Eth. ገብአ፡

II. አገባ፡ *trs.* "he introduced."

III. ተገባ፡ "it was proper," "becoming," "it belonged."

IV. አጋባ፡ *act.* "he married."

V. ተጋባ፡ *pass.* "was married."

VI. አስገባ፡ *caus.* "made go in," "introduced."

VII. በቃቃ፡ *intens.* "was quite sufficient."

VIII. አገባባ፡ *reiter.* "used to marry," "frequently cohabited," "behaved properly."

IX. አጸናና፡ *intens.* "he comforted."

X. ተጸናና፡ *pass.* "was comforted." ተከፋፋ፡ *recipr.* "quarrelled with each other."*

---

* Of the same class are the following: ገባ፡ ከፋ፡ ገፋ፡ ነፋ፡ ጸላ፡ ጸራ፡ መራ፡ ነሣ፡ ለማ፡ ለካ፡ መላ፡ በላ፡ መታ፡ መጣ፡ ነካ፡ ነቃ፡ መኛ፡ መካ፡ ሠራ፡ ሰራ፡ ሠዋ፡ ረሳ፡ ረባ፡ ረታ፡ ረካ፡ ረዳ፡ ረጋ፡ ሰላ፡ ሰማ፡ ሠሣ፡ ሰባ፡ ሰካ፡ ሰፋ፡ ቀላ፡ ቀማ፡ ቀባ፡ ቀና፡ ቀዳ፡ ቀጣ፡ በራ፡ በሳ፡ በቃ፡ በካ፡ በዛ፡ በዣ፡ በጣ፡ ተላ፡ ተጋ፡ ተፋ፡ ነዳ፡ ነጸ፡ ነጋ፡ ሓማ፡ ከሳ፡ ከዳ፡ ወቃ፡ ወዛ፡ ወራ፡ ወጋ፡ ወጣ፡ ዘማ፡ ዘራ፡ ዘጋ፡ ደፋ፡ ጎሣ፡ ገራ፡ ገዛ፡ ፈራ፡ &c.

2. *Verbs with Absorbed Guttural in the middle.*

I. ማለ፡ Eth. መሐለ፡ "he swore."

II. አማለ፡ *trs.* "made swear," "administered an oath."

III. ተማለ፡ *pass.* "was sworn."

IV. አስማለ፡ *trs.* "made swear."

V. አጣጣለ፡ *frequentat.* "distributed by casting lots."

VI. ተማማለ፡ *recipr.* "mutually swore," "conspired."

VII. ተማለለ፡ *intens.* "besought," "adjured." *

3. *Verbs with an Absorbed* የ፡ *in the middle.* †

I. ሼጠ፡ *act.* "he sold." ሔደ፡ *neutr.* "he went."

II. አሔደ፡ *trs.* "he made go," "drove the threshing oxen."

III. ተሼሔ፡ *pass.* "was sold."

IV. ተሻየጠ፡ "he traded." ተካየደ፡ "made a treaty."

V. አስሔደ፡ *caus.* "made go."

4. *Verbs with an Absorbed* ወ፡ *in the middle* ‡.

I. ቆመ፡ *neut.* "he stood.

II. አቆመ፡ *trs.* "made to stand," "erected."

III. ተቆመ፡ *pass.* "was erected.

IV. ተቃወመ፡ *intens.* "he withstood," "resisted."

V. አስቈየ፡ *caus.* "he detained," "caused to wait.

VI. ተቋቈመ፡ } *intens.* "ultimately resisted."
VII. ተቋቋመ፡ }

5. *Verbs with two Absorbed Gutturals,* derived from Quadriliterals. They are but few in number, and only three Conjugations have been discovered §.

I. ላላ፡ "to be loose," "lax."

II. አላላ፡ *act.* "to loosen," "slacken."

III. ተጋጫ፡ *intens.* "to stamp," "pound," "clapper," "to chatter."

---

* See also the following Verbs: ላሰ፡ ላቀ፡ ላከ፡ ላጠ፡ ላፈ፡ ማለ፡ ማረ፡ ማሰ፡ ናቀ፡ ማገ፡ ማፀ፡ ሣለ፡ ራቀ፡ ራበ፡ ሳለ፡ ሳማ፡፡ ሳቀ፡ ሳበ፡ ሳተ፡ ሳነ፡ ሻለ፡ ሻረ፡ ሻተ፡ ቻለ፡ ናደ፡ ካሰ፡ ካደ፡ ዋለ፡ ዋሰ፡ ዋኘ፡ ዋጠ፡ ዛገ፡ ዳረ፡ ዳሰ፡ ዳነ፡ ጋለ፡ ጋተ፡ ጋዘ፡ ጣለ፡፡

† ሼጠ፡ ሔደ፡ (ኼደ፡) ሌለ፡ ሼነ፡ ጤሰ፡ ፌዘ፡፡

‡ ሆነ፡ ሞቀ፡ ሞተ፡ ሮጠ፡ ሾመ፡ ቆመ፡ ቆየ፡ ኖረ፡ ኰረ፡ ዞረ፡ ጾመ፡፡

§ ላላ፡ ራራ፡ ሳሳ፡ ባባ፡፡ ዋጀ፡፡

6. *Verbs doubly imperfect.*

(*a*) Beginning with an አ: and having an Absorbed Guttural at the end. There are but few (አየ: and አለ: not being included): አጣ: አማ: አጪ::

I. አጣ: *negat.* "to want."

II. ታጣ: *neg. pass.* "to be wanted."

III. አሳጣ: *caus.* "to deprive."

(*b*) *Beginning with* የ: *which absorbs a Guttural.*

I. ያዘ: Eth. አኀዘ:: *act.* "to seize."

II. አያዘ: *trs.* "caused another to seize."

III. ተያዘ: *pass.* "was seized."

IV. አስያዘ: *caus.* "caused to seize," "betrayed."

V. ተያያዘ: *pass. frequentat.* & *recipr.* "was frequently or alternately seized," "seized frequently," "completely," or "reciprocally."

(c) *Various forms of the Verb* አለ: "*To say.*"

Not to be confounded with the Auxiliary አለ: "To be." Its forms are partly derived from አለ:, partly from ብህለ: Eth.

I. አለ: "he said."

II. አበለ: "to deceive by talking."

III. ተባለ: "to be said," "called."

IV. ታበለ: "to be deceived."

V. ተባላ: "to rumour in public."

VI. ተባበለ: } *recipr.* "to say to each other."
VII. ተባባለ: }

VIII. አባበለ: "he persuaded."

IX. ታለለ: "he was talked into any thing," "was persuaded."

X. አታለለ: "he persuaded," "cheated by talking."

(*d*) Conjugation of the Verb ቶወ:: and መጣ::

VII. VARIOUS CONJUGATIONS OF QUADRILITERAL AND PLURILITERAL VERBS.

1. *Reduplicated and Transposed Biliterals.*

Stems: ለመለመ: "to be green." ለቀለቀ: "to bedaub." ነቀነቀ: "to shake." በደበደ: "to cudgel." ቀሰቀሰ: "to excavate." ቀጠቀጠ: "to bruise." (ከረከረ::)

I. ለመለመ: *neut.* "it was green," "fresh."

II. አለመለመ: *trs.* "he made green," "verdant," "refreshed."

III. ተለቀለቀ፡ *pass.* "he was bedaubed."

IV. አነቃነቀ፡ *act. intens.* "he shook."

V. ተለቃለቀ፡ *refl.* "bedaubed," "washed himself."

VI. አስለቀለቀ፡ *caus.* "he caused bedaubing."

VII. አንበደበደ፡ *act.* "beat," "shook."

VIII. ተንቀጠቀጠ፡ *pass.* & *neutr.* "trembled."

IX. አንቀሳቀሰ፡ *act.* "he stirred," "moved."

X. ተንቀሳቀሰ፡ *pass.* & *neutr.* "was moved," "moved."

XI. አሳንቀሳቀሰ፡ *trs.* "he moved."*

2. *Derivates from Triliterals having one Radical doubled and transposed.*

I. ደሎደመ፡ *neut.* "it was blunt."

II. አደሎደመ፡ *trs.* "he blunted."

III. ተደሎደመ፡ *pass.* "was blunted."

IV. አከናወነ፡ *trs.* "he gave success."

V. ተከናወነ፡ *neut.* "he succeeded," "prospered."

VI. አንገረገበ፡ *neutr.* "it became knotty."

But few verbs belong to this class.

3. *Geminants.*

We rank under this class only such forms as cannot, with our present knowledge of the language, be considered to belong to Form XVI. of the regular Triliteral Verb. This class is but small:

I. ኰበለለ፡ *intrans.* "he fled," "escaped."

II. ተደመሰሰ፡ *pass.* "was destroyed."

---

* The Verbs of this class are very numerous. The following do belong to them:
መረመረ፡ መነመነ፡ ረበረበ፡ ሰበሰበ፡ ቀለቀለ፡ ቈረቈረ፡ ቈሰቈሰ፡ በረበረ፡ በሰበሰ፡ ጠመጠመ፡ ጐበጐበ፡ በዘበዘ፡ በጠበጠ፡ ተረተረ፡ ጠቀጠቀ፡ ጐነጐነ፡ ተበተበ፡ ተከተከ፡ ጠረጠረ፡ ተፈተፈ፡ ጠበጠበ፡ ገዘገዘ፡ ጠፈጠፈ፡ ጐደጐደ፡ ነሰነሰ፡ ነዘነዘ፡ ገለገለ፡ ከለከለ፡ ጠለጠለ፡ ከረከረ፡ ኰረኰረ፡ ኰደኰደ፡ ወለወለ፡ ወዘወዘ፡ ጨመጨመ፡ ጨበጨበ፡ ጦሎጦለ፡ ወረወረ፡ ዘበዘበ፡ ዘፈዘፈ፡ ደለደለ፡ ደረደረ፡ ደበደበ፡ ጨፈጨፈ፡ ደፈደፈ፡ ደነደነ፡ ጀፈጀፈ፡ ገመገመ፡ ጐረጐረ፡ ገሰገሰ፡ ፈለፈለ፡ ፈረፈረ፡ ፈገፈገ። And the Augmented Forms: አሽከረከረ፡ (for አስከረከረ፡) ተቅበዘበዘ።

III. ተኈማለለ: *neutr.* "walked nimbly," "affectedly," "proudly."
IV. አስጠነቀቀ: *trs.* "he warned," "cautioned."
V. አንኸባለለ: *act.* "he rolled about."
VI. ተንኸባለለ: *pass.* "was rolled about."

4. *Quadriliterals and Pluriliterals of different Radicals.*

I. መሰገነ: *neutr.* "was glorious."
II. አመሰገነ: *trs.* "he glorified."
III. ተመሰገነ: *pass.* "he was glorified."
IV. አሰናበተ: *intens.* "he dismissed."
V. ተሰናበተ: *pass.* "he was dismissed," "took his leave."
VI. አስመሰገነ: *caus.* "he caused to glorify."
VII. ገለባበጠ: *intens.* "he overthrew completely."
VIII. ተገለባበጠ: *pass. intens.* "he was completely overthrown."
IX. ተሰናባበተ: *recipr.* & *reiter.* "took leave from each other." *

Section III.

On the Flexion of Verbs.

The Flexion of Verbs treats on their *Moods, Tenses, Numbers,* and *Persons.*

1. *Moods of the Amharic Verb.*

The Amharic Verb has Seven Moods: (*a*) the *Indicative;* (*b*) the *Contingent;* (*c*) the *Subjunctive;* (*d*) the *Constructive;* (*e*) the *Imperative;* (*f*) the *Infinitive;* (*g*) the *Participle.*

---

* 1. This class is most numerous, and comprises a great variety of Verbs, as the following List will show: መረኮዘ: መሰኸረ: መሰኸወ: መነኩሰ: መነዘሀ: ሰበቀለ: ሰንከለ: ሰነዘረ: ሰነገለ: ሰነጠቀ: ሸመገለ: ሸነከረ: ሸነገለ: ቀለበሰ: ቀለወጠ: ቀለጠፈ: ቀመጠለ: ቁረጠመ: ቀባጠረ: በረኸተ: ተረጉመ: ተነኩለ: ቸነከረ: አመለከ: አነከሰ: አነጠሰ: ወነጀለ: (ወነገለ:) ዘነበለ: ዘነጉረ: ደነቁረ: ደነገዘ: ደነገጠ: ጉለመሰ: ጉነቁለ: ጉነበሰ: ጉነደለ: ጉነጸፈ: ጠረቀመ: ጠየወተ: ጨነገፈ: ጸወለገ: ፈነተረ: ፈነቀለ።

2. Most of the forms comprised in this List are Derivative; either from Nouns, as መሰኸረ: መነኩሰ: ቸነከረ: በረኸተ: or, as most of the rest, from Triliteral Verbs. The use of the liquid ነ: in this amplification of forms, is remarkable; *e.g.* አነጠሰ: is from the Arabic عطس, ሰነበተ: from the Hebrew שבת, ሰነጠቀ: from the Eth. ሰጠቀ:: ሰነዘረ: from the Eth. ሰዘረ: &c.

A. The *Indicative* Mood has nothing particular. It has two Tenses, the Preterite and the Present (or Future); besides which, other Tenses are formed by the Contingent and the Constructive, in connexion with Auxiliaries.

B. The *Contingent* is the simple verbal form with the Personal Preformatives and Terminations, and serves for the Indicative as well as for the Subjunctive, according as it is either, (1) Simple; or (2) has Conjunctions prefixed, and what the nature of those Conjunctions is; or (3) whether any, and what sort of Auxiliary, is attached to it. (See pp. 66, 67.)

C. The *Conjunctive* or *Subjunctive* Mood is not used in the Amharic, except for the purpose of expressing a desire, or request, or obligation. Its peculiarity consists in its Radicals, after the prefixion of the Personal Serviles, assuming the form of the Imperative. (See pp. 68, 69.)

D. A curious Mood, and peculiar to the Amharic and Tigrê languages, having its beginning undeveloped in the Ethiopic Infinitive, is the *Constructive*. It is formed by the simple root of the verb with Personal Afformatives; and has four forms; one simple, one augmented, and two compound forms. (See pp. 70, 71.)

E. The form of the *Imperative* (its nature being the same as in other languages) is short. (See p. 71.)

F. The *Infinitive*, or Verbal Substantive, is formed by the prefixion of መ: to the Simple Form.

G. The *Participle* presents five; viz. three Simple, and two Compound Forms. The three former, partaking of a nominal character, have been exhibited in the Table of Derivative Nouns: the two latter are formed by the Finite Verb Preterite and Contingent, to which certain Preformatives are prefixed; and they retain their flexibility, *i.e.* capability of being conjugated. Besides this, they are all declinable. (See pp. 72, 73.)

We come now to speak,

II. *Of the Tenses of the Amharic Verb.*

They are not so exactly distinguished in the Amharic as in our European Languages: in fact, the Abyssinians have not, strictly speaking, more than two divisions of time; *i.e.* the *Past* and the *Present;* the Present being used also for the Future. The Past is subdivided into the Perfect, and Imperfect or Pluperfect; the Perfect being rendered by the simple Preterite form, and the Imperfect or Pluperfect, (which are not distinguished from each other) being composed either of the Contingent or the Simple Constructive, with the Preterite Auxiliary ነበረ:: The Present, which might be, perhaps with propriety, called Aorist, because it is applicable to the Future as well as to the Present Tense, is a form composed of the Contingent and the Auxiliary አለ:: In order to distinguish the Future from the Present, where the context is not in itself clear enough, certain phrases are adopted which leave no doubt that the time is yet to come in which the action &c. of the subject is to take place. But more of this afterwards. (See p. 66.)

3. The *Number* of Conjugation is but twofold, Singular and Plural.

4. *The Persons.*

There are, in reality, not more than *three* for each Number; viz. the person speaking, the person spoken to, and the person spoken of; but the grammatical forms are more, as has been shown under the article of Pronouns, Chap. III.; namely, seven forms for the Singular, and three for the Plural. Now the Semitic Languages have this in common, that the personal distinctions in the Conjugations of Verbs are expressed by certain letters affixed or prefixed, or both, to the Radicals of the Verb; and in so doing, the act of Conjugation is accomplished. We call the prefixed letters *Preformatives,* and the affixed ones *Afformatives.* The following List exhibits them.

(*a*) *Preformatives.*

SINGULAR.			PLURAL. Com. Gender.	
3d pers.	masc.	ይ—:	3.	ይ—:
.. ..	fem.	ት—:		
2d ..	m. & f.	ት—:	2.	ት—:
.. ..	hon. 1.	ይ—:		
.. ..	.. 2.	ት—:		
1st ..	com.	እ—:	1.	እን—:

(*b*) *Afformatives.*

SINGULAR.	Pret.	Pres.	Subj.	Constr.	PLURAL. Com.	Pret.	Pres.	Subj.	Constr.
3. masc.	none.	none.		—o.	3.	—$\overset{3}{u}$,	—$\overset{3}{u}$,	—$\overset{3}{u}$,	—ăው:
.. fem.	—ች:	..	..	—ā.					
2. masc.	—ህ:	..	..	—ăህ:	2.	—āችሁ:	—$\overset{3}{u}$,	—$\overset{3}{u}$,	—āችሁ:
.. fem.	—ሽ:	..	ï	—ăሽ:					
.. hon. 1.	—$\overset{3}{u}$	..	$\overset{3}{u}$	—ăው:					
.. .. 2.	—āችሁ:	..	$\overset{3}{u}$	—āችሁ:					
1. com.	—ሁ:	..	..	—ê.	1.	—ን:	none		—ăን::

What hitherto has been said, may suffice for the preliminaries: we therefore now proceed to the *Conjugation of the Verbs.*

Section IV.

Conjugation of Verbs.

Before we enter upon the conjugation of the *Regular* Verb, we give the conjugation of the two *Auxiliary* Verbs:

አለ: he is. ነበረ: he was;

and of the Irregular and Defective Verb Substantive, ነው: "he is."

A. አለ: Eth. ሀለወ: contr. ሀሎ: "he is," "there is" (French, *il y a*), is used only in the Present; but that has a Preterite form.

	Singular. Masc.	Singular. Fem.	Singular. Common.	Plural. Common.
3d pers.	አለ: he is.	አለች: she is.		አሉ: they are, he (hon.) is.
2d ..	አለህ:	አለሽ: thou art.		አላችሁ: you are.
.. .. hon. 1.			አሉ: you are.	
.. .. .. 2.			አላችሁ: you are.	
1st ..			አለሁ: I am.	አለን: we are.

Note 1.—This verb is not to be confounded with the Irregular Verb አለ: "he said"; which will be given, when we treat of the Irregular Verbs in general.

2. The 3d pers. sing. and plur., combined with Suffixed Pronouns, have the same signification as "*est*" and "*sunt*" in the Latin, with the Dative of the Personal Pronoun; *e.g. Mihi est,* "I have." So in the Amharic,

ብር: አለኝ: I have (possess) money.

ልጆች: አሉት: he has (possesses) children.

3. As Auxiliary, the 3d pers. sing. masc. is changed into አል: *e.g.*

ይላል: for ይል: አል: he says.

ተቀምጦዋል: for ተቀምጦ: አል: he is sitting.

B. ነበረ: "he was," is used as Auxiliary for the Past Tenses in the Indicative and Subjunctive. It has only the Preterite.

	Singular. Masc.	Singular. Fem.	Singular. Com.	Plural. Common.
3.	ነበረ: (ነበር:) he was.	ነበረች: she was.		ነበሩ: they were.
2.	ነበርህ:	ነበርሽ: thou wast.		ነበራችሁ: you were.
.. hon. 1.			ነበሩ: you were.	
.. .. 2.			ነበራችሁ: you were.	
1.			ነበርሁ: I was.	ነበርን: we were.

NOTE.—When used as an Auxiliary, ነበር: serves often for any person Singular or Plural; *e.g.*

ተቀምጠው: ነበር: they were sitting.
ትመጣ: ነበር: thou wouldest come.

C. ነው: *He is.*

This verb is singularly anomalous. It consists of merely one radical letter ነ:, to which the Verbal Suffixes are attached, instead of Personal Afformatives. Is used only in one form, which we may call the Preterite of the Indicative, because it resembles that more than any other form.

	SINGULAR. Masc.	Fem.	Com.	PLURAL. Common.
3d pers.	ነው: he is.	ናት: she is.		ናቸው: they are
2d pers.	ነህ: thou art.	ነሽ: thou art.		ናችሁ: you are
.. .. hon. 1.			ናችሁ: } you are.	
.. .. .. 2.			ነዎ: } you are.	
1st pers.			ነኝ: I am.	ነን: we are.

This is the regular form of this anomalous verb. Deviations are these: ነዋ:, for the 3d pers. sing. masc. interrogative, "Is he?" In the Shoa Dialect, ነወይ: for the regular ነውን: *e.g.*

እንዴት: ነዋ: How is it? for እንዴት: ነው::

A second deviation is ነች:, in the Shoa Dialect, "She is," for ናት::

1. *Conjugation of the Perfect and Triliteral Verbs.*

A. FIRST CONJUGATION.

Simple form ከበረ: neut. "He was honourable." መለሰ: act. "he turned." intrs. "he answered." ሰደበ: trs. "he scolded," "blasphemed."

(*a*) *Indicative Mood.*

α. PRETERITE.

SINGULAR.

	Masc.		Fem.		Com.	
3d pers.	ከበረ:	he was honourable.	ከበረች:	she was honourable.		
2d ..	ከበርህ:		ከበርሽ:	thou wast honourable.		
.. hon. 1.					ከበሩ:	} you were honourable.
.. .. 2.					ከበራችሁ:	} you were honourable.
1.					ከበርሁ:	I was honourable.

PLURAL. Common.

3d pers.	ከበሩ:	they were honourable.
2d ..	ከበራችሁ:	you were honourable.
1st ..	ከበርን:	we were honourable.

β. PRESENT AND FUTURE.

SINGULAR.

	Masc.		Fem.		Common.	
3d p.	ይከብራል:	he is, will be hon.	ትከብራለች:	she is, will be hon.		
2.	ትከብራለህ:		ትከብሪያለሽ:	thou art, wilt be hon.		
.. hon. 1.					ይከብራሉ:	you are, or will be hon.
.. .. 2.					ትከብራላችሁ:	
1.					እከብራለሁ:	I am, shall be hon.

PLURAL.

Common.

3d pers. ይከብራሉ: they are, will be honourable.
2d .. ትከብራላችሁ: you are, will be honourable.
1st .. እንከብራለን: we are, shall be honourable.

NOTE 1.—Whether this form, when it occurs, is intended for the Present or for the Future Tense, generally depends on the context. In order, however, to leave no doubt when they speak of future things, they use the simple contingent form with additional particles; *e.g.* እከብር: ዘንድ: አለኝ: "I have (am) to be honourable." እከብር: ዘንድ: ጊዜ: አለኝ: "time is for me (to come) that I am to be honourable," &c.

2. Personal Suffixes, and sometimes the Conjunction ም:, are infixed between the Simple Form and the Auxiliary.

(b.) CONTINGENT.

α. *Simple.*

	SINGULAR. Masc.	Fem.	Common.	PLURAL. Common.
3d pers.	ይከብር:	ትከብር:		ይከብሩ:
2d ..	ትከብር:	ትከብሪ:		ትከብሩ:
.. hon. 1.			ይከብሩ:	
.. .. 2.			ትከብሩ:	
1st pers.			እከብር:	እንከብር:

As this form is used for both the Indicative and the Subjunctive, as well as for the formation of Participles, we have given no translation of it; but shall present a few instances here, to illustrate its use:

ይከብር፡ ዘንድ፡ in order that he may be honourable.

ሊከብር፡ that he may be honourable.

እንዲከብር፡ that he is honourable.

ቢከብር፡ or ይከብር፡ እንደሆን፡ if he is (be) honourable.

ኪከብር፡ than that he should be honourable.

ሲከብር፡ while he is honourable.

የሚከብር፡ he that is honourable.

አይከብርም፡ he is not honourable.

The Present and Future of the Indicative, also, is a composition of the Contingent with the Auxiliary አለ፡ which is omitted whenever the word receives any augmentation at the beginning or at the end, except Suffixes or Copulative Conjunctions.

β. COMPOUND.

SINGULAR.

	Masc.		Fem.	Common.
3 p.	ይከብር፡ ነበር፡	he was, had been hon.	ትከብር፡ ነበረች፡	she was, had been hon.
2	ትከብር፡ ነበርህ፡		ትከብሪ፡ ነበርሽ፡	thou wast, hadst been hon.
hon. 1.			ይከብሩ፡ ነበሩ፡	you were, had been hon.
.. 2.			ትከብሩ፡ ነበራችሁ፡	
			እከብር፡ ነበርሁ፡	I was, had been hon.

PLURAL.

Common.

3d pers. ይከብሩ፡ ነበሩ፡ they were, or had been honourable.

2d .. ትከብራችሁ፡ ነበራችሁ፡ you were, or had been honourable.

1st .. እንከብር፡ ነበርን፡ we were, or had been honourable.

This form is used for the Subjunctive, as well as for the Indicative.

(c) *Subjunctive Mood.*

Is characterized by having the form of the Imperative Mood with the Personal Preformatives.

SINGULAR.

	Masc.		Fem.		Com.	
3d pers.	ይክበር፡	let him be hon.	ትክበር፡	let her be hon.		
2. ..	ትክበር፡		ትክበሪ፡	mayest thou be hon.		
.. hon. 1.					ይክበሩ፡	may you be hon.
.. .. .. 2.					ትክበሩ፡	
1. ..					እክበር፡	let me, may I, be hon.

PLURAL.
Common.

3d pers.	ይክበሩ፡	may they, let them be honourable.
2. ..	ትክበሩ፡	may you be honourable.
1. ..	እንክበር፡	may we, let us be honourable.

NOTE 1.—As the Subjunctive is so nearly related to the Imperative, always expressing a wish, a request, or indirect command, it is natural that the Second Person Singular, in its direct form, and the same person in the Plural, is less frequently used than the remaining forms; for they use more generally the Imperative.

2. Several verbs are destitute of this form, and they use the Simple Contingent. It may therefore be of service to the Student, to give a list of those verbs of this class which have this form; and another of those which have not.

VERBS WITH THE SUBJUNCTIVE FORM.					VERBS WITHOUT IT.		
ለመጠ፡	ለቀጠ፡	ለበሰ፡	ለበጠ፡	ለገመ፡	ለመነ፡	ለመደ፡	ለሰነ፡
ለገሰ፡	ለገደ፡	ለገጠ፡	መለከ፡	መለጠ፡	ለቀመ፡	ለወሰ፡	ለወጠ፡
መረገ፡	መረጠ፡	መሰለ፡	መከረ፡	መከነ፡	ለዘበ፡	ለጐመ፡	መለሰ፡
መጠነ፡	ሠለጠ፡	ሠመረ፡	ሠረቀ፡	ሠረፀ፡	መረቀ፡	መረዘ፡	ሞከረ፡
ሠቀየ፡	ሠጠመ፡	ረከሰ፡	ረኰሰ፡	ረኰዘ፡	መዘነ፡	መገለ፡	መገበ፡
ረዘመ፡ ረገመ፡	ረገጠ፡	ረገፈ፡	ረጠበ፡	ረፈደ፡	መጐተ፡	ሰነጋ፡	ሰነፈ፡
ረፈቀ፡	ሰለበ፡	ሰማራ፡	ሰረቀ፡	ሰረየ፡	ሰወረ፡	ሸለመ፡	ሸመተ፡
ሰረፈ፡	ሰቀለ፡	ሰበረ፡	ሰበቀ፡	ሰበከ፡	ሸሸገ፡	ሸቀበ፡	ሸጐረ፡
ሰከረ፡	ሰደበ፡	ሰገደ፡	ሰፈረ፡	ሸመቀ፡	ሸፈነ፡	ቀለመ፡	ቀለበ፡
ሸመነ፡	ሸከረ፡	ሸኰረ፡	ሸገተ፡	ሸፈጠ፡	ቈለፈ፡	ቀቀለ፡	ቀደሰ፡
ቀለጠ፡	ቀመሰ፡	ቀሠጠ፡	ቀሠፈ፡	ቈረሰ፡	ቈራረ፡	በረታ፡	በቀለ፡
ቀረበ፡	ቈረበ፡	ቀረጠ፡	ቈረጠ፡	ቀረፈ፡	በቈለ፡	በደለ፡	በደረ፡

VERBS WITH THE SUBJUNCTIVE FORM.

ቍሰለ፡ ቀበረ፡ ቀዘነ፡ ቀዘፈ፡ ቀደመ፡
ቀጠለ፡ ቀጠረ፡ ቈጠረ፡ ቀጠነ፡ በለጠ፡
በረቀ፡ በረደ፡ በሰለ፡ በቀለ፡ (grow) በተነ፡
በጠሰ፡ ተመሰ፡ ተረዘ፡ ተረፈ፡ ተከለ፡
ነቀለ፡ ነቀሰ፡ ነቀዘ፡ ነቀፈ፡ ነከረ፡ ነከሰ፡
ነደለ፡ ነደቀ፡ ነደፈ፡ ነገረ፡ ነገሠ፡ ነገደ፡ ነጠረ፡
ነጠቀ፡ ነጸረ፡ ነጸፈ፡ ነፈሰ፡ ነፈቀ፡ ነፈገ፡
ከመረ፡ ከረመ፡ ከበረ፡ ከበደ፡ ከደነ፡
ከፈለ፡ ከፈተ፡ ከፈነ፡ ወለሰ፡ ወለደ፡
ወረሰ፡ ወረደ፡ ወሰነ፡ ወሰደ፡ ወቀረ፡
ወቀጠ፡ ወከለ፡ ወደሰ፡ ወደቀ፡ ወገረ፡
ወገዘ፡ ዘለቀ፡ ዘመረ፡ ዘመደ፡ ዘረፈ፡
ዘከረ፡ ዘገመ፡ ዘገነ፡ ዘገየ፡ ዘፈረ፡ ደረሰ፡
ደረቀ፡ ደበቀ፡ ደነዘ፡ ደነፈ፡ ደከመ፡ ደገመ፡
ደፈነ፡ ገለጠ፡ ገመረ፡ ገመደ፡ ገረመ፡ ጐረሰ፡
ገረፈ፡ ገበረ፡ ገበዘ፡ ጐበጠ፡ ገተረ፡ ጐተነ፡
ገነኘ፡ ገነዘ፡ ገዘረ፡ ገዘተ፡ ገደለ፡ ጐደለ፡
ገደመ፡ ገደረ፡ ገደፈ፡ ገጠመ፡ ገጸበ፡ ጠለቀ፡
ጠለፈ፡ ጠመቀ፡ ጠረቀ፡ ጠቀመ፡ ጠቀሰ፡
ጸደቀ፡ ጸደፈ፡ ፈለቀ፡ ፈለጠ፡ ፈረሰ፡ ፈረደ፡
ፈቀደ፡ ፈተለ፡ ፈተነ፡ ፈተገ፡ ፈጠረ፡ ፈጠነ፡
ፈጸመ።

VERBS WITHOUT IT.

ተኰሰ፡ ተከዘ፡ ቸኰለ፡
ቸገረ፡ ነወረ፡ ነወጠ፡
ወቀሰ፡ ወገደ፡ ወፈረ፡
ዘለፈ፡ ዘረጋ፡ ዘነመ፡
ዘነጋ፡ ዘፈነ፡ ደመቀ፡
ደረበ፡ ደቈሰ፡ ደነቀ፡
ደወለ፡ ደጐሰ፡ ደገፈ፡
ደፈረ፡ ደፈቀ፡ ጀመረ፡
ገመሰ፡ ገሠጸ፡ ጐበኘ፡
ገገረ፡ ጠረሰ፡ ጠቈረ፡
ጠበሰ፡ ጠበቀ፡ ጠየቀ፡
ጠገነ፡ ጨለመ፡ ጨለጠ፡
ጨመረ፡ ጨመተ፡ ጨረሰ፡
ጨበጠ፡ ጨነቀ፡ ጨከነ፡
ጨፈረ፡ ጨፈነ፡ ጸመደ፡
ጸረበ፡ ጸረገ፡ ጸየፈ፡ ጸገበ፡
ፀነሰ፡ ፈለሰ፡ ፈለገ፡
ፈወሰ።

3. In verbs whose first radical has a diphthong, the latter is shortened into that diphthong which answers the sixth vowel order; *e.g.* ይቈርጥ፡ "let him cut," from ቈረጠ። አትጕደል፡ "do not be deficient."

4. The Subjunctive is so nearly related to the Imperative, that it yields all its forms to serve the latter, where that is deficient. So in the negative orders, prohibitions or warnings, where the Imperative cannot be used for having no Servile Preformatives; *e.g.*

አትንገር፡ do not tell. አትውደቅ፡ do not fall.
አትግደል፡ do not kill. አትቈርጥ፡ do not cut.

(*d*) *Constructive Mood.*

This is a singular Mood, which has nothing corresponding, either in our European or in the other Semitic Languages; although its form, as far as the Simple one is concerned, answers the Ethiopic Infinitives ገቢር: and ጉብሮ:; but this Mood is not an Infinitive. It has nothing of a Substantive character; whereas the Infinitive is the first Verbal Substantive, possessing both the characters of Substantive and Verb. Nor is there any other Mood to which it exactly corresponds: neither Participle nor Gerund, nor Finite Verb, will answer it; although it may be occasionally translated by either, and sometimes by an Adverb. It occupies an intermediate station between the Infinitive and the Finite Verb; has four forms, one of which is Simple, one Augmented, and two Compound; and is flexible, like the Finite Verb, having Afformatives resembling the Suffixed Pronouns, partly of the Noun, and partly of the Verb. The Simple form is used for amplifying; the other forms, on account of the auxiliaries which are attached to them, for constituting sentences. When the nature of this Mood is understood, we hope the designation *Constructive* will be justified; not having been able to fix upon any better.

The Simple form ክቡር: (a modification of the radix ክብር: "honour"), which may be considered as containing the idea of an agent, and of an action, or a concrete being, and an abstract state or condition, &c., assumes peculiar forms of Pronouns; which must not be taken as Possessive (Nominal), but as Personal (Verbal); nor as the other Verbal Suffixes which are in the Accusative; but they are Nominatives. Here it is:

a. FIRST FORM OF THE CONSTRUCTIVE MOOD.

Simple Form.

	SINGULAR. Masc.	Fem. / Com	PLURAL. Com.
3d p.	ክቡር: he being hon.	ክቡሪ: she being honourable.	ክቡረው: they being honourable.
2.	ክቡረህ:	ክቡረሽ: thou being honourable	ክቡራችሁ: you being honourable.
.. hon. 1.	. . . .	ክቡረው: you being hon.	ክቡረን: we being honourable.
... .. 2.	. . . .	ክቡራችሁ: you being hon.	
1.	....	ክቡሬ: I being hon.	

The Augmented form has become Finite by the Auxiliary አለ: being attached to the Simple form; but not in the same manner as it attaches itself to the Contingent, in constituting the Present and Future Tense. It serves for the Past and the Present Tenses.

β. SECOND OR AUGMENTED FORM OF THE CONSTRUCTIVE MOOD.

Constructive Aorist (Present and Perfect).

	SINGULAR.			PLURAL.	
	Masc.	Fem.	Com.	Com.	
3.	ኩብርዋል: he is (was) hon.	ኩብራለች: she is (was) hon.		ኩብረዋል: they	are, or were honourable.
2.	ኩብረሃል:	ኩብረሻል: thou art (wast) hon.		ኩብራችኋል: you	
.. hon. 1.	. . . . .		ኩብረዋል: you were hon.		
.. .. 2.	. . . . .		ኩብራችኋል: you were hon.		
1.	. . . . .		ኩብርያለሁ: for ኩብሬ: አለሁ: I am (was) h.	ኩብረናል: we	

γ. COMPOUND CONSTRUCTIVE FORMS.

א Constructive Perfect.

	SINGULAR.			
	Masc.		Fem.	
3.	ኩብር: ነበር:	he was, or had been hon.	ኩብራ: ነበረች:	she was, or had been hon.
2.	ኩብረህ: ነበርህ:	thou wast, hadst been hon.	ኩብረሽ: ነበርሽ:	thou wast, hadst been hon.

	Common.	
.. hon. 1.	ኩብረው: ነበሩ:	you were, had been hon.
.. .. 2.	ኩብራችሁ: ነበራችሁ:	you were, had been hon.
1.	ኩብሬ: ነበርሁ: I was, had been h.	

PLURAL.

Common.

3d pers.	ኩብረው: ነበሩ: they	were, or had been honourable.
2d ..	ኩብራችሁ: ነበራችሁ: you	
1st ..	ኩብረን: ነበርን: we	

This form is used merely for the Indicative. Observe, also, that ነበር: may be used throughout, without any change, as remarked in the Note to the conjugation of ነበረ: p. 65.

ב. *Constructive Form of Uncertainty.*

SINGULAR.

3d masc.	ኩብር፡ ይሆናል፡ he may		probably be honourable.
.. fem.	ኩብራ፡ ትሆናለች፡ she may		
2d masc.	ኩብረህ፡ ትሆናለህ፡	thou mayest	
.. fem.	ኩብረሽ፡ ትሆኛለሽ፡		
.. hon. 1.	ኩብረው፡ ይሆናሉ፡	you may	
.. .. 2.	ኩብራችሁ፡ ትሆናላችሁ፡		
1st com.	ኩብሬ፡ እሆናለሁ፡ I may		

PLURAL.

3d masc.	ኩብረው፡ ይሆናሉ፡ they	may be honourable.
2d ..	ኩብራችሁ፡ ትሆናላችሁ፡ you	
1st com.	ኩብረን፡ እንሆናለን፡ we	

(*e*) *Imperative.*

The Imperative has two forms; one which has the first Radical in the sixth, and the second in the first order; and another which has the first Radical in the first, and the second in the sixth order. All those verbs which have the Subjunctive form, have the Imperative in the first; and the rest have it in the second form. As a specimen of the first, we take the Imperative of ከበረ፡፡; and of the other, that of ጠበቀ፡፡ It is used only in the Second Person Singular and Plural.

α. *Form* ህሀህ፡፡

SINGULAR.		PLURAL.
Masc. ክበር፡	be honourable.	Com. ክበሩ፡ be honourable.
Fem. ክበሪ፡		

Diphthong form: ቍጠር፡ ቍጠሪ፡ *sing.* ቍጠሩ፡ *pl.* "count."

β. *Form* ሀህህ፡፡

SINGULAR.		PLURAL.
Masc. ጠብቅ፡	do thou observe.	Com. ጠብቁ፡ do you observe.
Fem. ጠብቂ፡		

(*f*) *Infinitive Mood.*

Is formed by prefixing መ፡ to the Simple root; and it presents the two forms: መክበር፡ "to be honourable;" and መጠበቅ፡ "to observe." With Prima Rad. Diphthong: መቍጠር፡፡ "to number." መቈፈር፡ "to till," "dig."

(*g*) *Participles.*

α. Simple: *act.* ከባሪ፡ one who is honoured.
pass. ጥሙቅ፡ any thing dipped.
Eth. *pass.* ክቡር፡ honoured.

β. Compound Part., Adjective, or Relative Participle.

א *For the Preterite*—Is formed by prefixing the Relative Pronoun የ፡ to the Preterite.

SINGULAR.			PLURAL.
3. masc.	የከበረ፡	he who was hon.	3. የከበሩ፡ they who were hon.
.. fem.	የከበረች፡	she who was hon.	
2. masc.	የከበርህ፡	thou who wast hon.	2. የከበራችሁ፡ you who were hon.
.. fem.	የከበርሽ፡	thou who wast hon.	
.. hon. 1.	የከበሩ፡	you who were hon.	
.. .. 2.	የከበራችሁ፡	you who were hon.	
1. com.	የከበርሁ፡	I who was hon.	1. የከበርን፡ we who were hon.

ב *For the Present* — Is formed by prefixing the Relative Pronoun የም—፡ to the forms of the Contingent Mood.

SINGULAR.			PLURAL.
3. masc.	የሚከበር፡	he who is hon.	3. የሚከበሩ፡ they who are hon.
.. fem.	የምትከበር፡	she who is hon.	
2. masc.	የምትከበር፡	thou who art hon.	2. የምትከበሩ፡ you who are hon.
.. fem.	የምትከበሪ፡	thou who art hon.	
.. hon. 1.	የሚከበሩ፡	you who are hon.	
.. .. 2.	የምትከበሩ፡	you who are hon.	
1. com.	የምከበር፡	I who am hon.	1. የምንከበር፡ we who are hon.

OBSERVATIONS.

1. The Simple Participial forms are used in their verbal as well as in a nominal character. This is evident in Active Verbs; *e.g.* ጠባቂ፡ "observing," watching," guarding"; and "guardian," "observer": which may have its object connected with it either in the Genitive Case, when it is considered as a Noun, *e.g.* የበግ፡ ጠባቂ፡ "a keeper, guardian, of sheep," "shepherd"; or in the Accusative Case, በግን፡ ጠባቂ፡ "one keeping, watching the sheep." The Passive forms are resolvable by the two compound forms (א) and (ב) of the Passive Conjugations.

2. The two compound forms of the Relative or Adjective Participle evince their Participial character (which consists in partaking—*participiendo*—of the properties of the Verb as well as of the Noun, and forming a connecting link between both) by the position in which they stand when connected with Nouns, as Adjectives; by the treatment they experience from other Transitive Verbs, when being put into the Accusative Case; and by the influence they themselves exercise on Nouns and Pronouns. As this subject, however, belongs more properly to the Syntax, we shall leave it for the present.

Before we leave this subject, we beg to present to the Student those regular deviations which take place in those verbs whose third radical letter is liable to change, by the accession of the vowels ï and ê, according to the rule laid down Part I. Ch. VII. c. This occurs in verbs ending in ለ፡ ሠ፡ ሰ፡ ተ፡ ነ፡ ዘ፡ ደ፡ ጠ፡ ጸ፡ and ፀ፡, with (1) the Feminine of the 2d pers. masc. in (a) the Present Indicative; (b) the Contingent Simple and Compound; (c) Subjunctive; (d) Imperative; (2) with the 1st pers. sing. in the Constructive Simple and its Compounds. Instances:

1. ፈተለ፡ "He span." FOR

ትፈትያለሽ፡ thou (*fem.*) spinnest . . ትፈትልያለሽ።
ትፈትይ፡ . . . . ትፈትሊ፡
ትፈትይ፡ ነበርሽ፡ thou (*f.*) wast spinning, ትፈትሊ፡ ነበርሽ፡
ትፈትይ፡ ትሆኚለሽ፡ thou (*f.*) wilt be spinning, ትፈትሊ፡ ትሆኚ፡ አለሽ፡
ፍትይ፡ do thou (*f.*) spin . . . . . ፍትሊ፡
ትፍትይ፡ thou (*f.*) shalt, mayest thou spin, ትፍትሊ፡
ፈትዬ፡ I spinning . . . . ፈትሌ፡
ፈትያለሁ፡ I spin, span . . . . . ፈትሌ፡ አለሁ፡
ፈትዬ፡ ነበርሁ፡ I was spinning . . . ፈትሌ፡ ነበርሁ፡
ፈትዬ፡ እሆናለሁ፡ {I shall (may probably) be spinning} ፈትሌ፡ እሆናለሁ፡

2. ነገሠ፡ "He was king" (queen). መለሰ፡ "He returned." (*act.*)

ትነግሻለሽ፡ thou art queen . . . . ትነግሢ፡ አለሽ፡
ትነግሽ፡ . . . . ትነግሢ፡
ትመልሽ፡ ነበርሽ፡ thou was returning, ትመልሲ፡ ነበርሽ፡
ትምልሽ፡ ትሆኚለሽ፡ {thou wilt be returning} ትመልሲ፡ ትሆኚለሽ።
ትንገሽ፡ mayest thou reign as Queen . ትንገሢ፡
ንገሽ፡ be queen . . . . ንገሢ፡
መልሼ፡ . . . . መልሴ፡
መልሻለሁ፡ & መልሽያለሁ፡ መልሼ፡ ነበርሁ፡ መልሼ፡ እሆናለሁ፡ {መልስያለሁ፡ መልሴ፡ ነበርሁ፡ መልሴ፡ እሆናለሁ፡}

3. ከፈተ፡ "He opened."

ትከፍቻለሽ፡ thou openest . . . . ትከፍቲያለሽ፡
ትከፍች፡ . . . . ትከፍቲ፡

	FOR
ትከፍች፡ ነበርሽ፡ thou wast opening,	ትከፍቲ፡ ነበርሽ፡
ትከፍች፡ ትሆኛለሽ፡ { thou wilt be opening }	ትከፍቲ፡ ትሆኛለሽ፡
ትክፈች፡ mayest thou open	ትክፈቲ፡
ክፈች፡ do thou open	ክፈቲ፡
ከፍቼ፡ I opening	ከፍቴ፡
ከፍቻለሁ፡ I open	ከፍትያለሁ፡
ከፍቼ፡ ነበርሁ፡ & ከፍቼ፡ እሆናለሁ፡	ከፍቴ፡ እሆናለሁ፡ & ከፍቴ፡ ነበርሁ።

4. ለመነ፡ "He begged."

ትለምኛለሽ፡ thou beggest	ትለምንያለሽ፡
ትለምኚ፡ &c.	ትለምኒ፡
ለምኚ፡ do thou beg	ለምኒ፡
ለምኜ፡ I begging	ለምኔ፡
ለምኛለሁ፡ I am (was) begging . . .	ለምንያለሁ።

5. መረዘ፡ "He poisoned."

ትመርዣለሽ፡ thou poisonest	ትመርዝያለሽ፡
ትመርዢ፡ &c.	ትመርዚ፡
መርዢ፡ and መርዢ፡ do thou poison,	መርዚ፡
መርዤ፡ I poisoning	መርዜ፡
መርዣለሁ፡ I poison (poisoned) . . .	መርዝያለሁ፡

6. ወረደ፡ "He descended."

ትወርጃለሽ፡ thou descendest	ትወርድያለሽ፡
ትወርጂ፡ &c.	ትወርዲ፡
ትውረጂ፡ mayest thou descend . . .	ትውረዲ፡
ውረጂ፡ do thou descend	ውረዲ፡
ወርጄ፡ &c., I descending	ወርዴ፡
ወርጃለሁ፡ I was, am descending . .	ወርድያለሁ፡

7. ወገጠ፡ "he pounded."

ትወግጫለሽ፡ thou poundest	ትወግጥያለሽ፡
ትወግጪ፡ &c.	ትወግጢ።
ትውገጪ፡ mayest thou pound . . .	ትውገጢ፡
ውገጪ፡ do thou pound	ውገጢ፡

ወግጬ፡ I pounding &c. . . . . . . ወግጢ፡
ወግጪለሁ፡ I am (was) pounding . . ወግጥያለሁ።

8. ገሠጸ፡ "he reproved," "chastised." ሠረፀ፡ "he proceeded." The changes are the same as in No. 7.

B. SECOND CONJUGATION.

whose characteristic is a prolongation of the first radical, by which it is changed from the first into the fourth form. Its force is intensity of the idea of the original form.

ሳደበ፡ he scolded exceedingly.

Its difference in form, from the First Conjugation, is as follows:

1. It retains the first long radical throughout; on this acccount, it
2. Has no peculiar form for the Subjunctive, but is served by the Contingent Mood.
3. In the Imperative, the first radical is long, of the fourth: the second short, of the sixth order.
4. In the Infinitive, the first radical is of the fourth; the second, as in all the conjugations, of the first order.

The mode of conjugating being the same as in the first species, we shall give only the Third Person, Singular and Plural, in those Moods and Tenses which have it.

1. INDICATIVE.

Preterite.

3d pers. SINGULAR.	3d pers. PLURAL.
ሳደበ፡ he scolded exceedingly &c.	ሳደቡ፡ they scolded exceedingly &c.

Present and *Future.*

ይሳድባል፡ he scolds exceedingly &c.	ይሳድባሉ፡ they scold exceedingly &c.

2. CONTINGENT.

Simple.

ይሳድብ፡	ይሳድቡ፡

Compound Preterite.

ይሳድብ፡ ነበረ፡ he scolded, had scolded, was scolding, would scold, would have scolded exceedingly.	ይሳድቡ፡ ነበሩ። he scolded, &c.

Compound of Uncertainty.

ይሳድብ፡ ይሆናል፡ he may (perhaps) scold exceedingly &c.	ይሳድቡ፡ ይሆናሉ።

3. SUBJUNCTIVE.—None.

4. CONSTRUCTIVE.

Simple.

SINGULAR. PLURAL.

ሳድቦ: he, scolding exceedingly &c. | ሳድበው: they scolding &c.

Augmented Present and Perfect (Aorist).

ሳድብዋል: he scolds (scolded) exceedingly, &c. | ሳድበዋል: they scold, &c.

Comp. Preterite.

ሳድቦ: ነበረ: he scolded, was scolding exceedingly, &c. | ሳድበው: ነበሩ: they scolded, &c.

Comp. of Uncertainty.

ሳድቦ: ይሆናል: he may (perhaps) scold exceedingly, &c.

5. IMPERATIVE.

Masc. ሳድብ: Fem. ሳድቢ: do thou scold. | ሳድቡ: do you scold exceedingly, &c.

6. INFINITIVE.

መሳድብ: to scold, the scolding.

7. PARTICIPLES.

1. *Nominascens.*—ሳዳቢ: "a scolder," "one who scolds exceedingly."
2. *Adject.*—የሚሳድብ: &c. "one who scolds exceedingly," &c.

Of course, there is no Passive Participle of this form.

C. THIRD CONJUGATION.

Active and Transitive Voice.—The characteristic is an አ: prefixed to the radix; which puts the Personal Preformatives, excepting እ:, into the fourth order.

Form አከበረ: "he honoured."

1. INDICATIVE.

Preterite.

SINGULAR. PLURAL.

አከበረ: he honoured, &c. as ከበረ: | አከበሩ: they honoured, &c.

Present and Future.

ያከብራል: he honours. | ያከብራሉ: they honour, &c.
ታከብራለች: she honours, &c.

2. CONTINGENT.

Simple.

ያክብር: ታክብር: &c. &c. | ያክብሩ: &c.

Compound Preterite.

SINGULAR.	PLURAL.
ያከ·ብር፡ ነበረ፡ &c.	ያከ·ብሩ፡ ነበሩ፡ &c.

Compound of Uncertainty.

ያከ·ብር፡ ይሆናል፡ he may (perhaps) honour, &c.

3. SUBJUNCTIVE.

ያክብር፡ may he (let him) honour, &c. as ይክበር፡ &c.

4. CONSTRUCTIVE.

Simple.

አክ·ብሮ፡ he honouring.	አክ·ብረው፡ they honouring.
አክ·ብራ፡ she honouring.	
አክ·ብረህ፡ / አክ·ብረሽ፡ } thou honouring.	አክ·ብራችሁ፡ you honouring.
አክ·ብረው፡ / አክ·ብራችሁ፡ } you honouring.	
አክ·ብሬ፡ I honouring.	አክ·ብረን፡ we honouring.

Augmented Present and Preterite.

አክ·ብሮዋል፡ { he honours (honoured) &c.	አክ·ብረዋል፡ { they honour (honoured) &c.

Compound Preterite.

አክ·ብሮ፡ ነበረ፡ he honoured, &c.	አክ·ብረው፡ ነበሩ፡ they honoured, &c.

5. IMPERATIVE.

SINGULAR.	PLURAL.
Masc. አክብር፡ / Fem. አክብሪ፡ } do thou honour.	አክብሩ፡ do ye honour.

6. INFINITIVE.

ማክበር፡ to honour, the honouring.

7. PARTICIPLES.

1. *Nominal*, አክባሪ፡ the honourer, one who honours.
2. *Adject.* { የሚያከ·ብር፡ he who honours. / ያከበረ፡ he who honoured.

D. FOURTH CONJUGATION.

ተሰደበ፡ "he was reviled."

Its nature is pre-eminently *Passive* (objective), and reflective. Its characteristic is the Preformative ተ፡ to the original form in the Preterite, Constructive, and Imperative, which, in the same manner as in the cognate languages, gives way to the other Preformatives in the process of conjugations. The second radical remains unchanged in all the moods, tenses, and persons, except in the Constructive Moods. So does also the first radical in the Infinitive Mood. These two remarks serve to distinguish this and the other Passive Conjugations from the rest.

1. INDICATIVE.

Preterite.

	SINGULAR.	PLURAL.
3d pers. masc.	ተሰደበ: he was reviled.	ተሰደቡ: they were reviled,

&c. &c., the same as ከበረ: &c.

Present and Future.

	SINGULAR.			PLURAL.	
3d pers. masc.	ይሰደባል:	he is (will be) reviled.	3d p. c.	ይሰደባሉ:	they are (will be) reviled.
.... fem.	ትሰደባለች:	she is (will be) reviled.			
2d per. masc.	ትሰደባለህ:	thou art (wilt be) reviled.		ትሰደባላችሁ:	you are (will be) reviled.
.. .. fem.	ትሰደቢያለሽ:	thou art (wilt be) reviled.			
.. .. hon. 1.	ይሰደባሉ:	you are (will be) reviled.			
.. .. .. 2.	ትሰደባላችሁ:	you are (will be) reviled.			
1st .. com.	አሰደባለሁ:	I am (shall be) reviled.		አንሰደባለን:	we are (shall be) reviled.

2. CONTINGENT.

Simple.

	SINGULAR.			PLURAL.
3d per. masc.	ይሰደብ:	fem.	ትሰደብ:	ይሰደቡ:
2d	ትሰደብ:	fem.	ትሰደቢ:	ትሰደቡ:
.. .. hon. 1.	ይሰደቡ:	2.	ትሰደቡ:	
1st .. com.	አሰደብ:			አንሰደብ:

Compound Preterite.

3d pers. masc. SINGULAR.

ይሰደብ: ነበረ: he was (would be), had been (would have been), reviled, &c. &c.

PLURAL.

ይሰደቡ: ነበሩ: they were (would be), had been (would have been), reviled, &c. &c.

Compound of Uncertainty.

SINGULAR.		PLURAL.	
3d pers. masc. ይሰደብ: ይሆናል:	he may (perhaps) be reviled, &c. &c.	ይሰደቡ: ይሆናሉ:	they may (perhaps) be reviled, &c. &c.

3. SUBJUNCTIVE.—None.

4. CONSTRUCTIVE.

Simple.

	SINGULAR.		PLURAL.	
3d p. masc.	ተሰድቦ: he being reviled.		ተሰድበው: they being	reviled.
.. .. fem.	ተሰድባ: she being reviled.			
2d .. masc.	ተሰድበህ:	thou being reviled.	ተሰድባችሁ: you being	
.. .. fem.	ተሰድበሽ:			
.. .. hon. 1.	ተሰድበው:	you being reviled.		
.. .. .. 2.	ተሰድባችሁ:			
1st .. com.	ተሰድቤ: I being reviled.		ተሰድበን: we being	

Augmented Aorist.

	SINGULAR.			PLURAL.	
3d p. m.	ተሰድበዋል: he	is (was)	reviled.	ተሰድበዋል: they	are (were) reviled.
.. .. f.	ተሰድባለች: she				
2d .. m.	ተሰድበሃል:	thou art (wast)		ተሰድባችኋል: you	
.. .. f.	ተሰድበሻል:				
.. .. hon. 1.	ተሰድበዋል:	you are (were)			
.. .. .. 2.	ተሰድባችኋል:				
1st .. com.	ተሰድብያለሁ:	I am (was)		ተሰድበናል: we	

Compound Preterite.

	SINGULAR.		PLURAL.	
3d p. m.	ተሰድቦ: ነበረ:	he was (had been) reviled, &c. &c. &c.	ተሰድበው: ነበሩ:	they were (had been) reviled, &c. &c.

5. IMPERATIVE.

Masc.	ተሰደብ:	do thou be (submit to being) reviled.	ተሰደቡ:	do you be (submit to being) reviled.
Fem.	ተሰደቢ:			

6. INFINITIVE.

መሰደብ: to be reviled, the being reviled.

7. PARTICIPLES.

(*a*) *Nominal,* ተሰደቢ: one who is reviled.

(*b*) *Relative,* *α. Perf.* የተሰደበ: he who was (has been) reviled.

β. Pres. የሚሰደብ: he who is reviled.

E. FIFTH CONJUGATION.

አናገረ: He made (caused to) speak.

The nature of this verb is doubly transitive, or *causative*. It combines the characteristics of both the second and the third conjugations; the prolongation of the first radical giving intensity to the transitively (by **አ**:) augmented form.

1. INDICATIVE.

Preterite.

	SINGULAR.			PLURAL.	
3d p. masc.	አናገረ:	he made	to speak.	አናገሩ: they made	to speak.
.. .. fem.	አናገረች:	she made			
2d .. masc.	አናገርህ:	thou madest		አናገራችሁ: you made	
.. .. fem.	አናገርሽ:				
.. .. hon. 1.	አናገሩ:	you made			
.. .. .. 2.	አናገራችሁ:				
1st .. com.	አናገርሁ:	I made		አናገርን: we made	

Present and Future.

3d p. masc.	ያናግራል:	he makes (will make)	to speak.	ያናግራሉ: they	make (will, shall make) to speak.
.. .. fem.	ታናግራለች:	she makes (will make)			
2d .. masc.	ታናግራለህ:	thou makest (will make)		ታናግራላችሁ: you	
.. .. fem.	ታናግርያለሽ:				
.. .. hon. 1.	ያናግራሉ:	you make (will make)			
.. .. .. 2.	ታናግራላችሁ:				
1st .. com.	አናግራለሁ:	I make (shall make)		እናናግራለን: we	

2. CONTINGENT.

Simple.

3d pers.	ያናግር:	fem.	ታናግር:	ያናግሩ:
2d ..	ታናግር:	fem.	ታናግሪ:	ታናግሩ:
.. hon. 1.	ያናግሩ:	2.	ታናግሩ:	እናናግር::
1.	አናግር:			

Compound Preterite.

SINGULAR.		PLURAL.	
3d pers. masc. ያናግር: ነበር:	he made (would make), had made (would have made) to speak, &c.	ያናግሩ: ነበሩ:	they made &c. to speak &c.

Compound of Uncertainty.

3d pers. masc. SINGULAR.		PLURAL.	
ያናግር፡ ይሆናል፡	he may (perhaps) make to speak, &c.	ያናግሩ፡ ይሆናሉ፡	they may (perhaps) make to speak, &c.

3. NO SUBJUNCTIVE.

4. CONSTRUCTIVE.

Simple.

3d p. masc.	አናግር፡ he	making to speak.	አናግረው፡ they	making to speak.
.... fem.	አናግራ፡ she			
2d .. masc.	አናግረህ፡ thou		አናግራችሁ፡ you	
.... fem.	አናግረሽ፡ thou			
.... hon. 1.	አናግረው፡ you			
...... 2.	አናግራችሁ፡ you			
1st.. com.	አናግሬ፡ I		አናግረን፡ we	

Compound Aorist.

3d pers. masc.			
አናግርዋል፡	he makes (made) to speak, &c.	አናግረዋል፡	they make (made) to speak, &c.

Compound Preterite.

አናግር፡ ነበረ፡	he made (had made) to speak, &c.	አናግረው፡ ነበሩ፡	they made (had made) to speak, &c.

5. IMPERATIVE.

Masc. አናግር፡ Fem. አናግሪ፡	do thou make to speak.	አናግሩ፡ do ye make to speak.

6. INFINITIVE.

ማናገር፡ to make or cause to speak; the causing to speak.

7. PARTICIPLES.

(*a*) *Simple,* አናጋሪ፡ one who makes to speak.

(*b*) *Relative,*

α. *Perfect,* ያናገረ፡ he who made to speak, &c.

β. *Present,* የሚያናግር፡ he who makes to speak, &c.

F. SIXTH CONJUGATION.

ተናገረ፡ "He spoke."

The nature and force of this species is intensity, continuation, sometimes reciprocity, either of the original, or of the Fourth Conjugation. It combines the properties of the Second (long first radical) and Fourth (Preformative ተ:) Conjugations. The ተ: is found in the Preterite, Imperative, and Constructive Moods: the first radical is long throughout: the second is of the first order, in all moods, tenses, and persons, except in the Constructive.

1. INDICATIVE.

Preterite.

3d pers. masc. SINGULAR.	PLURAL.
ተናገረ: he spoke, &c.	ተናገሩ: they spoke, &c.

Present and Future.

ይናገራል: he speaks (will speak) &c.	ይናገራሉ: they speak (will speak) &c.

2. CONTINGENT.

Simple.

3d pers. masc.	
ይናገር: fem. ትናገር: &c.	ይናገሩ: &c. &c.

Compound Preterite.

ይናገር: ነበር: he spoke &c.	ይናገሩ: ነበሩ: they spoke &c.

Compound of Uncertainty.

ይናገር: ይሆናል: he may (perhaps) speak &c.	ይናገሩ: ይሆናሉ: they may (perhaps) speak &c.

3. NO SUBJUNCTIVE.

4. CONSTRUCTIVE.

Simple.

3d pers masc.	
ተናግር: he speaking &c.	ተናግረው: they speaking &c.

Compound Aorist.

ተናግርዋል: he speaks or spoke &c.	ተናግረዋል: they speak or spoke &c.

Compound Preterite.

ተናግር: ነበር: he spoke (had spoken), &c.	ተናግረው: ነበሩ: they spoke (had spoken), &c.

5. IMPERATIVE.

Masc. ተናገር: Fem. ተናገሪ: do thou speak.	ተናገሩ: do ye speak.

6. INFINITIVE.

መናገሩ: to speak, the speaking.

7. PARTICIPLES.

Simple, ተናጋሪ: a speaker, speaking.

Relative (*a*) *Perfect*, የተናገረ: he who spoke.

(*b*) *Present*, የሚናገር: he who speaks.

G. SEVENTH CONJUGATION.

ተምዋኸረ: he tried. **ተምዋገተ:** he disputed.

No other instances of this conjugation present themselves to us, except these two. The peculiarity of this conjugation, *i.e.* the change of a radical of the first or of the fourth order into two letters, into the radical of the sixth, with the **ዋ:** of the fourth order, is so frequent in Shoa in other instances, that we apprehend the use of this conjugation itself may be of no small extent. Its force differs not from the sixth conjugation, with which it is identical, except in the change of the first radical.

1. INDICATIVE.

Preterite.

3d pers. masc. SINGULAR.	PLURAL.
ተምዋኸረ: he tried, &c.	**ተምዋኸሩ:** they tried, &c.

Present and Future.

ይምዋኸራል: he tries (will try) &c.	**ይምዋኸራሉ:** they try (will try) &c.

2. CONTINGENT.

Simple.

ይምዋኸር: &c.	**ይምዋኸሩ:** &c.

Compound Preterite.

ይምዋኸር: ነበረ: he tried, &c.	**ይምዋኸሩ: ነበሩ:** they tried, &c.

Compound of Uncertainty.

ይምዋኸር: ይሆናል: he probably has tried, &c.	**ይምዋኸሩ: ይሆናሉ:** they probably have tried, &c.

3. NO SUBJUNCTIVE.

4. CONSTRUCTIVE.

Simple.

3d pers. masc.	
ተምዋኽር: he trying, &c.	**ተምዋኽረው:** they trying, &c.

Compound Aorist.

ተምዋኽርዋል: he tries or tried &c.	**ተምዋኽረዋል:** they try or tried, &c.

Compound Preterite.

ተምዋኽር: ነበረ: he tried, had tried, &c.	**ተምዋኽረው: ነበሩ:** they tried, had tried, &c.

5. IMPERATIVE.

Masc. **ተምዋኸር:** Fem. **ተምዋኸሪ:** do thou try.	**ተምዋኸሩ:** do ye try.

6. INFINITIVE.

መምዋኸር: to try, the trying, trial.

7. PARTICIPLES.

Simple, ተሞቃካሪ: one who tries.
Relative (*a*) *Perfect*, የተሞቃከረ: he who tried, &c.
(*b*) *Present*, የሚሞቃከር: he who tries, &c.

H. EIGHTH CONJUGATION.

አስከበረ: He caused to honour, caused to be honoured.

This is the most frequent form for the causative voice. Its characteristic is the prefixion of the two letters አስ: to the original form, with which it has nearly the same mode of conjugation. The second radical is, in the Contingent and all other forms derived from it, put into the sixth order. But it has no Subjunctive form. The Imperative has the Contingent form of the radicals. The Infinitive has the first and second radicals in the first order. The Personal Preformatives are put before the አስ: absorbing the አ::

1. INDICATIVE.

Preterite.

3d pers. masc. SINGULAR.	3d pers. PLURAL.
አስነበረ: he caused to be hon. &c.	አስከበሩ: they caused to be honoured, &c.

Present and Future.

	SINGULAR		PLURAL	
3d p. masc.	ያስከብራል: he causes &c.	to be honoured.	ያስከብራሉ: they	cause to be honoured.
.. .. fem.	ታከክብራለች: she causes &c.			
2d .. masc.	ታስከብራለህ: } thou causest &c.		ታስከብራላችሁ: you	
.. .. fem.	ታስከብርያለሽ: }			
.. .. hon. 1.	ያስከብራሉ: } you cause &c.			
.. .. .. 2.	ታስከብራላችሁ: }			
1st .. com.	አስከብራለሁ: I cause &c.		እናስከብራለን: we	

2. CONTINGENT.

Simple.

	SINGULAR.			PLURAL.
3d p. masc.	ያስከብር:	fem.	ታስከብር:	ያስከብሩ:
2d	ታስከብር:	fem.	ታስከብሪ:	ታስከብሩ:
.. .. hon. 1.	ያስከብሩ:	2d	ታስከብሩ:	
1st ..	አስከብር:			እናስከብር:

Compound Preterite.

3d pers. masc.			
ያስከብር: ነበረ:	he caused, &c. to be honoured, &c.	ያስከብሩ: ነበሩ:	they caused, &c. to be honoured, &c.

Compound of Probability.

3d pers. masc. SINGULAR.		PLURAL.	
ያስከብር፡ ይሆናል፡	he (probably) may cause to be hon. &c.	ያስከብሩ፡ ይሆናሉ፡	they (probably) may cause to be hon. &c.

3. NO SUBJUNCTIVE.

4. CONSTRUCTIVE.

3d pers. masc. *Simple.*

አስከብሮ፡	he causing to be honoured, &c.	አስከብረው፡	they causing to be honoured, &c.

Compound Aorist.

አስከብሮዋል፡	he causes (caused) to be hon. &c.	አስከብረዋል፡	they cause (caused) to be hon. &c.

Compound Preterite.

አስከብሮ፡ ነበር፡	he caused (had caused) to be honoured, &c.	አስከብረው፡ ነበሩ፡	they caused (had caused) to be honoured, &c.

5. IMPERATIVE.

Masc. አስከብር፡ Fem. አስከብሪ፡	do thou cause to be honoured.	አስከብሩ፡	do ye cause to be hon.

6. INFINITIVE.

ማስከበር፡ to cause to be honoured, the causing to be honoured, the procuring honour.

7. PARTICIPLES.

Simple, አስከባሪ፡ one who causes to be honoured.

Relative,

(*a*) *Pret.* ያስከበረ፡ he who caused &c.

(*b*) *Pres.* የሚያስከብር፡ he who causes to be honoured, &c.

I. NINTH CONJUGATION.

አስመሳለ፡ He caused to resemble; he flattered, dissimulated.

The difference of this conjugation from the preceding is so slight, that we do not find it necessary to give its flexion: it consists merely in the second radical being constantly long, except in the Constructive: in all the rest it is similar to the preceding አስከበረ፡ As to the third radical ለ፡ we refer to the deviations marked under the First Conjugation, No. 1. This conjugation, by the way, is very rare.

J. TENTH CONJUGATION.

አስተነገረ: He made to speak.

The force of this conjugation is Causative, as the two preceding ones. The difference consists in the form being augmented by three letters, **አስተ:** instead of the two **አስ::**

1. INDICATIVE.

Preterite.

3d pers. masc. SINGULAR.	PLURAL.
አስተነገረ: he made to speak, &c.	**አስተነገሩ:** they made to speak, &c.

Present and Future.

ያስተነግራል: he makes &c. to speak, &c.	**ያስተነግራሉ:** they make &c. to speak, &c.

2. CONTINGENT.

Simple.

3d pers. masc.	
ያስተነግር: &c.	**ያስተነግሩ:** &c.

Compound Preterite.

ያስተነግር: ነበረ: &c. he made &c. to speak, &c.	**ያስተነግሩ: ነበሩ:** they made &c. to speak, &c.

Compound of Probability.

ያስተነግር: ይሆናል: he may probably make to speak, &c.	**ያስተነግሩ: ይሆናሉ:** they may probably cause to speak, &c.

4. CONSTRUCTIVE.

Simple.

3d pers. masc.	
አስተነግር: he causing to speak, &c.	**አስተነግረው:** they causing to speak, &c.

Compound Aorist.

አስተነግርዋል: he causes (caused) to speak, &c.	**አስተነግረዋል:** they cause (caused) to speak, &c.

Compound Preterite.

አስተነግር: ነበረ: he caused &c. to speak, &c.	**አስተነግረው: ነበሩ:** they caused &c. to speak, &c.

3. SUBJUNCTIVE.

3d pers. masc.	
ያስተንገር: may he cause to speak, &c. the same as **ያክበር::**	**ያስተንገሩ:** may they cause to speak, &c.

5. IMPERATIVE.

Masc. **አስተንገር:** Fem. **አስተንገሪ:** do thou make to speak.	**አስተንገሩ:** do you make to speak.

6. INFINITIVE.

ማስተንገር፡ to cause (the causing) to speak.

7. PARTICIPLES.

Simple, አስተንጋሪ፡ one who causes to speak.
Relative Perfect, ያስተነገረ፡ he who caused to speak.
Present, የሚያስተነግር፡ he who causes to speak.

K. ELEVENTH CONJUGATION.

ተቀቀረደ፡ He was entirely humbled; humbled himself entirely.

The force of this conjugation is intensity added to forms D and F: its characteristic is reduplication of the prolonged first radical with the objective ተ፡ prefixed. As its conjugation is the same as ተናገረ፡ we abstain from detailing it.

L. TWELFTH CONJUGATION.

ሰባበረ፡ Broke to pieces.

The force of this conjugation is intense action, represented by a reduplication of the second radical.

1. INDICATIVE.

Preterite.

3d pers. masc. SINGULAR.	PLURAL.
ሰባበረ፡ he broke to pieces, &c.	ሰባበሩ፡ they broke to pieces, &c.

Present and Future.

ይሰባብራል፡ { he breaks, &c. to pieces, &c.	ይሰባብራሉ፡ { they break, &c. to pieces, &c.

2. SIMPLE CONTINGENT.

3d pers. masc.	
ይሰባብር፡ &c.	ይሰባብሩ፡ &c.

Compound Preterite.

ይሰባብር፡ ነበረ፡ { he broke, &c. to pieces, &c.	ይሰባብር፡ ነበሩ፡ { they broke, &c. to pieces, &c.

Compound of Probability.

ይሰባብር፡ ይሆናል፡ { he may probably break to pieces, &c.	ይሰባብሩ፡ ይሆናሉ፡ } they may probably break to pieces, &c.

3. SUBJUNCTIVE.

	SINGULAR.		PLURAL.	
3d p. m.	ይሰባብር: may he	break to pieces.	ይሰባብሩ: may they	break to pieces.
.. .. f.	ትሰባብር: may she			
2d p. m.	ትሰባብር: mayest thou		ትሰባብሩ: may you	
.. .. f.	ትሰባብሪ: mayest thou			
.. hon. 1.	ይሰባብሩ: may you			
.. hon. 2.	ትሰባብሩ: may you			
1st .. .	እሰባብር: may I		እንሰባብር: may we	

4. CONSTRUCTIVE.

Simple.

3d pers. masc.

ሰባብሮ: he breaking to pieces, &c.	ሰባብረው: they breaking to pieces, &c.

Compound Aorist.

ሰባብሮዋል: he breaks (broke) to pieces, &c.	ሰባብረዋል: they break (broke) to pieces, &c.

Compound Preterite.

ሰባብሮ: ነበረ: he broke, &c. to pieces, &c.	ሰባብረው: ነበሩ: they broke &c. to pieces, &c.

5. IMPERATIVE.

Masc. ሰባብር: / Fem. ሰባብሪ: do thou break to pieces, &c.	ሰባብሩ: do ye break to pieces, &c.

6. INFINITIVE.

መሰባበር: to break to pieces.

7. PARTICIPLES.

Simple, ሰባባሪ: one who breaks to pieces.

Rel. Pret. የሰባበረ: he that broke to pieces.

Pres. የሚሰባብር: he that breaks to pieces.

M. THIRTEENTH CONJUGATION.

አደራረገ: He performed great works.

The force of this conjugation is an addition of intensity to the Third Conjugation: this is represented by a reduplication and prolongation of the second radical, with the Preformative አ::

1. INDICATIVE.

Preterite.

3d pers. masc.

SINGULAR.	PLURAL.
አደራረገ: he performed great works, &c.	አደራረጉ: they performed great works, &c.

Present and Future.

SINGULAR.	PLURAL.
3d pers. masc. ያደራርጋል: he performs, &c. great works, &c.	ያደራርጋሉ: they perform great works, &c.

2. CONTINGENT.

Simple.

ያደራርግ: &c.	ያደራርጉ: &c.

Compound Preterite.

ያደራርግ: ነበረ: he performed &c. great works, &c.	ያደራርጉ: ነበሩ: they performed &c. great works, &c.

Compound of Probability.

ያደራርግ: ይሆናል: he may probably perform great works.	ያደራርጉ: ይሆናሉ: they may probably perform great works, &c.

3. SUBJUNCTIVE.

ያድራርግ: may he perform great works, &c.	ያድራርጉ: may they perform great works, &c.

4. CONSTRUCTIVE.

Simple.

አድራርጎ: he performing great works.	አድራርገው: they performing great works, &c.

Compound Aorist.

አድራርጓል: he performs (performed) great works &c.	አድራርገዋል: they perform (performed) great works, &c.

Compound Preterite.

አድራርጎ: ነበረ: he performed, &c. great works &c.	አድራርገው: ነበሩ: they performed, &c. great works, &c.

5. IMPERATIVE.

Masc. አድራርግ: Fem. አድራርጊ: do thou perform great works.	አድራርጉ: do ye perform great works.

6. INFINITIVE.

ማድራረግ: to perform (the performance of) great works.

7. PARTICIPLES.

Simple, አድራሪጊ: one who performs great works.
Rel. Perf. ያደራረግ: he who performed great works.
Pres. የሚያደራርግ: he who performs great works.

N. FOURTEENTH CONJUGATION.

ተመካከረ፡ He counselled with others, gave and took advice, advised frequently.

ተመላለሰ፡ He went and returned, went to and fro, *i.e.* walked.

The force of this conjugation is double intensity, reciprocity, and repetition of the action expressed in the verb. This is represented by reduplication and prolongation of the second radical. Its flexion and conjugation is quite the same as in the Sixth Conjugation.

O. FIFTEENTH CONJUGATION.

ተናገገረ፡ He conversed with another, spoke frequently.

The nature of this conjugation is the same as the preceding; and as to form, it differs only in having the first radical long, in conformity with the sixth species, which it resembles entirely in flexion and conjugation.

P. Q. R. S. SIXTEENTH, SEVENTEENTH, EIGHTEENTH, & NINETEENTH CONJUGATIONS.

ደነዘዘ፡ "To be stiff," "obdurate." *Intransitive.*

አደነዘዘ፡ "To stiffen." *Transitive.*

ተመለሰሰ፡ "He returned," "was returned." *Passive, & Reflective.*

ተሸማጠጠ፡ "He reviled." *Intensitive.*

The chief peculiarity of these four species consists in doubling the third radical, or gemination.—As we shall have an opportunity of treating more fully upon the Geminant Verbs, we merely mention these forms here ; and pass on to the remaining forms of the Regular Triliteral Verb.

T. TWENTIETH CONJUGATION.

አደናገረ፡ He talked one out of any thing, dissuaded.

This and the Twenty-first and Twenty-fourth species are rather remarkable for their singular Preformatives, which are not in use in the cognate dialects. The conjugation of አደናገረ፡ is similar to that of አደራረገ፡ we therefore proceed.

U. TWENTY-FIRST CONJUGATION.

አወሸናገረ፡ He folded his hands.

In what the peculiar force of this species consists, we cannot determine.

V. TWENTY-SECOND CONJUGATION.

ፈተለተለ፡ He rubbed thin between his fingers.

The reduplication of the second and of the third radical, which constitutes the peculiar character of this species, serves to express, as a sort of diminution, a peculiar modification of the original action.

1. INDICATIVE.

Preterite.

3d pers. masc. SINGULAR.	PLURAL.
ፈተለተለ: he rubbed thin between his fingers, &c.	ፈተለተሉ: they rubbed thin, &c.

Present and Future.

ይፈትለትላል: he rubs thin, &c.	ይፈትለትላሉ: they rub thin, &c.

2. CONTINGENT.

Simple.

3d pers. masc.	
ይፈትለትል: &c.	ይፈትለትሉ: &c.

Compound Preterite.

ይፈትለትል: ነበረ: he rubbed (&c.) thin, &c.	ይፈትለትሉ: ነበሩ: they rubbed (&c.) thin, &c.

Compound of Probability.

ይፈትለትል: ይሆናል: he may probably rub thin, &c. &c.	ይፈትለትሉ: ይሆናሉ: they may probably rub thin, &c.

3. SUBJUNCTIVE.

3d pers. masc.	
ይፍተልተል: may he rub thin, &c.	ይፍተልተሉ: may they rub thin, &c.

4. SIMPLE CONSTRUCTIVE.

3d pers. masc.	
ፈተልተሎ: he rubbing thin, &c.	ፈተልተለው: they rubbing thin &c.

Compound Aorist.

ፈተልተልዋል: he rubs (rubbed) thin, &c.	ፈተልተለዋል: they rub (rubbed) thin, &c.

Compound Preterite.

ፈተልተሎ: ነበረ: he rubbed (was rubbing) thin, &c.	ፈተልተለው: ነበሩ: they rubbed (were rubbing) thin, &c.

5. IMPERATIVE.

Masc. ፍተልተል: Fem. ፍተልተይ: do thou rub thin, &c.	ፍተልተሉ: do you rub thin, &c.

6. INFINITIVE.

መፍተልተል: to rub thin, the rubbing thin between the fingers.

7. PARTICIPLES.

Simple,	ፈተልታይ: one who rubs thin, &c.
Relative Perf.	የፈተለተለ: he who has rubbed thin, &c.
Pres.	የሚፈትለትል: he who rubs thin, &c. &c.

W. TWENTY-THIRD CONJUGATION.

ተፈተለተለ፡ It was rubbed thin between the fingers.

This is a Passive derivation from the preceding conjugation, to be treated entirely as the Fourth Conjugation.

X. TWENTY-FOURTH CONJUGATION.

አንጸበረቀ፡ It shone, glittered, sparkled, resplended.

This form seems to be derived from **በረቀ፡** "to fulminate," "to lighten"; and the Preformative **አንጸ—፡** appears to have either a diminutive or a frequentative effect.

---

2. *Conjugation of various Imperfect Forms of the Triliteral Verbs.*

Having thus exhibited the conjugation of the various forms of the Regular and Perfect Triliteral Verb, we now proceed to the consideration of the Imperfect Forms of Triliteral, of Perfect and Imperfect Forms of Biliteral, and of the various forms of Pluriliteral Verbs. We shall endeavour to point out, especially by paradigms, where it is necessary, and the peculiarities in the flexion and conjugation of each; not in order to accumulate materials for the memory, but to facilitate the comprehension of the structure of this part or the language. We notice,

---

I. TRILITERAL VERBS *whose First Conjugation is* A (**አ፡** *or* **ዐ፡፡**)

The chief peculiarity of these verbs consists in the liability under which they are to have the first radical contracted with every Preformative acceding to the Verb, according to the rule laid down in Part I. Chap. VII. 2. A.B. For the purpose of exemplifying, we select the two Verbs **አመነ፡** "he believed," and **አለፈ፡** "he passed."

A. FIRST CONJUGATION.

Simple Form, **አመነ፡** He believed.

1. INDICATIVE.

Preterite. Regular, as **ከበረ፡፡**

Present and Future.

	SINGULAR.		PLURAL.	
p. masc.	**ያምናል፡** he	believes, will believe.	**ያምናሉ፡** they believe, will believe.	
.. fem.	**ታምናለች፡** she	believes, will believe.		
.. masc.	**ታምናለህ፡**	thou believest, wilt believe.	**ታምናላችሁ፡** you believe, will believe.	
.. fem.	**ታምኛለሽ፡**	thou believest, wilt believe.		
.. hon. 1.	**ያምናሉ፡**	you believe, will believe.		
.. .. 2.	**ታምናላችሁ፡**	you believe, will believe.		
.. com.	**አምናለሁ፡**	I believe, shall believe.	**እናምናለን፡** we believe, shall believe.	

2. CONTINGENT,

As the Indicative Present, without the Auxiliary አለ:

3. SUBJUNCTIVE.

	SINGULAR.		PLURAL.
3d p. masc.	ይመን: may he	believe.	ይመኑ: may they believe.
.. .. fem.	ትመን: may she		
2d .. masc.	ትመን: } mayest thou		ትመኑ: may you believe.
.. .. fem.	ትመኚ: }		
.. .. hon. 1.	ይመኑ: } may you		
.. .. .. 2.	ትመኑ: }		
1st. . com.	እመን: may I		እንመን: may we believe.

4. CONSTRUCTIVE.

3d pers. masc.

አምኖ: he believing, &c. | አምነው: they believing, &c.

Regular; as, ኩበር: &c.

IMPERATIVE.

Masc. እመን: } do thou believe! | እመኑ: do ye believe!
Fem. እመኚ: }

6. INFINITIVE.

ማመን: to believe, the believing, faith, trust.

7. PARTICIPLES.

Simple, አማኝ: one who believes, a believer.

Relative Perfect, ያመነ: he who believed. ያመነች: she who believed, &c

Relative Present, የሚያምን: he who believes, &c.

የምታምን: she who believes, &c.

B. SECOND CONJUGATION.

Objective Voice.

ታመነ: He was believed, accredited, was trustworthy, faithful, entrusted himself.

Flexion and Conjugation according to the Fourth Conjugation of the Regular Triliteral Verb; with the exception, that the characteristic ተ: because it has joined to itself the vowel of the first radical, is not dropped, but retained in all the forms.

1. INDICATIVE.

Preterite.

3d pers. masc. SINGULAR. | PLURAL.

ታመነ: he was trusted, &c. | ታመኑ: they were trusted, &c.

Present and Future.

ይታመናል: he is trusted, &c. | ይታመናሉ: they are trusted, &c.

2. CONTINGENT.

SINGULAR.	PLURAL.
ይታመን: &c.	ይታመኑ: &c.

3. NO SUBJUNCTIVE.

4. CONSTRUCTIVE.

3d pers. masc.	
ታምኖ: he being trusted, &c.	ታምነው: they being trusted, &c.

5. IMPERATIVE.

Masc. ታመን: } Fem. ታመኚ: } be thou faithful.	ታመኑ: be ye faithful.

6. INFINITIVE.

መታመን: to be believed, faithfulness, &c.

7. PARTICIPLES.

Simple, ታማኝ: one who is believed.
Rel. Pret. የታመነ: he who was believed, faithful, &c.
Present, የሚታመን: he who is believed, &c.

C. THIRD CONJUGATION.

Transitive Voice.

አሳመነ: He made believe, persuaded.

This form corresponds with the Eighth Conjugation of the Perfect Verb አስከበረ:: The first radical አ: is absorbed by the characteristic Preformative አስ:: No Subjunctive form.

D. FOURTH CONJUGATION.

Transitive Voice.

አስታመነ: He accredited, attested, entrusted.

This form, which joins the characteristics of the Objective and of the Transitive Voice in nature and form, answers the Tenth Conjugation of the Perfect Triliteral Verb.

E. FIFTH CONJUGATION.

Intensive Voice.

ተላለፈ: Passed and repassed, trespassed, varied.

In this form, which corresponds with the Fourteenth Conjugation of the Regular Triliteral Verb, the first radical, አ:, is dropped; but the ተ: is retained when Prefixes are joined; *e.g.* Contingent, ይተላለፍ:: Infinitive, መተላለፍ::

F. SIXTH CONJUGATION.

Causative and Intensive Voice.

አስተላለፈ: He made pass in different ways.

In this form the Causative አስ: is joined to the preceding Conjugation.

II. SECOND CLASS OF IMPERFECT TRILITERALS.

Triliteral Geminants.

(See page 56, II.)

These verbs seem to have been derived from Biliterals which are lost, but whose second radical has been doubled. (See Part I. Ch. VII. 2. D.) In conjugating these verbs, the geminant letters are often contracted into one; but that letter, although the Abyssinians have no mark for distinguishing the accent, shows its origin, by having the tone.

It will be observed, that there are, among the ten different Conjugations of this class, four which have the ን:, either with the Transitive አ:, or the Intransitive ተ: prefixed.

In looking at the numerous verbs of this class, mentioned in the note, page 56, it will be seen that all classes of letters, except the gutturals and the vowel letters, are subject to gemination.

The general mode of conjugating being the same in this as in all other classes of verbs, attention is to be paid especially to those forms which have gemination, and to those which have the contraction.

After these preliminary remarks, we proceed to give the Paradigms.

A. FIRST CONJUGATION.

ለቀቀ: *neut.* He went away; *act.* He dismissed.

Gemination exists in this Conjugation—in the Indicative, Preterite, Subjunctive, Imperative, Infinitive and Simple, and Relative Preterite Participles: *Contraction* in the remaining Moods and Tenses.

1. INDICATIVE MOOD.

Preterite.

	SINGULAR.		PLURAL.
3d p. masc.	ለቀቀ:	he dismissed.	ለቀቁ: they dismissed.
.. .. fem.	ለቀቀች:	she dismissed.	
2d .. masc.	ለቀቅህ:	thou dismissedst.	ለቀቃችሁ: you dismissed.
.. .. fem.	ለቀቅሽ:		
.. .. hon. 1.	ለቀቁ:	you dismissed.	
.. .. .. 2.	ለቀቃችሁ:		
1st .. com.	ለቀቅሁ:	I dismissed.	ለቀቅን: we dismissed.

Present and Future.

SINGULAR.			PLURAL.
3d p. masc.	ይለቅል: he	dismisses.	ይለቃሉ: they dismiss.
. . . . fem.	ትለቃለች: she		
2d . . masc.	ትለቃለህ:	thou dismissest.	ትለቃላችሁ: you dismiss.
. . . . fem.	ትለቅያለሽ:		
. . . . hon. 1.	ይለቃሉ:	you dismiss.	
. . . . hon. 2.	ትለቃላችሁ:		
1st . . com.	እለቃለሁ: I dismiss.		እንለቃለን: we dismiss.

2. CONTINGENT.

3d p. masc.	ይለቅ:	fem. ትለቅ:	ይለቁ:
2d	ትለቅ:	fem. ትለቂ:	ትለቁ:
. . . hon. 1.	ይለቁ:	2. ትለቁ:	
1.	እለቅ:		እንለቅ:

3. SUBJUNCTIVE.

3d p. masc.	ይልቀቅ: may he		dismiss.	ይልቀቁ: may they dismiss.
. . . . fem.	ትልቀቅ: may she			
2d . . masc.	ትልቀቅ:	mayest thou		ትልቀቁ: may you dismiss.
. . . . fem.	ትልቀቂ:			
. . . . hon. 1.	ይልቀቁ:	may you		
. . . . . . 2.	ትልቀቁ:			
1st . . com.	እልቀቅ: may I			እንልቀቅ: may we dismiss.

4. CONSTRUCTIVE.

Simple.

3d p. masc.	ልቆ: he		dismissing.	ልቀው: they dismissing.
. . . . fem.	ልቃ: she			
2d . . masc.	ልቀህ:	thou		ልቃችሁ: you dismissing.
. . . . fem.	ልቀሽ:			
. . . . hon. 1.	ልቀው:	you		
. . . . . . 2.	ልቃችሁ:			
1st . . com.	ልቄ: I			ልቀን: we dismissing.

Compound Aorist.

3d p. masc.	ልቋል: he dismisses, &c.		ልቀዋል: they dismiss.
. . . . fem.	ልቃለች: she dismisses.		
2d . . masc.	ልቀሃል:	thou dismissest.	ልቃችኋል: you dismiss.
. . . . fem.	ልቀሻል:		
. . . . hon. 1.	ልቀዋል:	you dismiss.	
. . . . . . 2.	ልቃችኋል:		
1st . . com.	ልቅያለሁ: I dismiss.		ልቀናል: we dismiss.

Compound Preterite.

3d pers. masc. SINGULAR.	PLURAL.
ልቆ: ነበረ: he dismissed, &c.	**ልቀው: ነበሩ:** they dismissed, &c.

5. IMPERATIVE.

m. **ልቀቅ:** *fem.* **ልቀቂ:** do thou dismiss. | **ልቀቁ:** do ye dismiss.

6. INFINITIVE.

መልቀቅ: To dismiss, the dismission, dismissal.

7. PARTICIPLES.

Simple.

Simple Act. **ለቃቂ:** one who dismisses.
Pass. **ልቃቂ:** one who is dismissed.
Rel. Perf. **የለቀቀ:** he who has dismissed.
Pres. **የሚለቅ:** he who dismisses.

B. SECOND CONJUGATION.

Active or Transitive Voice.

አረቀቀ: He thinned, rarefied, refined.

We need scarcely to mention, that this form corresponds with the Third Conjugation of the Perfect Triliterals. Gemination prevails in the Preterite, Subjunctive, Infinitive, Simple, and Preterite Participles; Contraction in the Indicative Present, the Contingent, and Rel. Part. Present; both Gemination and Contraction in the Constructive and Imperative. Having presented a pretty full view of the preceding conjugation, it will suffice in the present one to give merely the leading types; *i.e.* 3d person masc. sing. and common plural of those paradigms which have all the Persons, besides the more simple Moods.

1. INDICATIVE.

Preterite.

3d pers. masc. SINGULAR.	PLURAL.
አረቀቀ: he refined, &c.	**አረቀቁ:** they refined.

Present and Future.

ያረቃል: he refines.	**ያረቃሉ:** they refine.

2. CONTINGENT.

ያረቅ:	**ያረቁ:**

3. SUBJUNCTIVE.

ያርቅቅ: may he refine.	**ያርቅቁ:** may they refine.

4. CONSTRUCTIVE.

Simple.

አርቆ: and **አርቅቆ:** he refining.	**አርቀው:** and **አርቅቀው:** they refining.

Compound Aorist.

3d pers. masc. SINGULAR.	PLURAL.
አርቋል: and አርቅቋል: } he refines.	አርቀዋል: and አርቀቀዋል: } they refine.

Compound Preterite.

አርቀ: ነበረ: and አርቅቀ: ነበረ:: he refined.	አርቀው: ነበሩ: and አርቅቀው: ነበሩ:: they refined.

5. IMPERATIVE.

Masc. አረቅ: and አርቅቅ: } do thou refine. Fem. አረቂ: and አርቅቂ: }	አረቁ: and አርቅቁ: do ye refine.

6. INFINITIVE.

ማርቀቅ: to refine, the refining, rarefaction.

7. PARTICIPLES.

Simple, አርቃቂ: a refiner.

Rel. Perf. ያረቀቀ: he who refined.

Pres. የሚያረቅ: he who refines.

C. THIRD CONJUGATION.

Passive or Objective Voice.

ተለቀቀ: He was dismissed.

This conjugation has no peculiar form for the Subjunctive. Contraction takes place only in the Constructive Mood. Besides this, it is regularly conjugated, after the manner of the Fourth Conjugation of the Perfect Triliteral Verbs.

D. FOURTH CONJUGATION.

Active and Intensive Voice.

አላቀቀ: He yawned. አሳደደ: He persecuted.

Both in nature and form, this conjugation resembles the Fifth of the Perfect Triliteral Verb. It preserves gemination in the Indicative Preterite, the Imperative, Infinitive, and Simple and Perfect Participle. In the other Moods and Tenses, it is contracted.

1. INDICATIVE.

Preterite.

3d pers. masc. SINGULAR.	PLURAL.
አሳደደ: he persecuted.	አሳደዱ: they persecuted.

Present and Future.

ያሳድዳል: he persecutes.	ያሳድዳሉ: they persecute.

2. CONTINGENT.

3d pers. masc. SINGULAR.	PLURAL.
ያሳድ:	ያሳዱ:

3. NO SUBJUNCTIVE.

4. SIMPLE CONSTRUCTIVE.

አሳደ: he persecuting.	አሳደው: they persecuting.

Compound Aorist.

አሳድዋል: he persecutes.	አሳደዋል: they persecute.

Compound Preterite.

አሳደ: ነበረ: he persecuted.	አሳደው: ነበሩ: they persecuted.

5. IMPERATIVE.

Masc. አሳድድ: } do thou perse- Fem. አሳድጅ: } cute.	አሳድዱ: do ye persecute.

6. INFINITIVE.

ማሳደድ: to persecute, the persecuting, persecution.

7. PARTICIPLES.

Simple, አሳደጅ: a persecutor.
Rel. Perf. ያሳደደ: he who persecuted.
Present, የሚያሳድ: he who persecutes.

E. FIFTH CONJUGATION.

Passive and Intensive Voice.

ተሳደደ: He was persecuted, habitually persecuted.

This form is conjugated after the Sixth Conjugation of the Perfect Verb; has no peculiar Subjunctive; and geminates and contracts after the third form of this class.

F. SIXTH CONJUGATION.

Causative Voice.

አስመረረ: He embittered.

Corresponds with the Eighth Conjugation of the Perfect Triliteral Verb, and is conjugated like the first form of this class.

G. SEVENTH CONJUGATION.

Intensive Voice.

አንሻተተ: He cheated.

A peculiar form, of which, as we have not hitherto had a similar one, we give here an outline.

1. INDICATIVE.

Preterite Regular.

3d pers. masc. SINGULAR.	PLURAL.
አንሳተተ: he cheated.	አንሻተቱ: they cheated.

Present and Future.

ያንሻታል: he cheats.	ያንሻታሉ: they cheat.

2. SIMPLE CONTINGENT.

ያንሻት:	ያንሻቱ:

3. SUBJUNCTIVE.—None.

4. SIMPLE CONSTRUCTIVE.

3d pers. masc.	
አንሻቶ: he cheating.	አንሻተው: they cheating.

Compound Aorist.

አንሻትዋል: he cheats.	አንሻትዋል: they cheat.

Compound Perfect.

አንሻቶ: ነበረ: he cheated.	አንሻተው: ነበሩ: they cheated.

5. IMPERATIVE.

Masc. አንሻትት: / Fem. አንሻትች: } do thou cheat.	አንሻትቱ: do ye cheat.

6. INFINITIVE.

ማንሻተት: to cheat, the cheating.

7. PARTICIPLES.

Simple, አንሻታች: a cheater.
Rel. Perf. ያንሻተተ: he who cheated.
Present, የሚያንሻት: he who cheats.

H. EIGHTH CONJUGATION.

Passive Voice.

ተንሻተተ: He was cheated.

This is the Passive form of the preceding derivation; and, in gemination, is regulated by the Third Conjugation of this class.

I. K. NINTH AND TENTH CONJUGATIONS.

Reflective Voice.

አንጠራራ: and ተንጠራራ: He stretched himself.

The peculiarity of these two forms, the power of which seems to be the same, consists in the length of both the geminating letters. On account of their length, they cannot be contracted. They assume, therefore, no Subjunctive form; and the Geminants retain their length, except in the

Constructive, which retains the last radical short, and enters a ቶ: which servile, also, is as a paragoge added in the Infinitive; thus:

SIMPLE CONSTRUCTIVE.

SINGULAR.	PLURAL.
አንጠራርቶ: he stretching himself, &c.	አንጠራርተው: they stretching themselves, &c.

INFINITIVE.

ማንጠራራት: the stretching, to stretch, oneself.

III. THIRD CLASS OF IMPERFECT TRILITERALS.

Geminants whose first radical is አ::

This class numbers only a few Verbs. They combine the imperfections of contraction in the beginning and at the end, *i.e.* the imperfections of both the preceding classes. For an exhibition, we select the Verbs አዘዘ: "he commanded," and አመመ: "it was painful."

This class has but four Conjugations; the first of which is Intransitive or Active; the second, Objective, Intransitive, or Reflective; the third, Causative; and the fourth, Intensive.

A. FIRST CONJUGATION.

አዘዘ: He commanded.

1. INDICATIVE.

Preterite.

3d pers. masc. SINGULAR. | PLURAL.

አዘዘ: he commanded. | አዘዙ: they commanded.

Present and Future.

ያዛል: he commands. | ያዛሉ: they command.

2. SIMPLE CONTINGENT.

3d pers. masc.

ያዝ: | ያዙ:

3. SUBJUNCTIVE.

3d pers. masc.

ይዘዝ: may he command. | ይዘዙ: may they command.

4. SIMPLE CONSTRUCTIVE.

3d p. masc. አዞ: he commanding. | አዘው: they commanding.

.. .. fem. አዛ: she commanding.

2d .. masc. አዘህ: } thou commanding. | አዛችሁ: you commanding.

.. .. fem. አዘሽ: }

.. .. hon. 1. አዘው: } you commanding.

.. .. hon. 2. አዛችሁ: }

1st .. com. አዤ: I commanding. | አዘን: we commanding.

Compound Aorist.

3d p. masc.	አዝዋል: he } commands.	አዘዋል: they command.
.. .. fem.	አዛለች: she } commands.	
2d .. masc.	አዛሃል: } thou commandest.	አዛችኋል: you command.
.. .. fem.	አዘሻል: } thou commandest.	
.. .. hon. 1.	አዘዋል: } you command.	
.. .. hon. 2.	አዛችኋል: } you command.	
1st.. com.	አዛለሁ: I command.	አዘናል: we command.

5. IMPERATIVE.

Masc. እዘዝ: } do thou command.	እዘዙ: do ye command.
Fem. እዘዢ: } do thou command.	

6. INFINITIVE.

ማዘዝ: to command, the commanding, command.

7. PARTICIPLES.

Simple, አዛዥ: one who commands, a commander.

Rel. Pret. ያዘዘ: he who commanded.

Present, የሚያዝ: he who commands.

B. SECOND CONJUGATION.

Passive, Reflective, and Intransitive.

ታመመ: He felt pain, was sick. ታዘዘ: He was commanded, he obeyed.

In this conjugation, the ታ: is retained throughout; and contraction of the second and third radical takes place in the Constructive Mood only. No Subjunctive. Second radical is treated as in all the Objective forms.

C. THIRD CONJUGATION.

Transitive and Causative Voice.

አሳመመ: He made sick, gave or caused pain.

The first radical አ:, absorbed in the Preformative ሳ:, undergoes no further change. Gemination prevails in the Preterite, Indicative, Imperative, Infinitive, and Simple and Preterite Participles; Contraction in the Indicative, Present, and Constructive; and both Gemination and Contraction in the Contingent. Respecting the latter, we think, that when it stands by itself, it is geminated; but when it receives any addition at the beginning or at the end, it is contracted.

D. FOURTH CONJUGATION.

Intensive Voice.

አስታመመ፡ He nursed sick persons.

This conjugation corresponds with the Tenth of the Perfect Triliterals, and with the Fourth of the First Class of Imperfect Triliterals. Contraction takes place only in the Constructive Mood.

---

3. *Conjugation of Biliteral Verbs.*

Biliteral Verbs are, in the Amharic Language, exceedingly numerous; owing especially, as will be seen hereafter, to the many contractions from Triliteral Verbs, by which they became Biliterals. In treating on these Verbs, it will be best to divide them into four distinct classes; namely, (*a*) Perfect; (*b*) Imperfect; (*c*) Contracted; (*d*) Irregular and Anomalous Biliteral Verbs.

I. FIRST CLASS.—*Perfect Biliterals.*

These are Verbs which have the two radical letters in the first form, do not begin with any vowel letter, and are conjugated regularly. They have this resemblance to some of the Contracted forms, that the paragogic **ት፡** is added to most of its Infinitives, and enters into the Constructives. They are conjugated through Eight different Species or Conjugations.

A. FIRST CONJUGATION.

Intransitive, Active, and Transitive Voice.

ገነ፡ He flourished. **ደገ፡** Was great. **ሰጠ፡** He gave.

1. INDICATIVE.

Preterite.

	SINGULAR.	PLURAL.
3d p. masc.	**ሰጠ፡** he gave.	**ሰጡ፡** they gave.
. . . . fem.	**ሰጠች፡** she gave.	
2d . . masc.	**ሰጠህ፡** } thou gavest.	**ሰጣችሁ፡** you gave.
. . . . fem.	**ሰጠሽ፡** } thou gavest.	
. . . . hon. 1.	**ሰጡ፡** } you gave.	
. . . . . . 2.	**ሰጣችሁ፡** } you gave.	
1st . . com.	**ሰጠሁ፡** I gave.	**ሰጠን፡** we gave.

Present and Future.

	SINGULAR.	PLURAL.
3d p. masc.	ይሰጣል: he gives.	ይሰጣሉ: they give.
.. .. fem.	ትሰጣለች: she gives.	
2d .. masc.	ትሰጣለህ: } thou	ትሰጣላችሁ: you give.
.. .. fem.	ትሰጫለሽ: } givest.	
.. .. hon. 1.	ይሰጣሉ: } you	
.. .. .. 2.	ትሰጣላችሁ: } give.	
1st .. com.	እሰጣለሁ: I give.	እንሰጣለን: we give.

2. CONTINGENT.

3d p. masc.	ይሰጥ: fem. ትሰጥ:	ይሰጡ:
2d .. masc.	ትሰጥ: fem. ትሰጪ:	ትሰጡ:
.. .. hon. 1.	ይሰጡ: 2. ትሰጡ:	
1st	እሰጥ::	እንሰጥ::

3. SUBJUNCTIVE.

3d p. masc.	ይስጥ: may he give.	ይስጡ: may they give.
.. .. fem.	ትስጥ: may she give.	
2d .. masc.	ትስጥ: } mayest thou	ትስጡ: may you give.
.. .. fem.	ትስጪ: } give.	
.. .. hon. 1.	ይስጡ: } may you	
.. .. .. 2.	ትስጡ: } give.	
1st .. com.	እስጥ: may I give.	እንስጥ: may we give.

4. CONSTRUCTIVE with ተ:

3d p. masc.	ሰጥቶ: he giving.	ሰጥተው: they giving.
.. .. fem.	ሰጥታ: she giving.	
2d .. masc.	ሰጥተህ: } thou	ሰጥታችሁ: you giving.
.. .. fem.	ሰጥተሽ: } giving.	
.. .. hon. 1.	ሰጥተው: } you	
.. .. .. 2.	ሰጥታችሁ: } giving.	
1st .. com.	ሰጥቼ: I giving.	ሰጥተን: we giving.

Compound Aorist.

3d p. masc.	ሰጥትዋል: he gives.	ሰጥተዋል: they give.
.. .. fem.	ሰጥታለች: she gives.	
2d .. masc.	ሰጥተሃል: } thou	ሰጥታችኋል: you give.
.. .. fem.	ሰጥተሻል: } givest.	
.. .. hon. 1.	ሰጥተዋል: } you	
.. .. .. 2.	ሰጥታችኋል: } give.	
1st .. com.	ሰጥቻለሁ: I give.	ሰጥተናል: we give.

Simple Form without ተ: (rare).

	SINGULAR.	PLURAL.
3d p. masc.	ድገ: he being great.	ድገው: they being great.
. . . . fem.	ድጋ: she being great.	
2d . . masc.	ድገህ: } thou being	
. . . . fem.	ድገሽ: } great.	ድጋችሁ: you being great.
. . . . hon. 1.	ድገው: } you being	
. . . . . . 2.	ድጋችሁ: } great.	
1st. . com.	ድጌ: I being great.	ድገን: we being great.

5. IMPERATIVE.

Masc. ስጥ: ሰጥ:	} do thou give.	ስጡ: ሰጡ: do ye give.
Fem. ስጪ: ሰጪ:		

6. INFINITIVE.

መስጠት: to give, the giving. መጠጥ: to drink, the drinking.

7. PARTICIPLES.

Simple, ሰጪ: and ሳጪ: a giver.
Rel. Pret. የሰጠ: he who gave.
Pres. የሚሰጥ: he who gives.

B. SECOND CONJUGATION.

Active, Transitive Voice.

አገነ: He beautified, praised. አደገ: He grew.

1. INDICATIVE.

Preterite.

	SINGULAR.	PLURAL.
3d p. masc.	አደገ: he grew.	አደጉ: they grew.
. . . . fem.	አደገች: she grew.	
2d . . masc.	አደግህ: } thou	
. . . . fem.	አደግሽ: } grewest.	አደጋችሁ: you grew.
. . . . hon. 1.	አደጉ: } you	
. . . . . . 2.	አደጋችሁ: } grew.	
1st. . com.	አደግሁ: I grew.	አደግን: we grew.

Present and Future.

3d pers. masc.	
ያድጋል: he grows, &c.	ያድጋሉ: they grow.

2. CONTINGENT.

ያድግ: &c.	ያድጉ: &c.

3. NO SUBJUNCTIVE.

4. CONSTRUCTIVE, with ት::

SINGULAR.	PLURAL.
አበጅቶ: he preparing.	አበጅተው: they preparing.

Without ት::

አድጎ: he growing.	አድገው: they growing.

5. IMPERATIVE.

Masc. አድግ: Fem. አድጊ: } do thou grow.	አድጉ: do ye grow.

6. INFINITIVE.

ማደግ: to grow, the growth.

ማብጀት: to prepare, the preparing, preparation.

7. PARTICIPLES.

Simple, አዳጊ: one who grows. አጣጪ: one who irrigates.

Rel. Pret. ያደገ: he who grew.

Pres. የሚያድግ: he who grows.

C. THIRD CONJUGATION.

Objective Voice.

ተሰጠ: He was given.

This has nothing peculiar. It is treated like other objective forms, and has the paragogic ት: uniformly.

D. FOURTH CONJUGATION.

Transitive or Causative Voice.

አስገነ: He beautified, glorified.

Has the paragogic ት::

1. INDICATIVE.

Preterite.

3d pers. masc. SINGULAR.	PLURAL.
አስገነ: he beautified.	አስገኑ: they beautified.

Present and Future.

ያስገናል: he beautifies.	ያስገናሉ: they beautify.

2. CONTINGENT.

ያስገን:	ያስገኑ:

3. SUBJUNCTIVE.

ያስግን: may he beautify.	ያስግኑ: may they beautify.

4. CONSTRUCTIVE.

አስገንቶ: he beautifying.	አስገንተው: they beautify.

5. IMPERATIVE.

Masc. አስግን: Fem. አስግኚ: } do thou beautify.	አስግኑ: do ye beautify.

6. INFINITIVE.

ማስገነት: to beautify, beautifying.

7. PARTICIPLES.

Simple, አስጋኝ: beautifier.
Rel. Pret. ያስገነ: he who beautified.
Present, የሚያስገን: he who beautifies.

E. FIFTH CONJUGATION.

Transitive or Causative Voice.

አሳደገ: He caused to grow, trained, reared, educated.

Differs only in form from the preceding conjugations. It has no paragogic ት:, and is conjugated like አሳመነ: in the Third Conjugation of the first class of Imperfect Triliteral Verbs.

F. G. H. The Sixth, Seventh, and Eighth Conjugations are treated like Triliteral Geminants.

II. SECOND CLASS.

Imperfect Biliterals, which have አ: *for the first Radical Letter.*

The first radical አ: undergoes the usual changes, as shown in the preceding conjugations. The paragogic ት: prevails through all the conjugations of this class, which contains but few verbs. The verb አየ: "He saw," containing all the different forms of Conjugations of this class, we have selected for exhibition.

A. FIRST CONJUGATION.

Subjective, Intransitive, and Transitive Voice.

አየ: He saw.

1. INDICATIVE.

Preterite.

አየ: he saw, &c., like ሰጠ::

Present and Future.

	SINGULAR.		PLURAL.
3d p. masc.	ያያል: he sees.		ያያሉ: they see.
. . . . fem.	ታያለች: she sees.		
. . . . masc.	ታያለህ:	thou seest.	ታያላችሁ: you see.
. . . . fem.	ታያለሽ:		
. . . . hon. 1.	ያያሉ:	you see.	
. . . . hon. 2.	ታያላችሁ:		
1st.. com.	አያለሁ: I see.		እናያለን: we see.

2. CONTINGENT.

	SINGULAR.		PLURAL.
3d p. masc.	ያይ:	fem. ታይ:	ያዩ::
2d .. masc.	ታይ:	fem. ታዪ:	ታዩ:
.. .. hon. 1.	ያዩ:	2. ታዩ:	
1st.. com.	አይ:		እናይ:

3. SUBJUNCTIVE.

3d p. masc.	ይይ: may he see.		ይዩ: may they see.
.. .. fem.	ትይ: may she see.		
2d p. masc.	ትይ:	mayest thou see.	ትዩ: may you see.
.. .. fem.	ትዪ:		
.. .. hon. 1.	ይዩ:	may you see.	
.. .. .. 2.	ትዩ:		
1st.. com.	እይ: may I see.		እንይ: may we see.

4. CONSTRUCTIVE.

Simple.

3d p. masc.	አይቶ: he seeing.		አይተው: they seeing.
.. .. fem.	አይታ: she seeing.		አይታችሁ: you seeing.
2d p. masc.	አይተህ:	thou seeing.	
.. .. fem.	አይተሽ:		
.. .. hon. 1.	አይተው:	you seeing.	
.. .. .. 2.	አይታችሁ:		
1st.. com.	አይቼ: I seeing.		አይተን: we seeing.

5. IMPERATIVE.

Masc.	እይ:	do thou see.	እዩ: do ye see.
Fem.	እዪ:		

6. INFINITIVE.

ማየት: the seeing, sight, aspect.

7. PARTICIPLES.

Simple, None. *Relative Preterite,* ያየ: he who saw.

Present, የሚያይ: he who sees.

B. SECOND CONJUGATION.

Passive, Reflective, or Intransitive Voice.

ታየ: He was seen, appeared.

1. INDICATIVE.

Preterite.

	SINGULAR.	PLURAL.
3d p. masc.	ታየ: he was seen.	ታዩ: they were seen.
.. .. fem.	ታየች: she was seen.	
2d p. masc.	ታየህ:	ታያችሁ:
.. .. fem.	ታየሽ:	
.. .. hon. 1.	ታዩ:	
.. .. .. 2.	ታያችሁ:	
1st .. com.	ታየሁ:	ታየን:

Present and Future.

3d p. masc.	ይታያል: he is seen.	ይታያሉ: they are seen.
.. .. fem.	ትታያለች: { she is seen, &c.	

2. SIMPLE CONTINGENT.

3d p. masc. ይታይ: fem. ትታይ: | ይታዩ::

3. NO SUBJUNCTIVE.

4. CONSTRUCTIVE.

3d p. masc. ታይቶ: he appearing, &c. | ታይተው: they appearing.

5. IMPERATIVE.

Masc. ታይ: } do thou appear. | ታዩ: do ye appear.
Fem. ታዪ: }

6. INFINITIVE.

መታየት: to be seen, the appearing, appearance.

7. PARTICIPLES.

Simple, None. *Relative Preterite*, የታየ: he who appeared.

Present, የሚታይ: he who appears.

---

c. THIRD CONJUGATION.

Transitive and Causative Voice.

አሳየ: He made to be seen, caused to appear, showed.

1. INDICATIVE.

Preterite.

	SINGULAR.	PLURAL.
3d p. masc.	አሳየ: he showed.	አሳዩ: they showed.
.. .. fem.	አሳየች: she showed.	
2d p. masc.	አሳየህ: f. አሳየሽ:	አሳያችሁ:
.. .. hon. 1.	አሳዩ: 2. አሳያችሁ:	
.. .. com.	አሳየሁ:	አሳየን:

Present and Future.

	SINGULAR.	PLURAL.
3d p. masc.	ያሳያል: he shows.	ያሳያሉ: they show.
. . . . fem.	ታሳያለች: she shows.	
2d p. masc.	ታሳያለህ:	ታሳያላችሁ:
. . . . fem.	ታሳያለሽ:	
. . . . hon. 1.	ያሳያሉ:	
. . . . . . 2.	ታሳያላችሁ:	
1st. . com.	አሳያለሁ:	እናሳያለን:

2. CONTINGENT.

3d pers. masc.

ያሳይ: fem. ታሳይ: &c.	ያሳዩ: &c.

3. SUBJUNCTIVE.

3d p. masc.	ያስይ: may he show.	ያስዩ: &c.
. . . . fem.	ታስይ: &c. may she show	

4. CONSTRUCTIVE.

3d p. masc.	አሳይቶ: he showing.	አሳይተው:
. . . . fem.	አሳይታ:: she showing.	

5. IMPERATIVE.

Masc. አስይ: Fem. አስይ:	} do thou show.	አስዩ: do ye show.

6. INFINITIVE.

ማሳየት: To show, the showing.

7. PARTICIPLES.

Simple, None.

Rel. Pret. ያሳየ: he who showed.

Pres. የሚያሳይ: he who shows.

D. FOURTH CONJUGATION.

Transitive and Causative Voice.

አስታየ: He made to be seen, brought into sight.

1. INDICATIVE PRETERITE.

3d pers. masc. SINGULAR.	PLURAL.
አስታየ: brought into sight.	አስታዩ: &c.
አስታየች: &c., like the preceding.	

Present and Future.

ያስታያል: he brings into sight.	ያስታያሉ: they bring into sight.

2. CONTINGENT.

ያስታይ: fem. ታስታይ: &c.	ያስታዩ: &c.

3. SUBJUNCTIVE.—None.

4. CONSTRUCTIVE.

SINGULAR.	PLURAL.
3d pers. masc. አስታይቶ: he bringing into sight.	አስታይተው: they bringing into sight.

5. IMPERATIVE.

SINGULAR.	PLURAL.
Masc. አስታይ: Fem. አስታዪ: do thou bring into sight.	አስታዩ: do ye bring into sight.

6. INFINITIVE.

ማስታየት: to bring into sight.

7. PARTICIPLES.

Simple, None.
Rel. Pret. ያስታየ: he who brought into sight.
Pres. የሚያስታይ: he who brings into sight.

E. FIFTH CONJUGATION.

Reciprocative Voice.

ተያየ: He was with another in reciprocal sight; Looked at each other.

As this is not used in our languages in the Singular, we shall omit the translation, and give merely the requisite forms in Amharic.

1. INDICATIVE.

Preterite.

3d pers. masc.	SINGULAR.	PLURAL.
ተያየ:	fem. ተያየች:	ተያዩ:

Present and Future.

ይተያያል:	fem. ትተያያለች:	ይተያያሉ:

2. CONTINGENT.

ይተያይ:	fem. ትተያይ:	ይተያዩ:

3. SUBJUNCTIVE.—None.

4. CONSTRUCTIVE.

ተያይቶ:	fem. ተያይታ:	ተያይተው:

5. IMPERATIVE.

Masc. ተያይ:	fem. ተያዪ:	ተያዩ:

6. INFINITIVE.

መተያየት: the being in sight of each other; relation to each other.

7. PARTICIPLES.

Simple.—None. *Rel. Pret.* የተያየ:: *Pres.* የሚተያይ::

F. SIXTH CONJUGATION.

Causative and Reciprocative.

አስታየየ: He made look at each other; placed over against each other.

Is not, in form, different from the preceding; save the prefixing of **አስ:** and the changes which that undergoes; and, that in the Imperative it has **አስትያይ::**

III. THIRD CLASS.—*Contracted Biliterals.*

This very numerous class is derived from Triliterals; which, in the Ethiopic and Tigrê Languages, have either a Vowel letter **አ: ዐ: የ:** or **ወ:**, or a Guttural **ሀ: ሐ: ኀ:** or **ኸ:** contracted with the preceding letter. The letter to which their vowel has thus been joined has been made long; whilst the verb itself has become a biliteral one. In some few cases of Quadriliterals, two contractions have been made; and we have therefore Biliteral Verbs of two long radicals. Verbs contracted from Triliterals differ, as to whether the lost letter stood formerly in the middle or at the end; and this materially determines their form of conjugation.

(*aa.*) Verbs with an absorbed Guttural at the end.

A. FIRST CONJUGATION.

Intransitive and Active Voice.

ገባ: *intrs.* He entered (went in). Eth. **ገብአ::**

The second radical is always long; except in the Constructive Mood, and in the Simple Participle.

1. INDICATIVE.

Preterite.

	SINGULAR.	PLURAL.
3d p. masc.	**ገባ**: he went in.	**ገቡ:** they went in.
.... fem.	**ገባች:** she went in.	
2d .. masc.	**ገባህ:** } thou wentst in.	**ገባችሁ:** you went in.
.... fem.	**ገባሽ:** } thou wentst in.	
.... hon. 1.	**ገቡ:** } you went in.	
...... 2.	**ገባችሁ:** } you went in.	
1st.. . .	**ገባሁ:** I went in.	**ገባን:** we went in.

Present and Future.

3d pers. masc.

ይገባል: he goes in, &c. | **ይገባሉ:** they go in, &c.

2. CONTINGENT.

ይገባ: fem. **ትገባ:** | **ይገቡ:**

3. SUBJUNCTIVE.

	SINGULAR.	PLURAL.
3d p. masc.	ይግባ: may he go in.	ይግቡ: may they go in.
. . . . fem.	ትግባ: may she go in.	
2d p. masc.	ትግባ: } mayest thou	ትግቡ: may you go in.
. . . . fem.	ትግቢ: } go in.	
. . . . hon. 1.	ይግቡ: } may you go	
. . . . . . 2.	ትግቡ: } in.	
1st. . com.	እግባ: may I go in.	እንግባ: may we go in.

4. CONSTRUCTIVE.

3d p. m.	ገብቶ: he entering.	ገብተው: they entering.
. . . . f.	ገብታ: she entering.	
2d . . m.	ገብተህ: fem. ገብተሽ:	ገብታችሁ:
. . hon. 1.	ገብተው: 2. ገብታችሁ:	
1st com.	ገብቼ:	ገብተን:

5. IMPERATIVE.

Masc. ግባ: }	do thou enter.	ግቡ: do ye enter.
Fem. ግቢ: }		

6. INFINITIVE.

መግባት: to go in, the going in, the entrance.

7. PARTICIPLES.

Simple, ጋቢ: *intrs.* one who enters in.

ግቢ: that which is entered into, *i.e.* the interior.

Rel. Pret. የገባ: he who entered.

Pres. የሚገባ: he who enters.

B. SECOND CONJUGATION.

Transitive Voice.

አገባ: He made go in, introduced.—(Is quite regular.)

1. INDICATIVE.

Preterite.

3d pers. masc. SINGULAR.	PLURAL.
አገባ: he introduced.	አገቡ: they introduced.

Present and Future.

ያገባል: he introduces.	ያገባሉ:

2. CONTINGENT.

ያገባ: fem. ታገባ:	ያገቡ:

3. SUBJUNCTIVE.

3d pers. masc. SINGULAR.	PLURAL.
ያግባ: may he introduce.	ያግቡ: may they introduce.

4. CONSTRUCTIVE.

አግብቶ: he introducing.	አግብተው: they introducing.

5. IMPERATIVE.

Masc. አግባ: Fem. አግቢ: } do thou introduce.	አግቡ: do ye introduce.

6. INFINITIVE.

ማግባት: the introducing, introduction.

7. PARTICIPLES.

Simple, አጋቢ: one who introduces.
Rel. Perf. ያገባ: he who introduced.
Pres. የሚያገባ: he who introduces.

C. THIRD CONJUGATION.

Passive and Intransitive.

ተገባ: *impersonal.* It was proper, It belonged.

Is treated like other Passives—has no Subjunctive. The Constructive has ተገብቶ: and in other respects it is like ገባ::

D. FOURTH CONJUGATION.

Active Voice.

አጋባ: He married.

The ጋ: is long throughout; and the Preformative አ: is treated as in all the Transitive forms.

E. FIFTH CONJUGATION.

Passive of the preceding.

ተጋባ: Was married.

F. SIXTH CONJUGATION.

Causative Voice.

አስገባ: He caused to go in; introduced.

Subjunctive, ያስገባ::	*Imperative,* አስገባ::
Constructive, አስገብቶ::	*Infinitive,* ማስገባት::

All the other Forms quite regular.

G. SEVENTH CONJUGATION.

Intensive Voice.

በቃቃ: (from **በቃ:** it sufficed) was quite sufficient.

A geminating form. The long middle letter is retained throughout, and the rest treated like **ገባ::**

H. EIGHTH CONJUGATION.

Intensive and Reiterative.

አገባባ: He frequently went in, often cohabited, behaved properly.

This conjugation is like a transitive of the preceding one: the long penultima is retained throughout, and the rest treated like **አገባ::**

I. NINTH CONJUGATION.

አጸናና: He comforted, strengthened.

The two middle letters remain long; **አ:** is treated as in all Transitive forms: there is no Subjunctive; and as to the rest, this conjugation is like the others of this class.

K. TENTH CONJUGATION.

Intense Passive.

ተጸናና: Was comforted.

Is treated like other Passives, retains the long penultima, and has the other peculiarities of this class.

(bb.) *Forms with an Absorbed Guttural in the Middle.*

In these forms, the original guttural having been in the middle, on its absorption, the first radical has become long. It retains, however, its length only in the Indicative Preterite, the Imperative, and the Infinitive Moods of the Active; and through the whole of the Passive forms, except the Constructive. It has no peculiar form for the Subjunctive; but uses, as is generally done in such cases, the Contingent for the purpose. It has, besides, the paragogic **ት:** extremely seldom; because it appears that letter is intended for compensation for final absorbed letters, of which there are none in this class.

This class has seven different Conjugations.

A. FIRST CONJUGATION.

ማለ: (Eth. **መሐለ:**) He swore, took an oath.

1. INDICATIVE PRETERITE.

Preterite.

	SINGULAR.	PLURAL.
3d p. m.	**ማለ:** he swore.	**ማሉ:** they swore.
. . . . f.	**ማለች:** she swore.	
2d . . m.	**ማልህ:** fem. **ማልሽ:**	**ማላችሁ:**
. . hon. 1.	**ማሉ:** 2. **ማላችሁ:**	
1st com.	**ማልሁ:**	**ማልን:**

Present and Future.

3d p. m.	**ይምላል:** he swears.	**ይምላሉ:** they swear.

2. CONTINGENT.

3d p. m.	**ይምል:** fem. **ትምል:**	**ይምሉ::**

3. SUBJUNCTIVE.—None.

4. CONSTRUCTIVE.

3d p. m.	**ምሎ:** he swearing.	**ምለው:**
. . . . f.	**ምላ:** she swearing.	
2d . . m.	**ምለህ:** fem. **ምለሽ:**	**ምላችሁ:**
. . hon 1.	**ምለው:** 2. **ምላችሁ:**	
1st com.	**ምዬ:**	**ምለን:**

5. IMPERATIVE.

Masc. **ማል:**
Fem. **ማይ:** } do thou swear. | **ማሉ:** do ye swear.

6. INFINITIVE.

መማል: to swear, the swearing.

7. PARTICIPLES.

Simple,	**ማይ:** one who swears.
Rel. Pret.	**የማለ:** he who swore.
Pres.	**የሚምል:** he who swears.

B. SECOND CONJUGATION.

Transitive Voice.

አማለ: He made swear.

Contingent, **ያምል::**	*Imperative,* **አምል:**
Constructive, **አምሎ::**	*Infinitive,* **ማማል::**

(See the above remarks.)

C. THIRD CONJUGATION.

Passive Voice.

ተማለ: He was sworn.

Contingent, ይማል:: | *Imperative,* ተማል:
Constructive, ተምሎ:: | *Infinitive,* መማል::

D. FOURTH CONJUGATION.

Transitive (Causative) Voice.

አስማለ: He made swear.

Contingent, ያስምል:: | *Imperative,* አስማል::
Constructive, ኣስምሎ:: | *Infinitive,* ማስማል::

E. FIFTH CONJUGATION.

Frequentative (Intensive) Voice.

ኣጣጣለ: Distributed by casting (lots). Radix, ጣለ: He cast.

Contingent, ያጣጥል:: | *Imperative,* ኣጣጣል:
Constructive, ኣጣጥሎ:: | *Infinitive,* ማጣጣል::

F. SIXTH CONJUGATION.

Reciprocative Voice.

ተማማለ: Mutually swore, conspired.

Contingent, ይማማል:: | *Imperative,* ተማማል::
Constructive, ተማምሎ:: | *Infinitive,* መማማል:

G. SEVENTH CONJUGATION.

Intensive Voice.

ተማለለ:: He adjured, earnestly entreated.

Contingent, ይማለል:: | *Imperative,* ተማለል:
Constructive, ተማሎ:: | *Infinitive,* መማለል::

(*cc.*) *Forms with an Absorbed* የ: *in the Middle.*

These forms are determined by the rule laid down, Part I. Ch. VII. 4. E. On the absorption of the የ: its corresponding vowel *ê* has been joined to the first radical; which, whenever it is shortened, changes *ê* into a short *i*; but when lengthened (as in the Fourth Conjugation), the first radical is put into the Fourth Order, and የ: is restored. No paragogic ት: is in this class.

We take the two Verbs, ሼጠ: He sold, and ሔደ: He went.

A. FIRST CONJUGATION.

ሼጠ፡ *Active,* He sold. Ethiopic, **ሠየጠ፡**

1. INDICATIVE.

Preterite.

	SINGULAR.	PLURAL.
3d p. masc.	ሼጠ፡ he sold.	ሼጡ፡ they sold.
.... fem.	ሼጠች፡ she sold.	
2d .. masc.	ሼጥህ፡ fem. ሼጥሽ፡	ሼጣችሁ፡
.. .. hon. 1.	ሼጡ፡ 2. ሴጣችሁ፡	
1st.. com.	ሼጥሁ፡	ሼጥን፡፡

Present and Future.

3d p. masc.	ይሼጣል፡ he sells.	ይሼጣሉ፡ they sell.

2. CONTINGENT.

3d p. masc.	ይሼጥ፡ fem. ትሼጥ፡	ይሼጡ፡
2d	ትሼጥ፡ fem. ትሼጪ፡	ትሼጡ፡
.. .. hon. 1.	ይሼጡ፡ 2. ትሼጡ፡	
1st .. com.	እሼጥ፡	እንሼጥ፡

3. SUBJUNCTIVE.

3d pers. masc.	
ይሽጥ፡ may he sell.	ይሽጡ፡ may they sell.

4. CONSTRUCTIVE.

3d p. masc.	ሽጦ፡ he selling.	ሽጠው፡
.... fem.	ሽጣ፡ she selling.	
2d .. masc.	ሽጠህ፡ fem. ሽጠሽ፡	ሽጣችሁ፡
.... hon. 1.	ሽጠው፡	
.... .. 2.	ሽጣችሁ፡	
1st.. com.	ሽጬ፡	ሽጠን፡

5. IMPERATIVE.

Masc. ሽጥ፡ } Fem. ሽጪ፡ } do thou sell.	ሽጡ፡ do ye sell.

6. INFINITIVE.

መሼጥ፡ to sell, the selling, sale.

7. PARTICIPLES.

Simple (*a.*) *Act.* **ሽያጪ፡** one who sells, a seller.
(*b.*) **ሽያጪ፡** a thing sold, merchandize.
Rel. Preterite, **የሼጠ፡** he who sold.
Present, **የሚሼጥ፡** he who sells.

B. SECOND CONJUGATION.

Active and Transitive Voice.

ኣሔደ: He made go, drove the threshing ox.

Contingent,	ያሔድ:	*Imperative,*	ኣሒድ:
Subjunctive,	ያሒድ:	*Infinitive,*	ማሔድ::
Constructive,	ኣሒደ::		

C. THIRD CONJUGATION.

Passive Voice.

ተሼጠ: He was sold.

Contingent,	ይሼጥ:	*Imperative,*	ተሼጥ:
No *Subjunctive.*		*Infinitive,*	መሼጥ::
Constructive,	ተሺጦ:		

D. FOURTH CONJUGATION.

Intensive Voice.

ተሻየጠ: He traded, dealt, carried on commerce.

Contingent,	ይሻየጥ:	*Imperative,*	ተሻየጥ:
Constructive,	ተሻይጦ:	*Infinitive,*	መሻየጥ::

E. FIFTH CONJUGATION.

Causative (Transitive) Voice.

ኣስሔደ: He made to go.

Contingent,	ያስሔድ::	*Imperative,*	ኣስሒድ::
Subjunctive,	ያስሒድ::	*Infinitive,*	ማስሔድ::
Constructive,	ኣስሒደ::		

(*dd.*) *Forms with an Absorbed* ወ: *in the Middle.*

According to the rules laid down in Part I. Ch. VII. 5, and 6. the middle letter ወ: has been absorbed; its vowel *o* attached to the first radical. This is further shortened, in the Subjunctive Constructive and Active Imperative, into ů. But in those forms which have long letters, ወ: is restored. In some of these, it forms diphthongs of the fourth order. Those forms of this class, whose first radical is a diphthong, as ቈየ: ቈላ: ቈጣ: ኰረ: ጐደ:, have the Causative form with ኣስ: and the paragogic ት::; which the forms with simple *o* have not.

A. FIRST CONJUGATION.

Intransitive, Active Voice.

ቆመ፡ He stood.

1. INDICATIVE.

Preterite.

SINGULAR.	PLURAL.
3d p. masc. ቆመ፡ he stood.	ቆሙ፡ they stood.
.. .. fem. ቆመች፡ she stood.	
2d .. masc. ቆምህ፡ fem. ቆምሽ፡	ቆማችሁ፡
.. .. hon. 1. ቆሙ፡ 2. ቆማችሁ፡	
1st .. com. ቆምሁ፡፡	ቆምን፡፡

2. CONTINGENT.

3d p. masc. ይቆም፡ fem. ትቆም፡	ይቆሙ፡
2d .. masc. ትቆም፡ fem. ትቆሚ፡	ትቆሙ፡
.. .. hon. 1. ይቆሙ፡ 2. ትቆሙ፡	
1st .. com. እቆም፡፡	እንቆም፡፡

3. SUBJUNCTIVE.

3d p. masc. ይቁም፡ may he stand.	ይቁሙ፡፡ may they stand.
.. .. fem. ትቁም፡ may she stand.	

4. CONSTRUCTIVE.

3d p. masc. ቁሞ፡ he standing.	ቁመው፡ they standing.
.. .. fem. ቁማ፡ she standing.	
2d .. masc. ቁመህ፡ fem. ቁመሽ፡	ቁማችሁ፡
.. .. hon. 1. ቁመው፡ 2. ቁማችሁ፡	
1st .. com. ቁሜ፡	ቁመን፡፡

5. IMPERATIVE.

Masc. ቁም፡ } stand! Fem. ቁሚ፡ }	ቁሙ፡ do ye stand.

6. INFINITIVE.

መቆም፡ to stand, the standing, station, state.

7. PARTICIPLES.

Simple, ቀዋሚ፡ one who stands (see Dictionary). ቁም፡ Eth. standing, straightforward.

Rel. Pret. የቆመ፡ he who stood.

Pres. የሚቆም፡ he who stands.

B. SECOND CONJUGATION.

Transitive Voice.

አቆመ: He made to stand, erected.

Contingent,	ያቆም:	*Imperative,*	አቁም:
Subjunctive,	ያቁም:	*Infinitive,*	ማቆም::
Constructive,	አቁሞ:		

C. THIRD CONJUGATION.

Passive Voice.

ተቆመ: He was erected.—No Subjunctive.

Contingent,	ይቆም: (ይቀወም:)	*Imperative,*	ተቆም: (ተቀወም:)
Constructive,	ተቁሞ::	*Infinitive,*	መቆም:: (መቀወም:)

D. FOURTH CONJUGATION.

Intensive Voice.

ተቃወመ: He withstood, resisted.

Contingent,	ይቃወም:	*Imperative,*	ተቃወም:
Constructive,	ተቃውሞ:	*Infinitive,*	መቃወም::

E. FIFTH CONJUGATION.

Causative Voice.

አስቈየ: He caused to wait.

Contingent,	ያስቈይ:	*Imperative,*	አስቍይ:
Subjunctive,	ያስቍይ:	*Infinitive,*	ማስቈየት::
Constructive,	አስቍይቶ:		

F. G. SIXTH AND SEVENTH CONJUGATIONS.

Intensive Forms.

ተቋቈመ: and **ተቋቋመ::** To resist to the end.

Contingent,	ይቋቈም: and ይቋቋም:	*Imperative,*	ተቋቈም: & ተቋቋም:
Constructive,	ተቋቍሞ:	*Infinitive,*	መቋቈም: and መቋቋም:

IV. FOURTH CLASS.—*Doubly Imperfect Biliterals.*

These are subdivided into three species:

(*aa*) Verbs doubly contracted.

(*bb*) Verbs beginning with አ: and terminating in an absorbed guttural.

(*cc*) Beginning with የ: which absorbs a guttural.

(*aa*) *Doubly Contracted Biliterals.*

These are but few in number; derived from Quadriliterals, and flexible through three Conjugations.

A. FIRST CONJUGATION.

Intransitive. (Active) Voice.

ላላ: He was loose, lax.

1. INDICATIVE.

Preterite.

	SINGULAR.		PLURAL.
3d p. masc.	ላላ: he was lax.		ላሉ: they were lax.
.... fem.	ላላች: she was lax.		
.... masc.	ላላሀ:	fem. ላላሽ:	ላላችሁ:
.... hon. 1.	ላሉ:	2. ላላችሁ:	
1st.. com.	ላላሁ:		ላላን:

Present and Future.

3d p. masc.	ይላላል: he is lax.	ይላላሉ: they are lax.
.... fem.	ትላላለች: she is lax.	
2d.. masc.	ትላላለሀ:	ትላላላችሁ:
.... fem.	ትላያለሽ:	
.... hon. 1.	ይላላሉ:	
...... 2.	ትላላላችሁ:	
1st.. com.	እላላለሁ:	እንላላለን ::

2. CONTINGENT.

3d p. masc.	ይላላ:	fem. ትላላ:	ይላሉ:
2d	ትላላ:	.. ትላይ:	
.. .. hon. 1.	ይላሉ:	2. ትላሉ:	ትላሉ:
1st.. com.	እላላ:		እንላላ:

3. SUBJUNCTIVE.—None.

4. CONSTRUCTIVE.

	Singular	Plural
3d p. masc.	ላልቶ: he being lax.	ላልተው:
. . . . fem.	ላልታ: she being lax.	
2d . . masc.	ላልተህ:	ላልታችሁ:
. . . . fem.	ላልተሽ:	
. . . . hon. 1.	ላልተው:	
. . . . . . 2.	ላልታችሁ:	
1st. . com.	ላልቼ:	ላልተን:

5. IMPERATIVE.

Masc. ላላ: fem. ላይ: be lax. | ላሉ: do ye be lax.

6. INFINITIVE.

መላላት: to be loose, lax.

7. PARTICIPLES.

Simple, None.
Rel. Pret. ያላላ: he who was lax.
Pres. የሚላላ: he who is lax.

B. SECOND CONJUGATION.

Active, Transitive Voice.

አላላ: To loosen, relax.

Contingent,	ያላላ:	*Imperative,*	አላላ:
Constructive,	አላልቶ:	*Infinitive,*	ማላላት::

C. THIRD CONJUGATION.

Passive Reflective Voice.

ተራራ: Was pitied.

Contingent,	ይራራ:	*Imperative,*	ተራራ:
Constructive,	ተራርቶ:	*Infinitive,*	መራራት:

(*bb*) *Biliterals beginning with* አ: *and terminating in an Absorbed Guttural.*

They are but few, and have only Three Conjugations. They have the Paragogic ት:

A. FIRST CONJUGATION.

Intransitive, Active Voice.

አጣ: He wanted, had not.

1. INDICATIVE.

Preterite.

SINGULAR.		PLURAL.
3d p. m.	**አጣ:** he wanted.	**አጡ:** they wanted.
. . . . f.	**አጣች:** she wanted.	
2d . . m.	**አጣህ:** fem. **አጣሽ:**	**አጣችሁ:**
. . hon. 1.	**አጡ:** 2. **አጣችሁ:**	
1st com.	**አጣሁ:**	**አጣን::**

3d pers. masc. *Present,* and *Future.*

ያጣል: he wants. fem. **ታጣለች:** | **ያጣሉ:** they want.

2. CONTINGENT.

ያጣ: fem. **ታጣ:** | **ያጡ:**

3. SUBJUNCTIVE.

ይጣ: fem. **ትጣ:** | **ይጡ::**

4. CONSTRUCTIVE.

አጥቶ: he wanting. fem. **አጥታ:** | **አጥተው:** they wanting.

5. IMPERATIVE.

እጣ: fem. **እጪ:** do thou want. | **እጡ:** do ye want.

6. INFINITIVE.

ማጣት: To want, the wanting, want.

7. PARTICIPLES.

Simple, None.
Rel. Pret. **ያጣ:** he who wanted.
Pres. **የሚያጣ::** he who wants.

B. SECOND CONJUGATION.

Passive, Intransitive Voice.

ታጣ: To be wanted.

Contingent,	**ይታጣ::**	*Imperative,*	**ታጣ::**
Constructive,	**ተጥቶ::**	*Infinitive,*	**መታጣት::**

C. THIRD CONJUGATION.

Transitive, Causative Voice.

አሳጣ: To deprive.

Contingent,	ያሳጣ:	*Imperative,*	አስጣ:
Subjunctive,	ያስጣ:	*Infinitive,*	ማሳጣት:
Constructive,	አሳጥቶ:		

(*cc*) *Verb beginning with* **የ:** *which absorbs a Guttural.*

Only one Verb has been discovered to belong to this class.

ያዘ: Eth. **አኀዘ:** To seize.

The **ያ:** is shortened into **ይ:** and even reduced to the mere vowel *ĭ*.

A. FIRST CONJUGATION.

Active Voice.

ያዘ: He seized.

1. INDICATIVE.

Preterite.

	SINGULAR.	PLURAL.
3d p. m.	ያዘ: he seized.	ያዙ: they seized.
. . . . f.	ያዘች: she seized.	
2d . . m.	ያዝህ: fem. ያዝሽ:	ያዛችሁ:
. . hon. 1.	ያዙ: 2. ያዛችሁ:	
1st com.	ያዝሁ:	ያዝን::

Present and Future.

	SINGULAR.	PLURAL.
3d p. m.	ይዛል: & ይይዛል: he seizes.	ይዛሉ: and ይይዛሉ: they seize.
. . . . f.	ቲዛለች: & ትይዛለች: she seizes.	
2d . . m.	ቲዛለህ: & ትይዛለህ:	ቲዛላችሁ: and ትይዛላችሁ:
. . . . f.	ቲዣለሽ: & ትይዣለሽ:	
. . hon. 1.	ይዛሉ: and ይይዛሉ:	
. . . . 2.	ቲዛላችሁ: & ትይዛላችሁ:	
1st com.	ኢዛለሁ: & እይዛለሁ:	እኒዛለን: and እንይዛለን:

2. CONTINGENT.

	SINGULAR.	PLURAL.
3d p. m.	ይዝ:	ይዙ:
. . . . f.	ቲዝ: and ትይዝ:	
2d . . m.	ቲዝ: and ትይዝ:	ቲዙ: and ትይዙ:
. . . . f.	ቲዥ: and ትይዥ:	
. . hon. 1.	ይዙ: 2. ቲዙ: & ትይዙ:	
1st com.	ኢዝ: and እይዝ::	እኒዝ: and እንይዝ::

3. SUBJUNCTIVE.

	SINGULAR.		PLURAL.
3d p. m.	ያዝ: may he seize.		ያዙ: may they seize.
. . . . f.	ትያዝ: may she seize.		
2d . . m.	ትያዝ:	fem. ትያዢ:	ትያዙ:
. . hon. 1.	ያዙ:	2. ትያዙ:	
1st com.	እያዝ:		እንያዝ::

4. CONSTRUCTIVE.

3d p. m.	ይዞ: he seizing.		ይዘው: they seizing.
. . . . f.	ይዛ: she seizing.		
2d . . m.	ይዘህ:	fem. ይዘሽ:	ይዛችሁ:
. . hon. 1.	ይዘው:	2. ይዛችሁ:	
1st com.	ይዤ:		ይዘን::

5. IMPERATIVE.

Masc. ያዝ: Fem. ያዢ:	do thou seize.	ያዙ: do ye seize.

6. INFINITIVE.

መያዝ: to seize, the seizing, seizure.

7. PARTICIPLES.

Simple, ያዥ: a seizer. *Rel. Pret.* የያዘ: he who seized.

Present.

SINGULAR.

3d p. masc.	የሚያዝ: and የሚይዝ:	he who seizes.
. . . . fem.	የምትይዝ: and የምትያዝ:	she who seizes.
2d . . masc.	የምትያዝ: and የምትይዝ:	thou who seizest.
. . . . fem.	የምትያዢ: and የምትይዢ:	thou who seizest.
. . . . hon. 1.	የሚያዙ: and የሚይዙ:	you who seize.
. . . . . . 2.	የምትያዙ: and የምትይዙ:	you who seize.
. . . . com.	የምይዝ:	I who seize.

PLURAL.

የሚያዙ: and የሚይዙ: they who seize.

የምትያዙ: and የምትይዙ: you who seize.

የምንያዝ: and የምንይዝ: we who seize.

B. SECOND CONJUGATION.

Transitive and Causative Voice.

አያዘ: He caused to seize.

Contingent,	**ያይዝ:**	*Imperative,*	**አያዝ:**
Subjunctive,	**ያያዝ:**	*Infinitive,*	**ማያዝ::**
Constructive,	**አይዘ:**		

C. THIRD CONJUGATION.

Passive Voice.

ተያዘ: He was seized.

Contingent,	**ይያዝ:**	*Imperative,*	**ተያዝ:**
Constructive,	**ተይዘ:**	*Infinitive,*	**መያዝ::**

D. FOURTH CONJUGATION.

Causative Voice.

አስያዘ: He caused to be seized, betrayed.

Contingent,	**ያሲዝ:** and **ያስይዝ::**	*Imperative,*	**አስያዝ:**
Subjunctive,	**ያስያዝ:**	*Infinitive,*	**ማስያዝ::**
Constructive,	**አሲዘ:** and **አስይዘ::**		

E. FIFTH CONJUGATION.

Active and Passive, Frequentative and Reciprocative.

ተያያዘ: He frequently, alternately, reciprocally, completely, seized, or was seized.

Contingent,	**ይያያዝ::**	*Imperative,*	**ተያያዝ::**
Constructive,	**ተያይዘ::**	*Infinitive,*	**መያያዝ::**

---

4. *Various Conjugations of Quadriliteral and Pluriliteral Verbs.*

I. FIRST CLASS.—*Reduplicated and Transposed Biliterals.*

This numerous class has Eleven Conjugations. (See pp. 56—60.)

A. FIRST CONJUGATION.

Intransitive and Active Voice.

ለመለመ: It was green. **ቀጠቀጠ:** He beat.

Contingent,	**ይለመልም:**	*Imperative,*	**ለምልም:**
Subjunctive,	**ይለምልም:**	*Infinitive,*	**መለምለም::**
Constructive,	**ለምልሞ:**		

B. SECOND CONJUGATION.

Active, Transitive Voice.

አለምለም: He made green, verdant, refreshed.

Contingent,	ያለመልም:	*Imperative,*	አለምልም:
Subjunctive,	ያለምልም:	*Infinitive,*	ማለምለም::
Constructive,	አለምልሞ:		

C. THIRD CONJUGATION.

Passive Voice.

ተለቀለቀ: He was bedaubed.

Contingent,	ይለቀለቅ:	*Imperative,*	ተለቀለቅ:
Constructive,	ተለቅልቆ:	*Infinitive,*	መለቀለቅ:

D. FOURTH CONJUGATION.

Intensely-Active Voice.

አነቃነቀ: He shook.

Contingent,	ያነቃንቅ:	*Imperative,*	አንቃንቅ:
Subjunctive,	ያንቃንቅ:	*Infinitive,*	ማንቃነቅ::
Constructive,	አንቃንቆ:		

E. FIFTH CONJUGATION.

Intensely-Passive, Reflective, and Intransitive Voice.

ተለቃለቀ: He bedaubed, washed himself.

Contingent,	ይለቃለቅ:	*Imperative,*	ተለቃለቅ:
Constructive,	ተልቃልቆ:	*Infinitive,*	መለቃለቅ::

F. SIXTH CONJUGATION.

Causative, Transitive Voice.

አስለቀለቀ: He caused bedaubing. (አሽከረከረ: He moved, crept.)

Contingent,	ያስለቅልቅ:	*Imperative,*	አስለቅልቅ:
Subjunctive,	ያስልቅልቅ:	*Infinitive,*	ማስለቅለቅ::
Constructive,	አስለቅልቆ:		

G. SEVENTH CONJUGATION.

Active Voice.

አንበደበደ: He beat, shook.

Contingent,	ያንበደብድ:	*Imperative,*	አንበድብድ:
Subjunctive,	ያንበድብድ:	*Infinitive,*	ማንበድበድ::
Constructive,	አንበድብደ:		

H. EIGHTH CONJUGATION.

Passive and Intransitive Voice.

ተንቀጠቀጠ: He trembled.

Contingent,	ይንቀጠቅጥ:	*Imperative,*	ተንቀጠቅጥ:
Constructive,	ተንቀጥቅጦ:	*Infinitive,*	መንቀጠቀጥ::

I. NINTH CONJUGATION.

Intensive and Active Voice.

አንቀሳቀሰ: He stirred up, moved.

Contingent,	ያንቀሳቅስ:	*Imperative,*	አንቅሳቅስ:
Constructive,	አንቀሳቅሶ:	*Infinitive,*	ማንቀሳቀስ::

K. TENTH CONJUGATION.

Passive, Reflective, and Intransitive Voice.

ተንቀሳቀሰ: He was stirred, He moved.

Contingent,	ይንቀሳቀስ:	*Imperative,*	ተንቀሳቀስ:
Constructive,	ተንቀሳቅሶ:	*Infinitive,*	መንቀሳቀስ::

L. ELEVENTH COJUGATION.

Causative, Transitive Voice.

አሳንቀሳቀሰ: He stirred, moved.

Contingent,	ያሳንቀሳቅስ:	*Imperative,*	አስንቅሳቅስ:
Subjunctive,	ያስንቅሳቅስ:	*Infinitive,*	ማሳንቀሳቀስ::
Constructive,	አሳንቅሳቅሶ:		

II. SECOND CLASS.—*Derivates from Triliterals, having one Radical Reduplicated and Transposed.*

This class is not numerous, and it has Six Conjugations.

A. FIRST COJUGATION.

Intransitive Voice.

ደሎደሞ: He was blunt.

1. INDICATIVE.

Preterite.

	SINGULAR.	PLURAL.
3d p. masc.	ደሎደሞ: he was blunt.	ደሎደሙ: they were blunt.
.. .. fem.	ደሎደመች:	
2d .. masc.	ደሎደምህ:	ደሎደማችሁ:
.. .. fem.	ደሎደምሽ:	
.. .. hon. 1.	ደሎደሙ:	
.. .. hon. 2.	ደሎደማችሁ:	
1st.. com.	ደሎደምሁ:	ደሎደምን:

Present and Future.

ይደሎደማል: he is blunt. | ይደሎደማሉ: they are blunt.

2. CONTINGENT.

ይደሎደም: fem. ትደሎደም: | ይደሎደሙ:

3. NO SUBJUNCTIVE.

4. CONSTRUCTIVE.

ደሎዲምቶ: he being blunt. | ደሎዲምተው:

5. NO IMPERATIVE.

6. INFINITIVE.

መደሎደመት: to be blunt, the being blunt, bluntness.

7. PARTICIPLES.

Rel. Pret. የደሎደሞ: he who was blunt.
Pres. የሚደሎደም: he who is blunt.

B. SECOND CONJUGATION.

Active, Transitive, and Intransitive Voice.

አደሎደሞ: He blunted. አጉረመረመ: He murmured.

Contingent,	ያጉረመርም:	*Imperative,*	አጉሪምረም:
Subjunctive,	ያጉረምረም:	*Infinitive,*	ማጉረምረም:
Constructive,	አጉሪምርሞ:		

c. THIRD CONJUGATION.

Passive Voice.

ተደሎደመ፡ Was blunted.

Contingent,	ይደሎደም፡	*Imperative,*	ተደሎደም፡
Constructive,	ተደሎዲሞቶ፡	*Infinitive,*	መደሎደሙት፡፡

---

d. FOURTH CONJUGATION.

Intensive Voice.

አከናወነ፡ He gave success.

Contingent,	ያከናውን፡	*Imperative,*	አክናወን፡
Subjunctive,	ያክናወን፡	*Infinitive,*	ማክናወን፡፡
Constructive,	አክናውኖ፡		

---

e. FIFTH CONJUGATION.

Intransitive and Intensive Voice.

ተከናወነ፡ He had success, succeeded, prospered.

Contingent,	ይከናወን፡	*Imperative,*	ተከናወን፡
Constructive,	ተክናውኖ፡	*Infinitive,*	መከናወን፡፡

---

f. SIXTH CONJUGATION.

Intransitive Voice.

ተንገረገበ፡ It became knotty.

Contingent,	ይንገረገብ፡	*Imperative,*	ተንገረገብ፡
Constructive,	ተንገረግቦ፡	*Infinitive,*	መንገረገብ፡፡

III. THIRD CLASS.

Geminants, probably derived from Triliterals, but having their original verb lost, so as not to be reckoned to the geminating Conjugation of the Triliteral Regular Verb. This class is but small—is inflected through six conjugations, similar to other Geminants.

A. FIRST CONJUGATION.

Intransitive.

ኰበለለ: He escaped.

Contingent,	ይኰብል:	*Imperative,*	ኰብልል:
Subjunctive,	ይኰበልል:	*Infinitive,*	መኰበልል::
Constructive,	ኰበሎ:		

B. SECOND CONJUGATION.

Passive Voice.

ተደመሰሰ: He was destroyed.

Contingent,	ይደመስስ:	*Imperative,*	ተደመሰስ:
Constructive,	ተደምስሶ:	*Infinitive,*	መደመሰስ::

C. THIRD CONJUGATION.

Intransitive and Intensive Voice.

ተጐማለለ: Walked nimbly, affectedly, proudly.

Contingent,	ይጐማለል:	*Imperative,*	ተጐማለል:
Constructive,	ተጐማሎ:	*Infinitive,*	መጐማለል::

D. FOURTH CONJUGATION.

Transitive Voice.

አስጠነቀቀ: He cautioned.

Contingent,	ያስጠነቅቅ:	*Imperative,*	አስጠንቀቅ:
Subjunctive,	ያስጠንቅቅ:	*Infinitive,*	ማስጠንቀቅ::
Constructive,	አስጠንቅቆ:		

E. FIFTH CONJUGATION.

Active Voice.

አንከባለለ: He rolled about.

Contingent,	ያንከባል:	*Imperative,*	አንከባልል:
Constructive,	አንከባሎ:	*Infinitive,*	ማንከባለል:

F. SIXTH CONJUGATION.

Passive Voice.

ተንከባለለ: He was rolled about.

Contingent,	ይንከባለል:	*Imperative,*	ተንከባለል:
Constructive,	ተንከባሎ:	*Infinitive,*	መንከባለል::

IV. FOURTH CLASS.

Quadriliterals and Pluriliterals of different Radicals.

A. FIRST CONJUGATION.

Intransitive Voice.

መሰገነ: Was glorious.

Contingent,	ይመሰግን:	*Imperative,*	መስግን:
Subjunctive,	ይመስግን:	*Infinitive,*	መመስገን::
Constructive,	መስግኖ:		

B. SECOND CONJUGATION.

Active and Transitive Voice.

አመሰገነ: He glorified.

Contingent,	ያመሰግን:	*Imperative,*	አመስግን:
Subjunctive,	ያመስግን:	*Infinitive,*	ማመስገን::
Constructive,	አመስግኖ:		

C. THIRD CONJUGATION.

Passive Voice.

ተመሰገነ: He was glorified.

Contingent,	ይመሰገን:	*Imperative,*	ተመሰገን:
Constructive,	ተመስገኖ:	*Infinitive,*	መመሰገን::

D. FOURTH CONJUGATION.

Intensive Voice.

አሰናበተ: He dismissed.

Contingent,	ያሰናብት:	*Imperative,*	አሰናብት:
Constructive,	አሰናብቶ:	*Infinitive,*	ማሰናበት::

E. FIFTH CONJUGATION.

Intensive and Passive Voice.

ተሰናበተ: He was dismissed.

Contingent,	ይሰናበት:	*Imperative,*	ተሰናበት:
Constructive,	ተሰናብቶ:	*Infinitive,*	መሰናበት:

F. SIXTH CONJUGATION.

Causative Voice.

አስመሰገነ: He causes to be glorious or glorified.

Contingent,	ያስመሰግን:	*Imperative,*	አስመስግን:
Subjunctive,	ያስመስግን:	*Infinitive,*	ማስመሰገን:
Constructive,	አስመስግኖ:		

G. SEVENTH CONJUGATION.

Intensive Voice.

ገለባበጠ: He overthrew completely.

Contingent,	ይገለባብጥ:	*Imperative,*	ገልባብጥ:
Subjunctive,	ይገልባብጥ:	*Infinitive,*	መገልባበጥ::
Constructive,	ገልባብጦ:		

H. EIGHTH CONJUGATION.

Intensely Passive Voice.

ተገለባበጠ: He was completely overthrown.

Contingent,	ይገለባበጥ:	*Imperative,*	ተገለባበጥ:
Constructive,	ተገልባብጦ:	*Infinitive,*	መገለባበጥ::

I. NINTH CONJUGATION.

Reciprocative and Reiterative Voice.

ተሰናባበተ: Took leave from each other.

Contingent,	ይሰናባበት:	*Imperative,*	ተሰናባበት:
Constructive,	ተሰናባብቶ:	*Infinitive,*	መሰናባበት:

---

5. *Defective and Anomalous Verbs..*

Three of them—viz. I. The Auxiliary **አለ:** "He is"; II. **ነበረ:** "He was"; III. **ነው:** "He is,"—have been conjugated before we entered upon the Regular Triliteral Verb. (See pp. 64, 65.) We proceed to give here the rest.

IV. *Various Conjugations of the Verb* **አለ:** "He said."

The irregularities in this verb are caused by the mixing together of the two forms **አለ:** and **ባለ:** Eth. **ብህለ:** "To say." This verb has Ten Conjugations.

A. FIRST CONJUGATION.

Active Voice.

1. INDICATIVE.

Preterite.

	SINGULAR.	PLURAL.
3d p. masc.	አለ: he said.	አሉ: they said.
.... fem.	አለች: she said.	
2d .. masc.	አልህ: fem. አልሽ:	አላችሁ:
.... hon. 1.	አሉ: 2. አላችሁ:	
1st .. com.	አልሁ:	አልን::

Present and Future.

3d p. masc.	ይላል: he says.	ይላሉ: they say.
.... fem.	ትላለች: she says.	
2d .. masc.	ትላለህ: f. ትያለሽ:	ትላላችሁ:
.... hon. 1.	ይላሉ: 2. ትላላችሁ:	
1st .. com.	እላለሁ:	እንላለን::

2. CONTINGENT.

3d p. masc.	ይል: and ይበል:	ይሉ: and ይበሉ:
.... fem.	ትል: and ትበል:	
2d .. masc.	ትል: and ትበል:	ትሉ: and ትበሉ:
.... fem.	ትይ: and ትበይ:	
.... hon. 1.	ይሉ: and ይበሉ:	
.... .. 2.	ትሉ: and ትበሉ:	
1st .. com.	እል: and እበል:	እንል: and እንበል:

3. NO SUBJUNCTIVE.

4. CONSTRUCTIVE.

3d p. masc.	ብሎ: he saying.	ብለው:
.... fem.	ብላ: she saying.	
2d .. masc.	ብለህ: fem. ብለሽ:	ብላችሁ:
.... hon. 1.	ብለው: 2. ብላችሁ:	
1st .. com.	ብዬ:	ብለን:

5. IMPERATIVE.

Masc. በል:
Fem. በይ: } do thou say. | በሉ: do ye say.

6. INFINITIVE.

ማለት: To say, the saying, meaning, intention.

7. PARTICIPLES.

Simple, ባይ: one who says.

Rel. Pret. ያለ: he who said.

Pres. የሚል: he who says.

B. SECOND CONJUGATION.

አበለ: To deceive by talking.

Contingent, ያብል:	*Imperative,* አብል:
Constructive, አብሎ:	*Infinitive,* ማብል::

C. THIRD CONJUGATION.

ተባለ: *pass.* To be said, called, named.

1. PRETERITE.

	SINGULAR.	PLURAL.
3d p. m.	ተባለ: he was called.	ተባሉ: they were called.
. . . . f.	ተባለች: she was called.	
2d . . m.	ተባልህ: f. ተባልሽ:	ተባላችሁ:
. . hon. 1.	ተባሉ: 2. ተባላችሁ:	
1st com.	ተባልሁ:	ተባልን::

Present and Future.

3d p. m.	ይባላል: he is called.	ይባላሉ: they are called.
. . . . f.	ትባላለች: she is called.	

Contingent, ይባል:	*Imperative,* none.
Constructive, ተብሎ:	*Infinitive,* መባል::

D. FOURTH CONJUGATION.

ታበለ: *pass.* from አበለ: To be deceived.

Contingent, ይታበል:	*Imperative,* ታበል:
Constructive, ታብሎ:	*Infinitive,* መታበል::

E. FIFTH CONJUGATION.

ተባላ: To rumour in public.

Whether any more than the Preterite Indicative is extant of this form, we do not know.

T

F. SIXTH CONJUGATION.

አባበለ: He persuaded.

Contingent,	ያባብል:	*Imperative,*	አባብል:
Constructive,	አባብሎ:	*Infinitive,*	ማባበል::

G. SEVENTH CONJUGATION.

ተባበለ: To be persuaded, to say to each other.

Contingent,	ይባበል:	*Imperative,*	ተባበል:
Constructive,	ተባብሎ:	*Infinitive,*	መባበል::

H. EIGHTH CONJUGATION.

ተባባለ: *recipr.* To say to each other.

Contingent,	ይባባል:	*Imperative,*	ተባባል:
Constructive,	ተባብሎ:	*Infinitive,*	መባባል:

I. NINTH CONJUGATION.

ታለለ: He was talked into any thing, was persuaded, duped.

Contingent,	ይታለል:	*Imperative,*	ታለል:
Constructive,	ታሎ:	*Infinitive,*	መታለል::

K. TENTH CONJUGATION.

አታለለ: He persuaded, cheated.

Contingent,	ያታል:	*Imperative,*	አታልል:
Constructive,	አታሎ:	*Infinitive,*	ማታለል::

V. First Conjugation of the Verb አከለ: "To be equal," "amount to."

The remainder of this verb, ተካከለ: and አስተካከለ: is regular. The anomaly of the First Conjugation consists in its assuming more of the form ኣኸለ: or አሀለ: than of አከለ:, and in its not having all the Moods and Tenses. We give here all that is, as far as we know, extant.

1. INDICATIVE.

Preterite, none.

Present and Future.

	SINGULAR.	PLURAL.
3d p. masc.	ያሀል: he is equal,	ያሀላሉ:

The other Persons are wanting.

2. CONTINGENT.

3d Person Masculine, ያህል: Feminine, ታህል:

These two personal forms only are used with the signification, "Amounting to," "equal to;" *e.g.* የሚሰጠውን: ያህል: "*equal to* what he gives."

SUBJUNCTIVE, CONSTRUCTIVE, and IMPERATIVE—none.

INFINITIVE, ማኸል: *i.q.* መካከል: and መኻከል: "the middle."

PARTICIPLES—Eth. ኧኩል: "equal," "half."

Rel. Pres. የሚያህል: "what is equal to," "amounts to, about, almost"; *e.g.* ሶስት: ሺህ: የሚያህ:ል "*amounting to* (*about*) three thousand."

VI. *Negative Verb* ሌለ: "Is not."

All that exists of this verb is this: ሌለ: "it (he) is not." fem. ሌለች:: Participle, የሌለ: fem. የሌለች: "that which is not," "has not," "is without;" "without," "besides," "exclusively," "not including."

VII. Of the verb ላቀ: (Eth. ልህቀ:) "To be greater," "larger," "excel;" in the First Conjugation, nothing is extant but the 3d pers. masc. Conting. ይልቅ: which is used as a sort of Comparative, "more," "greater," "especially"; and Participle, የሚልቅ: የምትልቅ: "he, she, or it, who (which) is greater," "superior," "excels."

The Transitive form of this verb ኣላቀ: "he raised," "made excellent," is quite regular.

VIII. Verb መጣ: "He came," is, in its First Conjugation, destitute of an Imperative; whilst all the rest is regular and perfect. The Imperative is supplied by the form ና: Eth. and Tigr. ንዓ:: Sing. masc. ና: fem. ኒ: and ንዪ: "do thou come." Pl. ኑ: "do ye come." Only in very rare instances they use a regular form ምጣ: ምጪ: ምጡ:; but it is against the custom.

IX. ተወ: "He left," "omitted," "abandoned," "left off."

1. INDICATIVE MOOD.

Preterite.

	SINGULAR.		PLURAL.
3d p. masc.	ተወ:	fem. ተወች:	ተዉ:
2d .. masc.	ተውህ:	fem. ተውሽ:	
.. .. hon. 1.	ተዉ:	2. ተዋችሁ:	ተዋችሁ:
1st.. com.	ተውሁ:		ተውን::

SINGULAR. *Present and Future.* PLURAL.

3d p. masc.	ይተዋል: he abandons.	ይተዋሉ: they abandon.
.. .. fem.	ትተዋለች:	
2d .. masc.	ትተዋለህ:	
.. .. fem.	ትተያለሽ:	

(The rest is regular.)

2. CONTINGENT.

3d p. masc.	ይተው:	fem. ትተው:	ይተዉ:
.. .. masc.	ትተው:	fem. ትተይ:	

(The rest is regular.)

3. CONSTRUCTIVE.

3d p. masc.	ትቶ:	fem. ትታ:	ትተው:
2d .. masc.	ትተህ:	fem. ትተሽ:	ትታችሁ:
.. .. hon. 1.	ትተው:	2. ትታችሁ:	
1st .. com.	ትቼ:		ትተን:

4. IMPERATIVE.

masc. ተው: fem. ተይ: | ተዉ::

6. INFINITIVE. መተወት::

7. PARTICIPLES. የተወ:: የሚተው::

The Transitive Conjugation of this verb, አስተወ: "he caused to abandon," is analogous to the preceding; the ወ: being changed in the 2d Fem. Sing. of the Ind. Pres., Conting., and Imper. into የ:, and rejected in the Constr.

X. *Verb* ሻ: *and* እሻ: "to desire," "want," "seek."

1. INDICATIVE.

Preterite. Regular.

Present and Future.

SINGULAR.		PLURAL.
3d p. masc.	ይሻል: he wants.	ይሻሉ: they want.
.. .. fem.	ትሻለች: she wants.	
2d .. masc.	ትሻለህ: f. ትሻለሽ:	ትሻላችሁ:
.. .. hon. 1.	ይሻሉ: 2. ትሻላችሁ:	
1st. . com.	እሻለሁ:	እንሻለን::

2. CONTINGENT.

3d p. masc.	ይሻ:	fem. ትሻ:	ይሹ:
2d .. masc.	ትሻ:	fem. ትሺ:	ትሹ:
.. .. hon. 1.	ይሹ:	2. ትሹ:	
1st .. com.	እሻ:		እንሻ::

3. CONSTRUCTIVE.

	SINGULAR.	PLURAL.
3d p. masc.	ሽቶ፡ he wanting.	ሽተው፡ they wanting.
.. .. fem.	ሽታ፡ she wanting.	
2d .. masc.	ሽተህ፡ fem. ሽተሽ፡	ሽታችሁ፡
.. .. hon. 1.	ሽተው፡ 2. ሽታችሁ፡	
1st .. com.	ሽቼ፡	ሽተን።

4. IMPERATIVE.

Masc. ኣሻ፡ } do thou seek. Fem. ኣሺ፡ }	ኣሹ፡ do ye seek.

5. INFINITIVE.

መሻት፡ to want, &c. the want, desire, request.

6. PARTICIPLES.

Simple, none. *Perfect*, የሻ፡ he who wanted.

Present, የሚሻ፡ he who wants.

The Transitive form of this verb, ኣሻ፡ is only used impersonally, in the 3d person singular masc. and fem., with the signification, "to be requisite," or, in the mind of an Abyssinian, "to produce a feeling of want by absence"; *e.g.* ኣያሻኝም፡ "I do not want (it)." The forms used are these:

Preterite, ኣሻ፡	*Contingent*, ያሻ፡
Present, ያሻል፡	*Infinitive*, ማሻት።

XI. Of the verb የለም፡ which is negative to the verb ኣለ፡ "He is," nothing is extant but the 3d person singular masc. የለም፡ "he (it) is not," fem. የለችም፡ "she (it) is not," and plural የሉም፡ "they are not." With Suffixes, it signifies "has (have) not," *e.g.* የለውም፡ "he has not." የላትም፡ "she has not." የለንም፡ "we have not," &c.

XII. The negative ኣይደለም፡ "Is not," is the negative answering the substantive verb ነው፡ "He is." Whence it is derived, we know not. It is used only in the Preterite of the Indicative and Participle, which we give here.

INDICATIVE.

Preterite.

	SINGULAR.	PLURAL.
3d p. masc.	ኣይደለም፡ he is not.	ኣይደሉም፡ they are not.
.... fem.	ኣይደለችም፡	
2d .. masc.	ኣይደለህም፡	ኣይደላችሁም፡
.... fem.	ኣይደለሽም፡	
.... hon. 1.	ኣይደሉም፡	
.... .. 2.	ኣይደላችሁም፡	
1st .. com.	ኣይደለሁም፡	ኣይደለንም።

Relative Participle Preterite.

	SINGULAR.	PLURAL.
3d p. masc.	ያይደለ: he who is not.	ያይደሉ: they who are not.
.. .. fem.	ያይደለች:	
2d .. masc.	ያይደለህ:	ያይደላችሁ:
.. .. fem.	ያይደለሽ:	
.. .. hon. 1.	ያይደሉ:	
.. .. .. 2.	ያይደላችሁ:	
1st .. com.	ያይደለሁ:	ያይደለን::

አይደለም: also is used for the Adverb of Negation, "No."

Section V.

On the Connexion of Pronouns with Verbs.

1. In other languages, this subject would be referred to the Syntax; but in the Semitic family, the Pronouns governed by Verbs are so closely joined to them, that it would be improper to do so, as the form of the verb is modified in no slight degree by this combination. We conceive it to be here the best place for exhibiting the mode in which it is performed, after having explained all the other processes to which the Amharic Verbs are subjected.

2. Before we entered on the consideration of the Verb, in the preceding Chapter, Sect. VIII. we mentioned those Pronouns which are joined to Verbs. We now give a brief statement of the regulations under which they are joined.

(*a*) All the forms of Verbs assume the Verbal Suffixes, except the two nominal forms, the Infinitive and the Simple Participle, which assume Nominal Suffixes; *e.g.* እርሶን: መጠበቄ: "my keeping him." ጋሻ: ጦርን: ተሸካሚው: "his armour-bearer."

(*b*) All the forms which assume the Verbal Suffixes do receive them at the end, except the two forms which are inflected with the Auxiliary አለ: *i.e.* the Present and Future Indicative, and the Aorist of the Constructive Mood; which place the Pronoun between the radical letters and the Auxiliary, so as to render it rather an Infix than a Suffix.

(*c*) With regard to the different degrees of power the Suffixes possess, of changing the letter to which they are joined, they are divided into light (*levia*) and heavy (*gravia*) Suffixes. The light Suffixes are those which are not preceded by a long ā: those which are preceded by a long ā are heavy Suffixes.

(*d*) The *light Suffixes* attach themselves to *ultimæ radicales* of the first order, without change; and to ult. rad. of the sixth order, by converting the latter into the first order, sometimes without change. The heavy suffixes convert ult. rad., in either of those two orders, into the fourth order.

(*e*) Ultima radicalis of the second and of the seventh order, in accordance with Part I. Ch. VII. 5 & 6.

α. changes ው: into ት::

β. is changed, if it is a guttural or palatine, into a diphthong of the fourth order: if not, the vowel is detached from the consonant; the latter being put into the sixth, and the former becoming ዋ: of the fourth order, before all the heavy suffixes. Before suffix 2d pers. hon. 1., it is either left unchanged, or changed into the sixth order, leaving the suffix as it is.

(*f*) Ult. rad. of the third and of the fifth order changes none of the light suffixes; but agreeably to Part I. Ch. VII. 4. D., when being attached to the heavy suffixes, it is generally changed into the sixth order; and ያ: is added, to assume the long ā of the suffix.

(*g*) Ult. rad. of the fourth order neither suffers nor produces any change.

(*h*) With regard to the *insertion* or *infixion* of Pronouns, only this needs to be observed; that አ: of the Auxiliary አለ: being absorbed by the Pronoun, the latter, or, if it consists of more than one letter, its last letter, is put into the fourth order, ሁ: being changed into ኗ: or ኟ::

These rules are illustrated by the following Table:

TABLE OF A VERB WITH SUFFIXES.

መገበ: He has fed.

I. SIMPLE FORMS.

A. *Preterite.*

THIRD PERSON SINGULAR.

Masculine.		Feminine.	
መገበኝ:	he has fed me.	መገበችኝ:	she has fed me.
መገበህ:	he has fed thee (*m*.).	መገበችህ:	she has fed thee (*m*.).
መገበሽ:	he has fed thee (*f*.).	መገበችሽ:	she has fed thee (*f*.).
መገበዎ:	he has fed you (hon. 1).	መገባቸዎ:	she has fed you (h.1).
መገባችሁ:	he has fed you (hon. 2).	መገበቻችሁ:	she has fed you (h.2).
መገበው:	he has fed him.	መገበችው:	she has fed him.
መገባት:	he has fed her.	መገበቻት:	she has fed her.
PL.		PL.	
መገበን:	he has fed us.	መገበችን:	she has fed us.
መገባችሁ:	he has fed you.	መገበቻችሁ:	she has fed you.
መገባቸው:	he has fed them.	መገበቻቸው:	she has fed them.

SECOND PERSON SINGULAR.

Masculine.		Feminine.	
መገብሀኝ፡	thou hast fed me.	መገብሽኝ፡	thou (*f.*) hast fed me.
መገብሀው፡	thou hast fed him.	መገብሽው፡	thou (*f.*) hast fed him.
መገብሃት፡	thou hast fed her.	መገብሽኝ፡	thou (*f.*) hast fed her.
	PL.		PL.
መገብህን፡	thou hast fed us.	መገብሽን፡	thou hast fed us.
መገብሃቸው፡	thou hast fed them.	መገብሻቸው፡	thou hast fed them.

SECOND PERSON SINGULAR, HONORIFIC, like the Third and Second Plural.

FIRST PERSON COMMON.

መገብሁህ፡	I have fed thee (*m.*)
መገብሁሽ፡	I have fed thee (*f.*)
መገብሁዎ፡	I have fed you (hon. 1).
መገብኋችሁ፡	I have fed you (hon. 2).
መገብሁት፡	I have fed him.
መገብኋት፡	I have fed her.
	PL.
መገብኋችሁ፡	I have fed you.
መገብኋቸው፡	I have fed them.

PLURAL.

THIRD PERSON.		SECOND PERSON.	
መገቡኝ፡	they have fed me.	መገባችሁኝ፡	you have fed me.
መገቡህ፡	they have fed thee (*m.*)	መገባችሁት፡	you have fed him.
መገቡሽ፡	they have fed thee (*f.*)	መገባችኋት፡	you have fed her.
			PL.
መገብዎ፡	they have fed you (h.1).	መገባችሁን፡	you have fed us.
መገብዋችሁ፡	they have fed you (h.2).	መገባችኋቸው፡	you have fed them.
		FIRST PERSON.	
መገቡት፡	they have fed him.	መገብንህ፡	we have fed thee (*m.*)
መገብዋት፡	they have fed her.	መገብንሽ፡	we have fed thee (*f.*)
	PL.		
መገቡን፡	they have fed us.	መገብንዎ፡	we have fed you (h.1).
መገብዋችሁ፡	they have fed you.	መገብናችሁ፡	we have fed you (h.2).
መገብዋቸው፡	they have fed them.	መገብነው፡	we have fed him.
		መገብናት፡	we have fed her.
			PL.
		መገብናችሁ፡	we have fed you.
		መገብናቸው፡	we have fed them.

B. *Contingent.*

THIRD PERSON SINGULAR.

Masculine.

ይመግበኝ፡ let him feed me.
ይመግብህ፡ let him feed thee (*m.*)
ይመግብሽ፡ let him feed thee (*f.*)
ይመግብዎ፡ let him feed you. (h. 1.)
ይመግባችሁ፡ let him feed you. (h. 2.)
ይመግበው፡ let him feed him.
ይመግባት፡ let him feed her.

PL.

ይመግበን፡ let him feed us.
ይመግባችሁ፡ let him feed you.
ይመግባቸው፡ let him feed them.

Feminine.

ትመግበኝ፡ let her feed me, &c &c. quite like ይመግበኝ፡ &c.

SECOND PERSON MASCULINE.

ትመግበኝ፡ like the 3d pers. fem.

SECOND PERSON FEMININE.

ትመግቢኝ፡ mayest thou (*f.*) feed me.
ትመግቢው፡ mayest thou feed him.
ትመግብያት፡ mayest thou feed her.
ትመግቢን፡ mayest thou feed us.
ትመግብያቸው፡ mayest thou feed them.

FIRST PERSON.

እመግብህ፡ &c., assumes the Suffixes, like the 3d pers. masc.

PLURAL.

THIRD PERSON.

ይመግቡኝ፡ let them feed me.
ይመግቡህ፡ let them feed thee.
ይመግቡሽ፡ let them feed thee.
ይመግብዎ፡ let them feed you. (h. 1.)
ይመግብዋችሁ፡ let them feed you. (hon. 2.)
ይመግቡት፡ let them feed him.
ይመግቡት፡ let them feed her.

PL.

ይመግቡን፡ let them feed us.
ይመግብዋችሁ፡ let them feed you.
ይመግብዋቸው፡ let them feed them.

SECOND PERSON.

ትመግቡ፡ the same as with the 3d pers. plural.

FIRST PERSON.

እንመግብ፡ the same as with the 3d pers. sing.

C. The *Imperative* joins the Suffixes in the same manner *as the Contingent.*

D. *Simple Constructive.*

THIRD PERSON SINGULAR.

Masculine.		Feminine.	
መግቦኝ:	he feeding me.	መግባኝ:	she feeding me.
መግቦህ: / መግቦሽ:	he feeding thee.	መግባህ: / መግባሽ:	she feeding thee.
መግቦዎ: / መጉቡዋችሁ:	he feeding you.	መግባዎ: / መግባችሁ:	she feeding you.
መግቦት:	he feeding him.	መግባው:	she feeding him.
መጉቡዋት:	he feeding her.	መግባት:	she feeding her.
መግቦን:	he feeding us (PL.)	መግባን:	she feeding us. (PL.)
መጉቡዋችሁ:	he feeding you.	መግባችሁ:	she feeding you.
መጉቡዋቸው:	he feeding them.	መግባቸው:	she feeding them.

SECOND PERSON SINGULAR.

መግበህኝ: thou feeding me.	መግበሽኝ: thou feeding me.

Assume the Suffixes like the same Persons in the Preterite.

Second Pers. Sing. honor. 3d and 2d Plural, the same as Preterite 3d and 2d Plural.

FIRST PERSON SINGULAR.		FIRST PERSON PLURAL.	
መግቤህ: / መግቤሽ:	I feeding thee.	መግበንህ: / መግበንሽ:	we feeding them.
መግቤዎ: / መጉቢያችሁ:	I feeding you.	መግበነዎ: / ምግበናችሁ:	we feeding you. (*sing.*)
መግቤው:	I feeding him.	መግበነው:	we feeding him.
መጉቢያት:	I feeding her.	መግበናት:	we feeding her.
መጉቢያችሁ:	I feeding you. (*pl.*)	መግበናችሁ:	we feeding you. (*pl.*)
መጉቢያቸው:	I feeding them.	መግበናቸው:	we feeding them.

NOTE.—Constructive Forms with the paragogic ተ: differ in nothing concerning the affixion of the Pronoun.

E. The Relative Participle treats the Suffixes like the Preterite Indicative and the Contingent.

2. *Forms with the Auxiliary* አለ። *Infixion.*

INDICATIVE.

Present and Future.

THIRD PERSON SINGULAR MASCULINE.
(See Contingent.)

ይመግበኛል፡	he feeds me.
ይመግብሃል፡ } ይመግብሻል፡ }	he feeds thee.
ይመግበዋል፡ } ይመግባችኋል፡ }	he feeds you.
ይመግበዋል፡	he feeds him.
ይመግባታል፡	he feeds her.
ይመግበናል፡	he feeds us.
ይመግባችኋል፡	he feeds you.
ይመግባቸዋል፡	he feeds them.

THIRD PERSON PLURAL.

ይመግቡኛል፡	they feed me.
ይመግቡሃል፡ } ይመግቡሻል፡ }	they feed thee.
ይመግብዋችኋል፡ } ይመግቡታል፡ }	they feed you.
ይመግቡታል፡	they feed him.
ይመግብዋታል፡	they feed her.
ይመግቡናል፡	they feed us.
ይመግብዋችኋል፡	they feed you.
ይመግብዋቸዋል፡	they feed them.

3d p. Sing. Fem.
2d .. .. Masc.
1st.. .. & P.
{ in the same manner as the 3d pers. sing. masc. with necessary termination of አለ።

SECOND PERSON SINGULAR FEMININE.

ትመግቢኛለሽ፡	thou feedest me.
ትመግቢዋለሽ፡	thou feedest him.
ትመግብያታለሽ፡	thou feedest her.
ትመግቢናለሽ፡	thou feedest us.
ትመግብያቸዋለሽ፡	thou feedest them.

SECOND PERSON PLURAL.

ትመግቡኛላችሁ፡ &c., the same with regard to Infixes as 3d p. pl.

Constructive Aorist.

THIRD PERSON SINGULAR.

Masculine.		Feminine.	
መግቦኛል፡	he feeds (fed &c.) me.	መግባኛለች፡	she feeds me.
መግቦሃል፡ } መግቦሻል፡ }	he feeds (fed &c.) thee.	መግባሃለች፡ } መግባሻለች፡ }	she feeds thee.
መግቦታል፡ } መግብዋችኋል፡ }	he feeds (fed &c.) you (s. hon.)	መግባዋለች፡ } መግባችኋለች፡ }	she feeds you.
መግቦታል፡	he feeds (fed &c.) him.	መግባዋለች፡	she feeds him.
መግብዋታል፡	he feeds (fed &c.) her.	መግባታለች፡	she feeds her.
መግቦናል፡	he feeds (fed &c.) us.	መግባናለች፡	she feeds us.
መግብዋዋችል፡	he feeds (fed &c.) you.	መግባችኋለች፡	she feeds you.
መግብዋቸዋል፡	he feeds (fed &c.) them.	መግባቸዋለች፡	she feeds them.

SECOND PERSON SINGULAR.

Masculine.	Feminine.
መግበሀኛል፡ thou feedest me, &c.	መግበሽኛል፡ thou feedest me.
FIRST PERSON SINGULAR.	FIRST PERSON PLURAL.
መግቤሃለሁ፡ I feed thee, &c.	መግበንሃል፡ we feed thee.
SECOND PERSON PLURAL.	THIRD PERSON PLURAL.
መግባችሁኛል፡ you feed me.	መግበውኛል፡ they feed me.

Note.—The connexion of Negative as well as other Particles, Conjunctions, and Prepositions, will be noticed in the next Chapter.

CHAP. V.

ON THE ADVERBS.

1. The Amharic Adverbs are either *Separable* or *Inseparable*; and the Separable Adverbs are either *Simple* or *Compound*. The Simple Adverbs, again, are either Original or Derived. We have to consider, first, the *Simple Original* Adverbs.

2. The Simple Original Adverbs are to be subdivided into two classes; the first of which comprehends such Adverbs as express their ideas by themselves; the second, such as are usually connected with the Verbs አለ: "to say," አደረገ: or አሰኘ: "to do," "to make," "to induce."

(*a*) *First Class.*

መቼ: "when?"

ስንት: "how much?" "how many?"

ቀስ: "calmly," "cautiously," "quietly."

ብቻ: "but," "only," "singly." Is used also with Suffixes in the Accusative: ብቻየን: "I alone." ብቻህን: "thou alone," &c.

ቶሎ: "quickly," "speedily."

ትላንት: and ትላንትና: "yesterday."

አምና: "last year."

ዘንድሮ: "this year."

ገና: "yet." With neg. "not yet."

አሁን: "now."

እንኳ:: ስንኳ: Shoa, and Vulgar: እኮ: "indeed," "even."

እንኳን: "no!"

እንጂ: "but," "except," "not including."

እንጃ: "I do not know."

አወን: "yes!"

ከቶ: "thoroughly," "wholly," "fully." With negative "never," "nowhere," "not at all."

ወትር: "always."

ዛሬ: "to-day," "now," "at present."

(*b*) *Second Class.*

PARTICLE	INSTANCES.
መር: of leaping, jumping.	መር: ይላል: "he jumps."
ምር: of bitterness.	ምር: አለ: "it was bitter."
ልግም: of carelessness, idleness, and eye-service.	ልግም: ይላል: "he acts carelessly," "is an eye-servant."
ሲጢጥ: of cracking.	ሲጢጥ: ይላል: "it cracks."
ሰፌፍ: of soaring.	ሰፌፍ: ይላል: "it soars."
ሸተት: of gliding.	ሸተት: ይላል: "he slips."
ቀስ: of caution, silence.	ቀስ: ይላል: "he acts cautiously."

ብልጭ: of glimmering, glittering.	ብልጭ: ይላል: "it glimmers."
ብትን: of scattering.	ብትን: ይላል: "he scatters."
ቶሎ: of celerity.	ቶሎ: ይላል: "he does quickly."
ትፍ: of spitting from between the lips.	ትፍ: አለ: "he spat."
ቸል: of neglect.	ቸል: ይላዋል: "he neglects him."
እልል: of shouting.	እልል: በል: "shout!"
እምቢ: of refusing.	እምቢ: አለ: "he refused."
እሺ: of compliance.	እሺ: ይላል: "he yields, "is willing."
እፍ: of blowing, fanning.	እፍ: በል: "blow," "fan."
ክትት: of fulness, completion.	ክትት: ይላል: "it is full," "done."
ከፍ: of highness, elevation.	ከፍ: አደረገ: "he raised," "elevated," "made high."
ዝም: of silence.	ዝም: አሰኘው:: "he silenced him."
ዝቅ: of lowness.	ዝቅ: አለ: "he was low," "stooped."
ዘለግ: of tallness, &c.	ዘለግ: ይላል: "he is tall and stout."
ደስ: of joy.	ደስ: አሰኘው: "he rejoiced," "pleased him."
ደፀ: of slipperiness.	ደፀ: አለ: "it was slippery."
ግሥግሥ: of celerity.	ግሥግሥ: አለ: "he went quickly."
ጢ: of completion.	ጢ: አለ: "it was full," "entire."
ጭቅ: of spitting through the teeth.	ጭቅ: አለ: "he spat thro' the teeth."
ጸጥ: of silence, subsiding.	ጸጥ: አለ: "it became quiet."
ፊቅቅ: of moving forwards.	ፈቅቅ: አለ: "he proceeded," "went further."
ፊግምግ: of gliding.	ፊግምግ: አደረገ: "he made to glide."

Most of these particles seem to be originally intended for mere expressions of the natural sound of certain actions. Such is decidedly the case in ሲጢጥ: ትፍ: ጭቅ: እልል: እፍ: ዋይ: And their connexion with አለ: "to say," giving the idea that *e.g.* "to crack" is "to say *sit'it*"; to spit," is "to say *teff*" or "*tsh'ek*"; "to shout" is "to say *ellel*" (as is really the custom in the East*); "to blow" is "to say *eff*"; could lead us to rank the whole of this class rather with the Interjections, but that their connection with Verbs prohibits us, though several of these Particles are Interjections as well as Adverbs.

---

* See, in the Amharic Dictionary, እልል::

3. *Simple Derived* Adverbs are very numerous. They are derived from Nouns (Adjective and Substantive), and Verbs, and at least one Pronoun. Those derived from Nouns are not changed in form, but in the sense. Perhaps they may be considered as Accusatives, or having the Preposition በ፡ omitted. Such Nominal Adverbs are the following:

ORIGINAL SUBSTANTIVES.	ORIGINAL ADJECTIVES.
ሜዳ፡ { "outside," "abroad," "within."	መልካም፡ "well," "properly."
	ቅርብ፡ "near."
ነገ፡ "to-morrow."	ክፉ፡ "badly."
ማለዳ፡ "early in the morning."	ደህና፡ "well," "safely."
ቀድሞ፡ "before," "previously."	ታላቅ፡ "largely," "greatly."
	እጅግ፡ "much," "very."

Besides these, perhaps every other Adjective may be used adverbially.

Simple Adverbs derived from Verbs:

አይደለም፡ "no."	ይቅር፡ Particle of forgiveness; *e.g.*
ያህል፡ "nearly," "about."	ይቅር፡ ይላል፡ "he forgives."
ይልቅ፡ "more" (*magis*).	

The Simple Constructive Mood is altogether used for Adverbs; *e.g.*

ደግሞ፡ } "again."	በዝቶ፡ "more."
መልሶ፡ }	ቀድሞ፡ "before," "previously."
ማለዳ፡ "early in the morning."	አስቀድሞ፡ { "before," "in the beginning."
ቀርቦ፡ "near."	
ብሎ፡ "saying," "thinking."	ጐድሎ፡ "wanting," "but."
አብሮ፡ "together."	አድርጎ፡ "doing."

Adverbs of uncertain origin are:

በጄ፡ (Shoa, ባቡ፡ and ባሰኝ፡) "readily," "with pleasure!"

4. Compound Adverbs are formed, (*a*) by Prepositions and Nouns; (*b*) by Prepositions and Pronouns; (*c*) by Nouns and Nouns; (*d*) by Prepositions, Nouns, and Particles.

(*a*) *Adverbs formed by Prepositions and Nouns.*

በወሥጥ፡ "internally," "within," "inside."
በሜዳ፡ "externally," "without," "outside."
በደህና፡
በደህንነት፡ } "well," "safely," "in health," "successfully"
በጥቂት፡ "by little," "in a low degree."
በጥቂት፡ በጥቂት፡ "by little and little," "gradually."
በጅግ፡ "in a high degree," "in a great measure."
በልክ፡
ባቅሞ፡ } "with measure," "moderately."
በፍርሃት፡ "with fear," "fearfully," "shyly," "cowardly."
በድፍረት፡ "boldly," "courageously."
በደስታ፡ "joyfully."
ከለልብ፡ "from the heart," "heartily."
በፈቃድ፡ "willingly."
ባእምሮ፡ "rationally," "reasonably."
በቸርነት፡ "kindly."

በምህረት፡ "graciously," "mercifully."
በፊት፡ "before," "previously."
በጥዋት፡ "in the morning."
በቀትር፡ "at noon."
በማታ፡ "in the evening."
በሌት፡
በሌሊት፡ } "at night."
ከድሮ፡ "from time immemorial."
በኋላ፡ "after," "afterwards."
በቀድሞ፡ "before."
በሩቅ፡ "afar off," "at a distance."
በታች፡ "below."
ከታች፡ "from below."
ከበኋላ፡ "from behind."
በላይ፡ "above."
ከላይ፡ "from above."
በጣም፡ "entirely."
ለዘላለም፡ "for ever."
ከበፊት፡ "from before," "from a former time."
ከበላይ፡ "from above."
ከበታች፡ "from below."

(*b*) *Adverbs formed by Prepositions and Pronouns.*

በዚህ፡ (Shoa, በዲህ፡ & በዜህ፡) } "here," "herein."
ከዚህ፡ (Shoa, ከዲህ፡ & በዜህ፡) "here," "from here," "hence."
ወደዚህ፡
ወዲህ፡ } (Shoa, ወዲዲህ፡ & ሀዜህ፡) } "hither."
እንደዚህ፡
እንዲህ፡ } "so," "thus."
እንጊዲህ፡ "henceforth," "hence."

በዚያ፡ (Shoa, በያ፡ & በዛ፡) } "there," "therein."
ከዚያ፡ (Shoa, ሀዛ፡) "there," "from there," "thence."
ወደዚያ፡
ወዲያ፡ } "thither," "after," "beyond."
እስከዚያ፡
እስተዚያ፡ } "so far."
ከዚያ፡ ወዲያ፡ "afterwards."

ከንጊዲህ፡ ወዲህ፡ { "from henceforth."	እንዴት፡ "how?"
	እንዴታ፡ "to be sure!"
እስከዚህ፡ } "so far," "as far as this," "up to this."	በስቲያ፡ "after."
እስተዚህ፡	
በየት፡ } "where?"	ለምን፡ } "why?" "wherefore?" "on what account?"
ወዴት፡	ለመንድር፡
ከየት፡ } "whence?" "where-from?"	ስለ፡ ምን፡
ከወዴት፡	ስለ፡ ምንድር፡

(*c*) *Adverbs formed by Nouns* (Pronouns, Numerals) and *Nouns.*

ዕለት፡ ዕለት፡ { "every day," "daily."	ሁልጊዜ፡ { "always," "continually," "constantly."
አፍ፡ ላፍ፡ { "mouth to mouth," *i.e.* "by word of mouth," "*vivâ voce.*"	እንደጊዜ፡ "once." (See Numerals.)
	የዚያን፡ ጊዜ፡ { "then," "at that time."
ፊት፡ ለፊት፡ { "opposite," "over against each other."	ምናልባት፡ "perhaps."

(*d*) *Adverbs formed by Prepositions, Nouns,* and *Particles.*

በራስጌ፡ "by the head-side."	በግርጌ፡ "by the foot-side."
በጅጌ፡ "by the hand-side."	በደጅጋ፡ "near the door," &c.

5. *Inseparable Adverbs* are but few.

አ—፡ }
አል—ም፡ } "not."
አ—ም፡ }

አለ—፡ non—, un—, in—, &c. እየ—፡ Distributive Particle.

—ን፡ Interrogative Particle.

The *Negative* Particles አ—፡ አል—ም፡ and አ—ም፡ are joined to the Finite Verb. አል—ም፡ is used throughout the Preterite, and with the 1st pers. sing. of the Present Tense. In the other personal forms, the ል፡ is ejected, and አ—ም፡ remains. The mere አ—፡ is used in the Subjunctive, and in all cases where the Negative Verb receives any additional Prefixes; *e.g.*

PRETERITE.

አልመጣም: "he came not."
አልመጣችም: "she came not."
አልመጣህም: "thou (*m.*) } camest
አልመጣሽም: "thou (*f.*) } not."
አልመጣሁም: "I came not."
አልመጡም: "they }
አልመጣችሁም: "you } came not."
አልመጣንም: "we }

SUBJUNCTIVE.

አይምጣ: "let him not come."
አትምጣ: "let her not come."
አትምጣ: *m.* } "do not thou come."
አትምጪ: *f* }
አይምጡ: } "do not you (hon.) come."
አትምጡ: }
ላልመጣ: "I must not come."
አይምጡ: "let them not come."
አትምጡ: "do ye not come."
ላንመጣ: "let us not come.

PRESENT INDICATIVE.

አይመጣም: "he } does not
አትመጣም: "she } come."
አትመጣም: } "thou dost not
አትመጪም: } come."
አልመጣም: "I* }
አይመጡም: "they } do not
አትመጡም: "you } come."
አንመጣም: "we }

With additional Prefixes, which absorb the አ::

ባይሔድ: "if he do not go."
የማትመለስ: { "(thou) who doest not return."
እንዳታደርግ: { "that thou mayest not do."
ሳይበላ: { "without (his) eating," or "before he eats."
ሳልማር: "before I learn."

አለ—: is prefixed to Infinitives; *e.g.* አለማወቅ: "ignorance," *i.e.* the not knowing, non-intelligence. አለማመን: "unbelief." አለመታዘዝ: "disobedience," "insubordination," &c.

—ን: (in Shoa —ወይ:) is a Particle of Interrogation, and affixed to any part of speech; *e.g.* ደህና: ነህን: "Art thou well?" እርሱን: ይህነን: አደረገ: "Has he done this?"

CHAP. VI.

ON THE PREPOSITIONS, OR PARTICLES OF RELATION.

1. The term "Prepositions" for that part of speech which falls under the consideration of this Chapter, is not entirely suitable. It is a class which determines the relation between Nouns, Pronouns, or Verbs; and which, because in our European languages they are generally placed *before* the

* Mark the difference in pronunciation of the 1st pers. Present from the 3d pers. Preterite. The latter is pronounced "Almat'am"; the former "Alĕmat'am." In the 3d pers. sing. of the Preterite, the ል: is mute; but in the 1st pers. sing. of the Present, it is sounded, because in the latter the Preformative እ: which the ል: absorbs, must be heard.

object of relation, have been called Prepositions, but would be better called *Particles of Relation;* as this term would suit also in cases where the Particle is placed behind its object.

2. The Amharic Particles of Relation are partly *Simple*, partly *Compound*. The Simple ones are always *Pre*-positions; the Compound ones consist of Pre- and Postpositions. The Simple Prepositions are either Separable or Inseparable. The *Simple Separable Prepositions* are the following:

ስለ፡ "for," "for the sake of," "in behalf," "instead of," "in favour of," "because," "on account of," "concerning," "on."
ወደ፡ "to," "towards."
ያለ፡ "without."
እንደ፡ "as," "like as," "according to," "in proportion to."
እስከ፡ "to," "up to," "reaching to," "till," "until."

Inseparable Prepositions are, ለ—፡ በ—፡ ከ—፡ ተ—፡ ነ—፡ or ሀ—፡ እየ—፡፡

ለ—፡ "to," "unto," "in favour of," "to the benefit of," "belonging to."
በ—፡ "in," "on," "upon," "at," "by," "through," "with," "against," "for (in exchange)," "over."
ከ—፡ "of," "out of," "from," "(more) than," "to."
ተ—፡ "with (company)."
ነ—፡ or ሀ—፡ vulgar, instead of ከ—፡ and of በ—፡፡
እየ—፡ "in proportion to," "according to," &c., and Distributive.

Illustrations of the preceding Simple Prepositions.

(*a*) ስለ፡ እግዚአብሔር፡ "*For* God's *sake.*"
ስለ፡ ኃጢአቴ፡ እሞታለሁ፡ "I die *on account* (because) of my sins."
ስላንተ፡ መጣ፡ "He came *on* thy *account.*"
ስለ፡ ወዳጁ፡ ይደክማል፡ "He labours *for* (in behalf of) his friend."
ስለ፡ ምንድር፡ "where*fore?*"
ይህች፡ ምዕራፍ፡ ስለ፡ ሃይማኖት፡ ትናገራለች፡ "This chapter treats *on* faith."

(*b*) እንደ፡ ሰው፡ "*as* a man," "*according* to (the manner of) men."
እንደ፡ ጴጥሮስ፡ "like as," or "resembling Peter."
እንደ፡ ፈቃዱ፡ ያደርጋል፡ "He does *according to* his will," ("as he likes").
እንደ፡ ኃይሉ፡ "*In proportion to* his strength."

(*c*) ወደ፡ ሐበሻ፡ ሔደ፡ "He went *to* Abyssinia."
ፊቱን፡ ወደርሱ፡ አደረገ፡ "He set his face *towards* him."

(*d*) እስከ: (sometimes እስተ:) is seldom used without a following ድረስ:, but sometimes it is used by itself; *e. g.*

እስከ: ጎንደር: ይሔዳል: "It goes *as far as* Gondar," ("up to Gondar").

(*e*) ለ—: is used as a Universal Dative; *e.g.*

ለኔ: ሰጠው: "He gave it *to* me."

ለኔ: ነው: "It belongs *to* me."

ለምን: (ለምንድር:) "what *for*?" ("wherefore?")

ላክልኝ: signifies both "send *to* me," and "send *for* me," (in my favour, or behalf, to somebody else).

(*f*) በቤት: "*in* the house."

በእግዚአብሔር: ያምናል: "He believes *in* God."

በወንጌል: ያስተምራል: "He teaches (*in*) the Gospel."

በጥዋት: "*in* the morning."

በቀትር: "*at* noon."

በምድር: "on earth," "on the ground."

በድንገት: "*on* a sudden."

በሎንደን: "*at* (in) London."

በደጅ: "*at* the door."

ጻድቅ: በሃይማኖት: ይድናል: "The just shall live *by* faith."

በባሕርና: በምድር: "*By* sea and *by* land."

በሚያስችለኝ: በክርስቶስ: "*Through* him that strengtheneth me; *through* Christ."

በወርቅና: በብር: ገዛው: "*With* gold and *with* silver did he purchase it."

ጸላቴ: መጣብኝ: "My enemy came *upon* (against) me."

ይፈርድበታል: "He judges *over* him" (or, in contrast with —ለ—: "pronounces judgment *against*, condemns him.")

ይቅር: በለን: በኛ: ያለውን: "Forgive us that which is *against* us;" *i.e.* "forgive us our debts," Matt. vi. 12.

በስድስት: ብር: ይሼጠዋል: "He sells it *for* six dollars."

ድል: ነሣበት: "He gained the victory *over* him."

(*g*) ከቤቱ: ወጣ: "He went *out of* his house."

ከርሱ: ወሰድሁት: "I took it *from* him."

ከኔ: ይበልጣል: "He is greater *than* I."

ከርሱ: ያንሳል: "He is inferior *to* him."

(*h, i*) ተ: and ኋ: or ሀ: are frequently used in vulgar, but not in good language. (See the Dictionary.)

(*k*) እየ—: is a Preposition, Distributive and of Proportion. It is related to እንደ: and has been mentioned already with the Numerals as a Distributive Particle. Other instances are these: እየዘመዱ: "according to its kind." እየሥርዓቱ: "in his respective order."

3. The Compound Particles of Relation are formed by any of the Simple Prepositions, connected with Nouns, or other Particles. The latter (Postpositions) are either directly joined to the former, or follow after the Noun or Pronoun to which they refer. We shall first give here a list of Postpositions; then show how they are combined with Simple Prepositions; and afterwards exhibit their use, by expressions of daily occurrence in conversation.

List of Postpositions.

ውሥጥ: "the inside."
ኋላ: "what is behind."
ላይ: "high," "upper," "elevated."
ፊት: "face," "fore-part," "surface."
ታች: "that which is below."
አጠገብ: "the side."
መኻከል: "the middle."
ዙርያ: "surrounding place."
አንጻር: "front."

ዘንድ:, ጋራ: } particles of company.
ድረስ: particle of extent.
መጠን: "proportion."
ልክ: "measure."
በቀር: particle of omission.
እኩል: "equal," "equality."
መክንያት: "reason," "cause."
ፈንታ: "portion," "stead," "part."

They are thus combined with Simple Prepositions:

በውሥጥ: and በ—: ውሥጥ: "within," "inside."
በኩል: "about," "in the vicinity," "direction."
በዙርያ: and በ—: ዘርያ: "surrounding," "round about."
በፊት: "before," "previous to," "in sight of," "in front of."
በኋላ: and ከ—: በኋላ: "behind," "after."
በታች: and ከ—: በታች: "below," "under."
በ—: ዘንድ: "by," "with."
ከ—: ዘንድ: "from," "from with."
እስከ: —: ድረስ: "till," "up to," "to," "as far as."
በ—: ልክ: "in proportion to."
በመክንያት: and በ—መክንያት: "for the sake of," "on account of," "because of."

በላይ፡ and ከ—፡ በላይ፡ "on," "upon," "abovc," "over," "against."
ባጠገብ፡ "beside," "by."
በመኻከል፡ and በ—፡ መኻከል፡ "among," "between."
ከ—፡ ጋራ፡ "with," "together with."
በመጠን፡ and በ—፡ መጠን፡ "in proportion to."
ከ—፡ በቀር፡ "without," "excepting."
በ—፡ ፈንታ፡ "instead of."
ባንጻር፡ and በ—፡ አንጻር፡ "in front of," "opposite."

Instances for illustration:

በውሥጡ፡ "*within* him."
ባገር፡ ውሥጥ፡ "*within* the country."
በሎንደን፡ በኩል፡ "*in the vicinity* of London."
ከቀትር፡ በኋላ፡ "*after* midday," *i.e.* "in the afternoon."
በታቻችን፡ "*under* us."
ከሳድቃ፡ በታች፡ "*under* the table."
በኔ፡ ዘንድ፡ "*with* or *by* me."
ከጌታው፡ ዘንድ፡ መጣ፡ "He came *from* (from with) his master."
እስከ፡ ዛሬ፡ ድረስ፡ "*to* this day."
እስከ፡ ነጋ፡ ድረስ፡ "*till* to-morrow."
በዚያ፡ ልክ፡ "*in* that measure," *i.e.* so large &c. as that.
በመክንያትህ፡ "*on* thy *account*," "*for* thy *sake*."
በልጁ፡ መክንያት፡ "*because of* his son."
በዙርያው፡ "*round about* him."
ባገር፡ ዙርያ፡ "*in* the environs of (round about) the town."
በፊታቸው፡ ሔደ፡ "he went *before* them."
በምድር፡ ላይ፡ "*on* the earth."
ከቤቱ፡ በላይ፡ "*above* his house."
በስፍራ፡ አጠገብ፡ "*by the side* of the place."
በንጉሥ፡ ላይ፡ ተነሣ፡ "He rose *against* the king."
በሰዎች፡ መኻከል፡ "*among* men."
በኔና፡ በርሱ፡ መኻከል፡ "*between* me and him."
ካባቱ፡ ጋራ፡ ሔደ፡ "He went *with* his father."
በውቀቱ፡ መጠን፡ "*in proportion to* his knowledge."
ሁላቸው፡ ከርሱ፡ በቀር፡ ይጽፋሉ፡ "They all write *excepting* him."
በኔ፡ ፈንታ፡ ይቀበለዋል፡ "He receives it, *instead of* mc."
በቤት፡ አንጻር፡ "*opposite* the house."

CHAP. VII.

ON THE CONJUNCTIONS.

1. The *Amharic Conjunctions* are either Separable or Inseparable.

2. The *Separable Conjunctions* are as follows:

(*a*) *Copulative,* and *Reiterative:* ደግሞ: "also," "again."

(*b*) *Adversative,* ግን: "however," "but."

ደሮ:
ነገር: ግን: } "but."
ደሮ: ግን:

ሳይቀር: { "notwithstanding," "nevertheless."

እንጂ: "but," unless."

(*c*) *Disjunctive:*

ወይ:
ወይም: } "or."
ወይስ:

ወይስ: —: ወይስ: —: "either—," "or—": with Negation, "neither."

(*d*) *Causal:* እንድ: "that." ዘንድ: "in order that," "in order to."

(*e*) *Conditional,* እንደሆን: (Shoa, እንደ:) "if."

(*f*) *Conclusive,* ስለዚህ: "therefore."

3. The *Inseparable Conjunctions* are these:

(*a*) *Copulative,* —ም: —ና: "and," "also."
ካ—: ተ—: "and," "by," (in counting).

(*b*) *Copulative* and *Adversative:*— ስ: — ሳ:: "as for," "but," "indeed," "but."

(*c*) *Conditional:*

በ—:
ከ—: } "if." With the Negative አ: (ባ:) "if not," "unless."
ቢ—:

(*d*) *Conjunction of time,* ስ —: "when," "while."
Negat. ሳ —: "ere," "before," "without."

(*e*) *Final* and *Conditional:* እንድ —: "that," "if," "to."
ል—: "that," "in order that."

(*f*) *Intensive,* እስክ—: "so that," "so as to."
እስክ—: ድረስ: "until," "till."

(*g*) *Comparative,* ከ—: "than that."

(*h*) *Causal,* —ና: "for," "because."

NOTE.—The junction of these Particles to Verbs is effected according to the rules laid down in Part I. Ch. VII.

ILLUSTRATIONS:

ንጉሥና፡ ንግሥት፡ መጡ፡ ሔዱም፡ "The king *and* the queen came *and* went."

ደግሞ፡ ሎሌታቸው፡ ተቀመጡ፡ "*But* their servants remained"; or, ሎሌታቸው፡ ግን፡ ተቀመጡ።

መቶ፡ ካምሳ፡ "One hundred and fifty."

እርሱ፡ ደግሞ፡ እንደህ፡ አለኝ፡ "He *also* told me so."

ይህ፡ ሁሉ፡ ሳይቀር፡ "*Notwithstanding* all this."

ይህነን፡ አልሻም፡ ያነን፡ እንጂ፡ "I do not want this, *but* that."

ምንን፡ ትፈልጋለህ፡ መጽሐፉን፡ ወይስ፡ ብሩን፡ "What doest thou want, the book *or* the money?"

ወይስ፡ ይህነን፡ ወይስ፡ ይህነን፡ ልታድርግ፡ "Either this *or* that must thou do (art thou *to* do)."

እርሱስ፡ እንደ፡ ሔደ፡ አየሁ፡ ነገር፡ ግን፡ አንተ፡ እንድታከት፡ አል ሔደም። "*Indeed, that* he has gone, I have seen; *but* in order *that* thou shouldst be lazy, he did not go," ("was not his object in going").

እማር፡ ዘንድ፡ (or ልማር፡) እወዳለሁ፡ "I like *to* learn."

መጽሐፍ፡ ባገኝ፡ በወደድሁ፡ "I should like *to* get a book."

ከጫወት፡ ብትማረ፡ ይሻልሃል፡ "*If* thou learnest, that will be better for thee *than if* thou playest."

አንተ፡ ብትለምን፡ እርሱ፡ ቢሰጠህ፡ ነበር፡ "*If* thou wouldest ask, he would give thee."

ጌታው፡ ሲቀመጥ፡ ሎሌ፡ ይሔደል፡ "*While* the master remains, the servant goes."

እስከመጣ፡ ድረስ፡ ቆይልኝ፡ "Wait for me *till* I come."

መምጣትስ፡ እመጣለሁ፡ "*As for* coming, I shall come."

አንተሳ፡ "*But* thou?" (emphatic, "what wilt thou do?")

ታምዋልና፡ አይመጣም፡ "*Because he* is sick, he does not come."

CHAP. VIII.

ON THE INTERJECTIONS.

1. We notice first those Particles which, when combined with the Verbs አለ: አደረገ: and አሰኘ:, constitute Verbs (See Ch. V. 2.); but when used by themselves, are Interjections. They are the following:

Particles		Signification.	Particles		Signification.
ዝም:	of silence,	"tush!" "quiet!"	እሺ:	of compliance,	"yes," "readily."
ቀስ:	of caution,	"mind!" "softly!"	እምቢ:	of refusing,	"I will not!"
ቶሎ:	of haste,	"quickly!"	እልል:	of exultation,	"hurrah!" "huzzah!"
ክትት:	of completion	"done!" "finished!" "full!"			

2. The remaining Particles of Exclamation are as follows:

ሆይ:	of address,	"oh!"	አይ:	of commiseration,	"oh!"
ቀላ:	of expulsion,	"begone!"			
እሠይ:	of joy,	"eh!" "aha!"	ወዮ:	of lamentation,	"alas!" "woe!"
እነሆ:	of attention,	"look!" "behold!"	ዋይ:	of lamentation & abhorrence,	"woe!" "alas!" "fie!"
እረግ:	contradiction, complaint, abhorrence,	"oh!" "far be it!" "fie!"	ዕፁብ: ወይ: ጉድ:	of astonishment	"oh wonder!" "dear me!"
አቤት:	of courtesy, of address,	"Sir!" "O Lord!"			
እኮ: እንዴታ:	of assent,	"to be sure!" "no doubt!"			

ቤዛ: { of sudden sympathy, { "I hope you have not hurt yourself!" *lit.* "substitute," *i.e.* I should have preferred the accident to have happpened to me, instead of you!

Part III.—SYNTAX.

ON THE ARRANGEMENT OF WORDS,

AND THEIR

CONSTRUCTION INTO SENTENCES.

CHAP. I.

ON THE NATURE OF SENTENCES, ESPECIALLY IN THE AMHARIC LANGUAGE.

1. A *sentence* is an aggregate of words expressing a judgment of the mind. It is either simple, complex, or compound. The constituent parts of every sentence are, a subject, an attribute, a copula, and an object; the latter, however, being less necessary than the three former. *Simple* sentences are such as have nothing but these parts; *e.g.*

ምድር፡ ሰፊ፡ ናት፡ "The earth is spacious."

ንጉሥ፡ መጣ፡ "The king has come."

አንበሳ፡ ፈረስን፡ ገደለ፡ "The lion killed a horse."

Note.—The Copula, or Joining Verb, which connects the subject with the attribute, is frequently joined with the latter in one and the same verb; *e.g.* ንጉሥ፡ መጣ። Here መጣ፡ contains the attribute of ንጉሥ፡ ("king"), which is, "one that came," together with the Copulative Verb "is."

2. *Complex* sentences are such as are amplified by qualifying words in connection with either the subject or the attribute; *e.g.*

ልጄ፡ ዛሬ፡ መጣ፡ "My son came to-day."

Here is the subject, ልጅ፡ "son," qualified by the pronoun ê, "my," and the attribute "who came," (contained in the verb መጣ፡ "came," with the copula "is,") by the adverb ዛሬ፡ "to-day."

3. Compound sentences are such as have either the subject, or the attribute, or the object, or all of them, augmented by additional or explanatory parts; *e.g.*

ወታደርና፡ ነጋዴ፡ ገበሬም፡ የሚጠቅሙ፡ ሰዎች፡ ናቸው፡

"The soldier, the merchant, and the farmer, are useful men."

CHAP. II.

ON THE SUBJECT AND THE ATTRIBUTE, AND THEIR RELATION TO EACH OTHER.

SECTION I.—*On the Subject.*

1. The *subject* is the principal or the reigning part of every sentence: it therefore stands always in the *Nominative* Case: *e.g.*

ሰው፡ ይሞታል፡ "man dies."

2. The ideal subject is always a Noun Substantive: the grammatical subject may be a Substantive, Adjective, Numeral, Pronoun, an Infinitive, or Participle: for words which express no perfect ideas by themselves, *i.e.* which are not substances, cannot form subjects of thought, unless they be at least ideally converted into substantives.

3. In every sentence, the subject precedes; the attribute and the copula follow; *e.g.*

እርሱ፡ ደህና፡ ነው፡ "He is good."

This is always the case, whether the Subject be simple, defined, complex, or compound.

4. When the Subject is specified by a Substantive, an Adjective, a Numeral, Pronoun, or Participle, the specifying words precede; *e.g.*

የሰው፡ ልብ፡ ክፉ፡ ነው፡ "Man's heart is evil."

በጎ፡ ሰው፡ ይከብራል። "A good man is honoured."

ሰባት፡ ቀን፡ አለፈ፡ "Seven days passed."

ይህ፡ ቤት፡ ሰፊ፡ ነው፡ "This house is spacious."

የተሠራ፡ ቤት፡ ሰፊ፡ ነው፡ "The house which has been built, is spacious."

እግዚአብሔርን፡ መፍራት፡ ከላንት፡ ጋራ፡ ይሁን፡
"May the fear of the Lord be with you."—2 Chron. xix. 7.

5. A Compound Subject, which consists of several Nouns, Numerals, or Pronouns, has all these parts in the Nominative Case; *e.g.*

ሰማይና፡ ምድር፡ ያልፋሉ፡ "Heaven and earth shall pass away."

እልያ፡ መቶ፡ ከሰማንያ፡ ሰዎች፡ ሔዱ፡ "Those hundred and eighty men have gone."

6. Where the Subject is connected with subordinate explanatory parts, it follows after them; *e.g.* Luke xii. 47.

የጌታውን፡ ፈቃድ፡ አውቆ፡ ያልተዘጋጀ፡ እንደ፡ ፈቃዱም፡ ያላደረገ፡ ባርያ፡ እጅግ፡ ይገረፋል፡

Literally: "His Lord's will knowing who prepared not himself, according to his will and did not the servant, much shall be scourged;" *i.e.* "That servant who knew his Lord's will, and prepared not himself, neither did according to his will, shall be severely scourged."

These two rules, No. 4, and 6, are so peculiarly in the Amharic idiom, that they cannot fail to impress themselves at once upon the mind of the Student.

SECTION II.

On the Attribute, and its relations to the Subject.

1. The Attribute may be a Substantive, or an Adjective, or Pronoun, or Participle: it may be separate, or implied in the Verb.

EXAMPLES.

እግዚአብሔር፡ መንፈስ፡ ነው፡ "God is *a Spirit.*"
ይህ፡ ሰው፡ አዋቂ፡ ነው፡ "This man is *intelligent.*"
ነገሩ፡ ይህ፡ ነው፡ "The matter is *this.*"
ፈቃዱ፡ የተቈረጠ፡ ነው፡ "His resolution is *decided.*" Acts xix. 7.
ሰዎችም፡ አሥራ፡ ሁለት፡ ነበሩ፡ "And the men were *twelve.*"
እርሱ፡ ይፈራል፡ "He fears," *i.e.* "is *fearing.*"

2. Complex Attributes (see Ch. I. 2.) have their subordinate parts before them.

EXAMPLE.

ይህ፡ ሰው፡ በሥራው፡ ሁሉ፡ ተንኰለኛ፡ ነው፡

Lit. "This man, in his work all, is cunning."—"is cunning in all his doings."

3. The Attribute always follows the Subject. This is evident from the preceding instances.

4. It often agrees with the Subject in Gender, Number, and Case: often does not. As to the Gender, the concordance may be assumed, most of the Nominal forms being of Common Gender; and, in the Adjective Participles at least, the Gender is strictly attended to. Concerning Number, the Singular is more used in Adjectives than the Plural; which may be accounted for by the supposition, that they are regarded as an abstract mass, of which the individual subjects have their share; *e.g.*

እሌህ፡ ሰዎች፡ ደህና፡ ናቸው፡ "These men are good."

But when the Attribute is a Relative Participle, it must agree in Number, as well as in Gender, Case, and Person, (see Page 73.) with its subject; *e.g.*

ሎሌሎቹ፡ የታመኑ፡ ናቸው። "His servants are faithful."

The Number is especially uncertain, when the Subject is a Collective Noun; *e.g.*

ሰው፡ ሁሉ፡ ይሞታል፡ "All men (or every man) dies."

ሕዝቡ፡ ተሰበሰበች፡ (Sing.) or ተሰበሰቡ፡ (Pl.) "The people was (or were) gathered together."

With regard to Case, we remember but one instance where the Subject and the Attribute do not agree; ብቻ፡ with Suffixes; *e.g.*

እኔ፡ ብቻየን፡ ነኝ፡ "I am alone."

Here is the Subject እኔ፡ in the Nominative, and the Attribute ብቻየን፡ in the Accusative Case.

CHAP. III.

VARIOUS USES AND CONSTRUCTION OF THE NOUN.

A. *Construction of Substantives with Substantives.*

1. Two or more Substantives connected together, denoting the same thing, are in a state of apposition, and must agree in Gender and Number; *e.g.*

እግዚአብሔር፡ አምላክ፡ "The Lord God."

ወንድ፡ ባርያ፡ "a man-slave."

ንጉሥ፡ ዳዊት፡ "King David," & ዳዋት፡ ንጉሥ፡ "David, the king."

ሻንክሎች፡ ባሮች፡ "Negroes," "slaves"; *i.e.* "Negro-slaves."

2. Nouns of *Quantity* are joined to other Substantives in the Nominative Case; *e.g.*

ጥቂት፡ ብር፡ "a little silver."

አንድ፡ ነጥር፡ ቡን፡ "one pound (of) coffee."

አንድ፡ ጎምቦ፡ ውኃ፡ "one jar (of) water."

3. Substantives of Quality, of Origin, or of Possession, are joined to other Substantives. They stand in the Genitive Case; *e.g.*

የድንጊያ፡ ቤት፡ "a house (made) of stone."

የጤፍ፡ ጣቢታ፡ "Têff-bread-cakes."

ያገር፡ ሰው፡ "a man of the country"; or the Ethiopic expression, ባላገር።

የገባሪ፡ ማረሻ፡ "the farmer's plough."

More about this when we come to speak of the Genitive Case. (See p. 167.)

4. On the construction of Object-Substantives with Subject-Substantives we shall speak when coming to consider the Verb. (See Ch. VIII.)

B. *Construction of Adjectives with Substantives.*

Adjectives may be connected with Substantives, (*a*) either as epithets to the Subject; or (*b*) as Attributes of the sentence; or (*c*) as modified by another accompanying Substantive.

1. As *Epitheton* of a Substantive, the Adjective generally *precedes* the latter; *e.g.* በጎ፡ ሰው፡ "a good man."

2. In Number and Gender, the Epithetic Adjective does not always agree with its Substantive; but the following rules are observed:

(*a*) The Substantive may be in the Plural, and the Adjective in the Singular Number; never the reverse; *e.g.*

ደህና፡ መጻሕፍት፡ "good books"; never ደህኖች፡ መጽሐፍ።

(*b*) In the same manner, the Adjective is most frequently used in the Masculine form, when the Substantive is of Feminine Gender; but a Feminine Adjective is never used for a Masculine Substantive; *e.g.*
ክፉ፡ ሴት፡ "a bad woman," but not ንጽሕት፡* ወንድ፡ "a pure man."

3. The preceding paragraph refers not to Participial Adjectives of the Relative form, as in them the strictest attention is paid both to Number and Gender. (See Page 163. §. 4.)

4. When the Adjective is *attribute* to the sentence, the rules laid down in the preceding Chapter, Sect. II. §§ 3, 4. obtain.

5. When another qualifying Substantive is connected with the Adjective, a Relative Participle is required as complement; *e.g.*

በልባቸው፡ ንጹሓን፡ ያሉ፡ ሰዎች፡ "Men who are pure in their hearts."

C. *Number of Nouns.*

There is a strong tendency in the Abyssinians to use the Singular Number, where we would use the Plural. We shall point out several cases where the latter never, and others where it but seldom is used, although it would be impossible, in the present stage of our knowledge of the

---

* We do not quote ክፊእት፡, the Feminine form of ክፉ፡, because it is not used in the Amharic, nor the Participle የከፉች፡; because, when Adjective-Participles are used, the Gender and Number is always strictly attended to. (See the preceding Chap. Sect. II. § 4.)

Amharic language, to give rules for every case, and would exceed the bounds which must be assigned to this head. The following classes are, some of them, never, others, seldom used in the Plural:

1. Nouns denoting a mass; as, gold, silver, corn, wheat, honey, fat, dust, &c.

2. Several parts of the animal body; *e.g.*

ልብ: "the heart."	ሥጋ: "flesh."
ሆድ: "the belly."	ጸጕር: "hair."
ደም: "blood."	

3. The soul, and several powers and faculties of the mind:

ነፍስ: "the soul."	ውድ: "love."
ፈቃድ: "the will."	ፍቅር: "charity."
አሳብ: "thought."	ደስታ: "joy."
ልቡና: "reason."	አለኝታ: hope."

4. Most Abstract Nouns, denoting quality, condition, action, quantity. We especially refer to the two Tables of Nominal Forms. Table I: Triliteral Radices of Verbs, No. 5. and Quadriliteral ones of No. 4.. Table II: Simple Forms of 3. A. *a.* 4. 6.; and Augmented Forms, 1. *a. c.*; some of *d.*; and almost all of *e.*

5. The following Collective Nouns are not often used in the Plural:

(*a*) Generical names of animals and of plants; *e.g.*

ጅብ: "hyæna." አበባ: "flower."

(*b*) Names of assemblages of men, or other beings; *e.g.* ወገን: "tribe," "sect," "kind," &c. The Plural of this word, ወገኖች: signifies the individuals belonging to the whole assemblage. ሸንጎ: "court of justice," አገር: "town," "country," and other words.

6. Certain periods of time: ቀን: "day." ሌት: and ሌሊት: "night." ሰዓት: "hour." ቀትር: "noon." ረፋድ: "forenoon." These are never used in the Plural number. Seldom: ጊዜ: "time." ዘመን: "time," "period." አመት: "year." ሳምንት: "week."

7. Several Nouns denoting confines, borders, shores, &c.; *e.g.* ዳር: "banks," "shores," "coast." ዳርቻ: "borders." ወሰን: "confines," "borders." ዘርፍ: "seam," "hem."

8. As to the agreement in Number between Nouns in the same sentence, either Subjects or Attributes, see the preceding Chapter, Sect. II. 4.; and in this Chapter, A. 1. and B. 2.

D. *On the Various Cases of Declension.*

1. The *Nominative* is, in common conversation, often improperly used

where the Preposition ወደ: should stand; *e.g.* አንጎለላ: ሔደ: "He went Angollala," omitting ወደ: "to."

2. It is applied in answer to the question, How long? How often? How much? *e.g.*

ሦስት: ቀን: ተቀመጠ: "He remained three days."
ብዙ: ጊዜ: መጣ: "He came many times."
አንድ: ማድጋ: ገብስ: "One mādĕga (a certain measure) barley."

3. The Genitive Case expresses:

(*a*) *Possession:*

ያባቴ: ቤት: "My father's house." የንጉሥ: ኃይል: "The king's power."

(*b*) *Origin:*

የምድር: ፍሬ: "The fruit of the earth."
የሐበሽ: ሰው: "A man of (from) Abyssinia," *i.e.* "An Abyssinian."

(*c*) *Quality:*

የብረት: ዕቃ: "Iron furniture." የድንጊያ: ቤት: "A house of stone."
Here it supplies the place of Adjectives.

(*d*) *Measure* of time, space:

የሰባት: አመት: ስራ: "The work of seven years."
የሁለት: ቀን: መንገድ: "Two days' journey."

(*e*) *Price and Quantity:*

ያንድ: ብር: ቡን: "One dollar's (worth) of coffee."

4. When Prepositions precede the word which stands in the Genitive Case, the የ: is dropped. See Part I. Ch. VII. 3. B.

5. When an Accusative follows the Genitive, the latter adopts the mark ን: of the former, so that the word seems to stand both in the Genitive and in the Accusative; *e.g.*

ያገርን: ከተማ: አየሁ: "I have seen the capital of the country."
የእግዚአብሔርን: የምላክህን: ስም: ከንቱ: አታድርገው:
"Thou shalt not use the name of the Lord thy God in vain." Ex. xx. 7.

6. When the Genitive belongs to several Substantives in apposition, its የ: is to be applied to each; when to a Substantive preceded by an Epithetical Adjective, it is applied only to the Adjective; *e.g.*

የዳዊት: የንጉሥና: የነቢይ: መዝሙራት: "The Psalms of David, (of) the King, and (of the) Prophet."

የደህና: ሰው: ነገር: "The words of a good man."

7. When the Genitive belongs to a Substantive having several Epithetic

Adjectives, the የ፡ is applied to each Adjective, and may, or may not, be applied to the Substantive also; *e.g.*

የታላቅና፡ የጠቢብ፡ የባለጠጋም፡ የሰሎሞን፡ ቤተ፡ መቅደስ፡
or የታላቅና፡ የጠቢብ፡ የባለጠጋም፡ ሰሎሞን፡ ቤተ፡ መቅደስ።
"The temple of the great, wise, and wealthy Solomon."

8. The Ethiopic Genitive, or Status Constructus, has been mentioned, Part II. Ch. I. Sect. I. 4. and Sect. V. 2.

9. The *Dative* being formed by the prefixion of the Preposition ለ፡ (*to, for, in favour, in behalf,* &c.) to the Noun, we need only to refer to what has been said, Part II. Ch. VI. 2. *e.*

10. The *Accusative* Case is formed by the annexion of ን፡ at the end: it serves to indicate the immediate or direct action of the Subject upon its object; and is required by all Active, Intensive, Transitive, and Causative Verbs; *e.g.*

ሰውን፡ ለደደ፡ "He sent a man."

Although this rule is very plain, it may not be superfluous to specify it a little. The Accusative is governed—

(*a*) By the Verb Finite; *e.g.*

መልእክትን፡ ይጽፋል፡ "He writes a letter."
ትግባርህን፡ አድርግ፡ "Do thy business."
በትሩን፡ ይዞ፡ ሔደ፡ "He took his stick, and went."

(*b*) By the Infinitive; *e.g.*

በጎውን፡ ስራ፡ መስራት፡ አያውቅም፡ "He knows not to perform (cannot perform) good works."

(*c*) By Relative Participles; *e.g.*

ይህነን፡ ያደረገ፡ "He who has done this."
ልጁን፡ የሚወድ፡ "He that loves his child."

(*d*) By Nominal Active Participles; *e.g.*

ቤትን፡ ሠሪ፡ "One that builds a house."

11. Besides Active Verbs, there are a few phrases in which the Accusative is used; *e.g.*

መንገዴን፡ እሔዳለሁ፡ "I go my way."
ቤቱን፡ ገባ፡ "He entered his house."

·ብቻ፡ "alone," "single," with Suffixes, assumes the Accusative form, when it is converted into an Adverb; *e.g.*

ብቻውን፡ ነበረ፡ "He was by himself."

12. When the Noun which stands in the Accusative terminates in a

letter of the third, fourth, fifth, or seventh order, a euphonic ው፡ is joined before the accusative ን፡፡ *e.g.*

ጠባቂውን፡ መንጋውንም፡ በሬውንም፡ ቀበሮውንም፡ አየሁ፡
"I saw the herdsman, the herd, the oxen, and the fox."

12. Relative Participles in ǔ, standing in the Accusative, have a euphonic ት፡ before the accusative ን፡; *e.g.*

ያየሁትን፡ የገደሉትንም፡ በሬ፡ "The ox which I saw, and which they killed."

13. Accusative Nouns ending in the sixth order are euphonically changed into the second; Accusative Participles, into the first order; the latter receiving a euphonic ው፡; *e.g.*

መልካሙን፡ ጸጅ፡ "good wine."

ያደረግሀውን፡ ኃጢአት፡ "The sin which thou hast committed."

14. When a Descriptive Adjective is connected with the Noun standing in the Accusative, the ን፡ is not generally affixed to both, but sometimes to the Substantive, sometimes to its epitheton; when the latter is a Participle, to the Participle: *e.g.* it is equally good to say ደህና፡ ሰውን፡ or ደህናውን፡ ሰው፡ "a good man," but with a Participle; *e.g.*

የበላሽውን፡ እንጀራ፡ "The bread which thou (*f.*) hast eaten."

15. When several Adjectives are connected with a Substantive in the Accusative Case, the ን፡ is put to each of the Adjectives, but not to the Substantive; *e.g.*

ታላቁን፡ ወፍራሙንም፡ በጎ፡ ፍሬንም፡ የምታፈራውን፡ ዛፍ፡ ቈረጡ፡ "They cut down a large, thick, and good-fruit-bearing tree," *i.e.* "a large and thick tree which bore good fruit."

16. Concerning the construction of the Genitive with the Accusative, see §. 5.

CHAP. IV.

ON THE DEGREES OF COMPARISON.

1. The Amharic Language has almost the same mode of comparing things with each other as the Hebrew; namely, especially by prefixing the Preposition ከ: "of," "from," to the Positive Noun or Pronoun; *e.g.*

ከመታከት: መማር: ይሻላል: "Learning is better than to be idle."

2. In many cases, they add the Postpositive Particle ይልቅ: which gives, however, no additional force to the idea of gradation already expressed by ከ:; but it stands generally at the end of a sentence, and is used more for Verbs than for Adjectives; *e.g.*

ይህች: ዛፍ: ትረዝማለች: ከዚያች: ይልቅ:
"This tree is tall, more than that one."

Here it would be equally good to say,

ይህች: ዛፍ: ከዚያች: ትረዝማለች: "This tree is taller than that one."

3. The Verbs በለጠ: "is greater," አነሰ: "is smaller," "less," and ተሻለ: "is better," are in themselves of a comparative nature: nevertheless, when brought together with other Adjectives or Verbs for comparison, they require the ከ—: as well as Adjectives or other Verbs; *e.g.*

ጥበብ: ከኩብት: ይሻላል: "Wisdom is better than wealth."
ዝሆን: ከአይጥ: ይበልጣል: "An elephant is larger than a mouse."
አንጎላላ: ከአንኮበር: ታንሳለች: "Angollala is smaller than Ankobar."

4. Besides the preceding, every verb of quality, condition, or even of action, is capable of expressing a comparison when constructed with ከ: for the adjective is contained in that verb; *e.g.*

ተራራ: ከዛፍ: ይረዝማል: "A mountain is higher than a tree."
ኃጢአት: ከሞት: ትከፋለች: "Sin is worse than death."

Verbs of action, however, require ይልቅ: *e.g.*

ከጴጥሮስ: ይልቅ: ጳውሎስ: ደከመ: "Paul laboured more than Peter."

5. The Superlative is rendered by ከሁሉ: (with Suffixes) and ከሁሉ: ይልቅ: *e.g.*

ምድር: ታላቅ: ናት: ዓለም: ይበልጣል: እግዚአብሔር: ግን: ከሁሉ: ይበልጣል: "The earth is great; the universe is greater; but God is greatest (of all)."

ከሁላቸው: ይልቅ: እርሱ: ተማረ: "He learned more than they all."

CHAP. V.

ON THE NUMERALS.

1. The Numeral does not, properly speaking, form a particular part of speech, but is either, as the Cardinals, a Substantive, or, as are the Ordinals, an Adjective, or, as the Distributive, an Adverb. We need therefore to say but little about their Syntax.

2. The Cardinal Numbers are always, when connected with other Nouns, to be considered as in apposition with them; and they always precede; *e.g.*

ሁለት፡ ሰዎች፡ "two men.

3. All the Numbers, from One upwards, seem to be considered as Plurals; wherefore they are of common gender, except አንድ፡ "one," which has in the feminine, አንዲት።

4. Notwithstanding this, the noun to which the numeral is joined, is not always used in the plural number. Although they use, in common language, the singular and the plural indiscriminately, the rule seems to hold good, that the round numbers, ten, twenty, &c. up to a hundred, and the large numbers, as hundred, thousand, ten thousand (እልፍ፡ μύριοι), are more frequently constructed with the noun in the singular than in the plural, and the numbers between every ten generally in the plural; *e.g.*

ሁለት፡ ሰዎች፡ "two men." ሀያ፡ ሰው፡ "twenty man."

5. The Numbers ሀያ፡ ሠላሳ፡ አርባ፡ አምሳ፡ ስድሳ፡ ሰብዓ፡ ሰማንያ፡ ዘጠና፡ መቶ። are generally used for Ordinals as well as for Cardinals; or rather, as they do not like to adopt the ordinal form for those numbers, they place the cardinal behind the noun as a predicate; *e.g.*

መጽሐፍ፡ ሀያ፡ "book twenty," instead of ሀያኛ፡ መጽሐፍ፡ "the twentieth book."

6. The form of the Ordinal Numbers is regularly derived from the Cardinals; except, as in our European and in other languages, the first; although in compound numbers that also is used in the regular form; *e.g.*

አሥራ፡ አንደኛ፡ "the eleventh."

When used in a simple form, አንደኛ፡ signifies "unique," "sole," "only." In enumeration, they use መጀመርያ፡ "the beginning," or ፊተኛ፡ "the foremost," "first."

7. As for the Distributives, nothing needs to be added to what has been said Part II. Ch. II. §. 4.

CHAP. VI.

SYNTAX OF THE SEPARABLE PRONOUNS.

1. The Separable Personal Pronoun isused,

(*a*) When it is the subject of a sentence. እኔ: እሔዳለሁ: "I go," although it is not necessary to use it.

(*b*) When an emphasis lies on the pronoun; *e.g.*

እርሱ: አላደረገውም: እኔ: አደረግሁት: እንጂ:
"He has not done it, but I have."

2. The third person singular and plural is used for demonstration; as is the reverse in the Latin and Greek; *e.g.*

አሁን: ያልህኝ: እርሱ: ነው: ያልሁህ: "That which thou hast now been telling me, is the same with what I told thee."

3. The Separable Possessive Pronoun is used only when a stress is laid upon it; *e.g.* ይህ: ቤት: የኔ: ነው: "This house is mine."
Cf. John xvii. 9, 10: ያንተ: ናቸውና:: ለኔም: የሆነ: ሁሉ: እርሱ: ላንተ: ነው:: ያንተውም: እርሱ: ለኔ: ነው: "For they are Thine. And all that is mine, the same is Thine; and Thine, the same is mine."
Where no such stress lies on the Possessive, Suffixes are used.

4. The Singular Masculine of both the *Demonstrative* Pronouns forms Adverbs, by the junction of Prepositions with the Genitive Case of those Pronouns. See Part II. Ch. V. 4. (*b*).

5. The *Interrogative* ማን: "who?" "which?" "what?" is used for persons: it is made use of, also, for inanimate subjects in the phrase ማን: ነው: ስሙ: or ስሙ: ማን: ነው: (ማነው:) "*What* is his (its) name?" On the contrary, the Impersonal ምን: is employed as a Personal Interrogative, by way of utter contempt, in the expression, ምን: አባቱ: "What is his father?" Both these expressions are elliptical.

6. The Indefinite ሁሉ:, which may be considered, as it is in the other Semitic languages, as a Noun, ሁል: (כֹּל, كُلّ) with suffixes, assumes no other suffix in the singular than the suffixes masculine and feminine of the third, person; but it takes all the suffixes of the plural: ሁሉ: ሁልዋ: ሁላቸው: ሁላችሁ: ሁላችን::

7. When ሁሉ: is absolute, it stands at the beginning of a sentence: when connected with Nouns or Participles, it follows them; *e.g.*

ሁሉ: ሔደ: "All is gone."
ሁሉን: አደረገ: "He has done all."
ሰው: ሁሉ: "All men," "every man," "people in general," &c.

8. ሁሉ:, as subject of the sentence, and without any other suffixes, may have its verb either in the singular or in the plural: when connected with nouns or participles, or with other suffixes, the number and person of the verb are determined by those nouns, participles, or suffixes; *e.g.*

ሁሉ: ይጠፋል: "All will (sing.) perish"; or,
ሁሉ: ይጠፋሉ: "All will (plur.) perish."
ሁላችን: ባንድ: ነን: "We are all together."
ነገሥታት: ሁሉ: ተሰበሰቡ: ሁላቸውም: ተዋጉ: "All the kings were assembled together, and all of them engaged in war."

9. አንዳች: "some," "something," "any thing"; with negation, "nothing"; *e.g.*

አንዳችን: ሰጠው: "Give him something."
አንዳችን: አልተቀበልሁም: "I received nothing."

10. አያሌ: signifies an indefinite number or quantity; *e.g.*

አያሌ: ሰዎች: ያምኑታል: አያሌ: ግን: ይጠራጠሩበታል: "Some men believe; others doubt it."

When it is predicate, it signifies a large quantity:

ከብቱ: አያሌ: ነው: "His property is considerable."

11. In order to express Reciprocity, the Abyssinians make use of the form እርስ: በርስ—:, with the Plural Suffixes āችን: āችሁ: and āቸው: and a Reciprocitive or other Verb; *e.g.*

እርስ: በርሳችሁ: ተዋደዱ: "Love one another!"

12. An Indefinite Pronoun is እንትን: which signifies, "The what's his name." Gr. ὁ δεῖνα; French, *chose;* German, *Dingerich;* *e.g.*

እንትን: አይሔድም: "The what's his name does not go."

CHAP. VII.

ON THE AFFIXED PRONOUNS.

1. As to their position, that is determined, the Nominal Suffixes being joined to the final letter of the Noun (or Adverb); the verbal to the last radical of the Verb, or to the Verbal Afformative. Adjectives do not assume suffixes, except when considered as Substantives.

2. The Nominal Suffixes are to be considered as possessive; the verbal ones as objective; *e.g.*

ልጄ: "*My* child." መታኝ: "He struck *me*."

Adverbs with Suffixes are treated by them as Substantives, the nominal Suffixes being joined to them; *e.g.*

በላዬ: "over me."

3. Concerning the Verbal Suffixes, enough has been said in the preceding part of this work, Ch. IV. sect. V. We add here, that the suffix of the first pronoun in the singular is sometimes used pleonastically; *e.g.*

ሒድሁኝ: "I am gone."

CHAP. VIII.

CONSTRUCTION OF THE VERB.

Having discussed the nature and use of the Verb, and its various parts, rather extensively in the preceding part of this work, Ch. IV., we need not here go through it at full length; but shall offer, in the first place, such additional remarks on the Moods, Tenses, and Persons, as are deemed necessary; and, in the second place, to show the agreement of one verb with another, and of the verb with the other parts of speech.

SECTION I.

On the Tenses of the Amharic Verb.

1. The following Tenses are used for the *past* time: the Simple Preterite of the Indicative, the Compound Preterite of the Contingent, and the Compound Preterite of the Constructive.

(*a*) The Simple Preterite of the Indicative is used,

α. For the Perfect Tense; *e.g.*

እንግዳ: መጣ: "A stranger has arrived."

ሕዝቡ: ተሰበሰቡ: "The people have gathered themselves together."

β. For the Historical Tenses, the Imperfect and Pluperfect; *e.g.*

ከተራራው: በወረደ: ጊዜ: ተከተሉት: ብዙ: አሕዛብ:

"And when he descended from the mountain, many people followed him."

Matt. viii. 1.

ትእዛዙን: ከፈጸመ: በኋላ: ከዚያ: አለፈ:

"When he had finished his command, he passed over from thence."

Matt. xi. 1.

γ. For the Present or Immediate Future, in a very few instances. So when visitors courteously ask leave to go, they do it by saying: ሒድሁ: "I am gone," *i.e.* "If you allow me, I go now." Or when a person is frequently called, and does not come, he at last answers: መፃሁ፡ መፃሁ፡ "I come! I come!"

δ. With Conjunction Prefixes, it serves for the Potential and Optative Moods.—See Sect. II. §. 5. and Isa. i. 9.

(*b*) The Compound Preterite of the Contingent is used,

α. For the Imperfect and Pluperfect of the Indicative; *e.g.*

እኔ፡ ሳልመጣ፡ እርሳቸው፡ ይበሉ፡ ነበረ፡ "Before I came, they had been eating."

β. For the Imperfect and Pluperfect of the Potential Mood:

ብትለምነው፡ ቢሰጥህ፡ ነበር፡ "If thou wouldst ask him, he would give thee."

ይህን፡ ካላደረግህ፡ ብወድህ፡ ነበርሁ፡ "If thou hadst not done this, I should have loved thee."

(*c*) The Compound Preterite of the Constructive is used chiefly for the Pluperfect, and sometimes for the Imperfect of the Indicative; *e.g.*

ሰጥቼ፡ ነበርሁ፡ "I had given."

2. Tenses used for the *Present*, are, the Present of the Indicative; the Second, or Aoristic Constructive; and the Contingent with Conjunctions.

(*a*) The Present Indicative and the Aoristic Constructive are both used for the Present Indicative; *e.g.*

እርሱ፡ ተጫውትዋልና፡ እኔ፡ ዝም፡ እላለሁ፡
"Whereas he is talking, I keep silence."

(*b*) The Present Indicative is used for both the Present and the Future tenses: the Aoristic Constructive serves especially for an action, condition, state, or suffering, which *continues;* and therefore, although it is more frequently used for the Present, it is likewise made use of for the Perfect. This peculiarity of both these forms is owing to the Auxiliary Verb Substantive አለ፡ with which they are composed.

(*c*) The Simple Contingent Mood serves for the Present as well as for the Future Tenses, when connected with Particles; *e.g.* the Participles የሚመጣ፡ "he that comes;" ሲመጣ፡ "when he comes;" ሳይመጣ፡ "before he comes;" Negative assertions: አይመጣም፡ "he comes not," "will not come;" Conditional expressions: ቢጨርስ፡ "if he end," or "if he ends;" Final and referential: እንዲጽፍ፡ "that he writes," or "write;" Final: ሊወጣ፡ ተነሣ፡ "he rose to go out," where it is for an Infinitive; ወንድሙን፡ ይረዳ፡ ዘንድ፡ ሔደ፡ "He went to assist (that he might assist) his brother."

3. The *Future* time is generally expressed by the same forms which serve for the Present, except the Aoristic Constructive. Vide 2. a.—In p. 66 of this work we pointed out another mode of a decidedly future form; besides which they make use of the Contingent with አለ፡ or with ይሆናል፡ The one is found in the negative expression, Ezek. xvii. 9: ሥሯ፡ ይመዘዝ፡ የለምን፡ ፍሬውስ፡ ይቈረጥ፡ የለምን፡ "Shall not its root be extracted; and its fruit, shall it not be cut off." But these two latter forms are not confined to the Future: they are also used for the Present Tense.

Section II.

On the Moods of the Amharic Verb.

On this head, we shall add but little to what has been stated Chap. IV. of the preceding part, and in the preceding Section of this Chapter.

1. The *Contingent* serves for the Indicative, Subjunctive, Potential, and Participial Moods; as is shown in the preceding Section.

2. The *Subjunctive* expresses a desire, or an indirect request, order, command, or obligation.—See p. 72.

3. The Infinitive, as Verbal Noun, assumes Nominal Suffixes; but relates to and acts upon other nouns in a verbal capacity; *e.g.*

ለንጉሡ፡ መታዘዜ፡ "My obeying the King," "my being obedient to the King."

It is, however, likewise constructed as a Noun; *e.g.*

የክርስቶስ፡ መምጣት፡ "The coming of Christ."

ፍሬን፡ ለማፍራት፡ ተተከለች፡ "In order to bear fruit was it planted."

4. The Participles are of the same character, partaking of the nature of Adjectives (as the Infinitive does of the nature of Nouns), and of the Verb, as has been shown in the preceding Part, pp. 72, 73. The Simple forms, however, have more of a nominal; the Augmented forms more of a verbal character. The Augmented forms are verbally flexible through all the persons; besides their being capable of receiving Prepositions, and the Accusative ን፡ marking them as Nouns. ልቡ፡ የጸና፡ ሰው፡ አንድ፡ ጊዜ፡ ያለውን፡ ነገር፡ መለወጥ፡ አይወድም፡ "A man of a *determined* character does not like to change his word *which he* once *has spoken.* ፍሬውን፡ ለቃሚ፡ ደስ፡ ይለዋል፡ ዘርን፡ ከሚዘሩት፡ ይልቅ፡ "*The gatherer* of the fruit rejoices, more than *those that sowed* the seed."

5. There is in the Amharic Language no peculiar form for the Optative Mood: they express it by circumscription; *e.g.*

ቢሆንስ፡ ባስተማርሀኝ፡ በወደድሁ፡ "If it had been, if thou hadst instructed me, I should have liked it."

Section III.

Construction of the Verb with the other parts of the Sentence.

1. The Amharic Verb having all the personal forms connected with it, it is capable of including the subject in itself; *e.g.*

ጠበቀ: "he observed." መታህ: "thou hast beaten."

And by the aid of Suffixed Pronouns and Prepositions, it is further capable of expressing a whole sentence in itself; *e.g.*

መጣብህ: "He came upon thee." መታሀው: "Thou hast struck him."

2. But when, as is more usual, the subject is separate from the Verb, the latter should agree with it in gender, number, and person; *e.g.*

ይህች: ሴት: አትሔድም: "This woman does not go."
ሎሌቹ: ተከተሉት: "His servants followed him."

3. Collective Nouns, however, which admit of a Plural, have the Verb sometimes in the Singular, sometimes in the Plural: *e.g.*

ሕዝቡ: ተሰበሰበች: "The people gathered itself together"; or
ሕዝብ: ተሰበሰቡ: "The people gathered *themselves* together."

4. When there are more than one subject in a sentence, the Verb stands either in the Third Person of the Plural, or it is determined by what is considered as the chief subject; *e.g.*

ወንድና: ሴት: መጣ: "Male and female came."
ንጉሥና: ሠራዊቱ: ተመቱ: "The king and his army were beaten."

When the person who is addressed forms one of the subjects, the Verb follows in the Second Person Plural; *e.g.*

ኪዳን: ገብሩም: አንተም: ልትማሩ: ናችሁ:
"Kiddan, Gabru, and thou, (you) are to learn."

When the speaker is included, the Verb is to be in the First Person Plural:

እርሳቸውና: እኛ: ተለየን: "They and we are separated."

5. When the subject consists of several Infinitives, the number is not multiplied, and the Verb is used in the singular; *e.g.*

መማርና: መሥራት: ይጠቅማል: "Learning and working is useful."

But when the subject consists of several Participles, which are considered as Nouns, the Verb must be in the plural; *e.g.*

ሰራቂና: ገዳይ: መጡበት: "A thief and a murderer came upon him."

6. Active and Transitive Verbs have their objects in the Accusative

Case: see Ch. III. 10. Transitive and Causative Verbs may have a double Accusative; *e.g.*

 መልእክትን፡ አስጻፈው፡ "He caused him to write a letter."

But as these Verbs may sometimes be used as Intransitive, the use of Prepositions is frequently applied; *e.g.*

ፈረደበት፡ "He judged *over* (or against) him."

ጻፈበት፡ "He wrote *in* it."

ሰውን፡ አስመጣለት፡ "He caused a man to come *for* (or *to*) him."

7. Intransitive Verbs are generally connected with their objects by Prepositions; *e.g.*

በቤት፡ ነበረ፡ "He was in the house."

ወደገሩ፡ ሔደ፡ "He went to his country."

በወምበሩ፡ ተቀመጠ፡ "He sat upon his chair."

8. When the object of the sentence is another Verb, that is expressed by the Infinitive, or by the Contingent with Conjunctions; *e.g.*

መማር፡ ይወዳል፡ "He likes to learn"; or,

ይማር፡ ዘንድ፡ ይወዳል፡ "He likes that he may learn."

መድገም፡ ያውቃል፡ "He can read."

9. The reigning Verb should be always at the end of the sentence, whether the object be simple, or complex, or compound; *e.g.*

ሰው፡ ያልወደደውን፡ ነገር፡ አያደርግም፡

"What man does not like, he will not perform."

እግዚአብሔር፡ በትእዛዙ፡ የከለከለውን፡ ነገር፡ ሰው፡ ያደርጋል፡

"What God in His law has prohibited, man does commit."

በእግዚአብሔር፡ ቃል፡ እናምን፡ ዘንድ፡ በኀጢአታችንም፡ አዝነን፡ የሱስ፡ ክርስቶስ፡ የሰራውን፡ መድኀኒት፡ በሃይማኖት፡ እንቀበል፡ ዘንድ፡ ወንጌል፡ ያስተምረናል፡ "The Gospel teaches us to believe in the Word of God, to repent of our sins, and to receive in faith the Salvation which Christ has wrought out for us."

CHAP. IX.

CONSTRUCTION OF THE REMAINING PARTS OF SPEECH.

As the doctrine of the Particles, *i.e.* Adverbs, Prepositions, Conjunctions, and Interjections, has been pretty fully exhibited in the Etymological Part, Ch. V. to Ch. VIII., we do not think it necessary to add any more: and so we finish here the Amharic Grammar, adding only a few Specimens of Common Conversation, and a few Exercises.

Part IV.

SOME SPECIMENS OF CONVERSATION, AND A FEW EXERCISES.

1. CONVERSATIONAL MODES OF SALUTATION.

In conversation, the Abyssinians are very polite towards each other, without using quite such a bombastic style as is common among the Arabs and other Eastern nations. When speaking of the Pronouns and under the Verb, we have mentioned two honorific distinctions for the second person in the singular, and that they speak of a third person of respect in the plural. A neglect of these distinctions is overlooked in foreigners, whilst learning their language; but amongst themselves it is taken as an offence, except with intimate friends, and in a few other instances. In saluting, the various times of the day, the state of health, frequency of intercourse, season of the year, and some other circumstances, are to be regarded as determining the mode of address.

As for the time of the day when persons meet, four times are distinguished, for which four separate Verbs are used; viz. (*a*) The *morning*, until the sun has finished half his course from the horizon to the meridian, *i.e.* between nine and ten o'clock A.M. During this time, when meeting, the verb አደረ፡ "to spend the night," "to rest," is used in the Preterite: when parting, the verb ረፈደ፡ "to spend the forenoon," አስረፈደ፡ "to make spend the forenoon," or ዋለ፡ "to spend (አዋለ፡ "to make spend) the middle of the day," in the Imperative or Subjunctive Mood. (*b*) The *forenoon*, from about nine to eleven o'clock A.M. At meeting, they salute each other with the verb ረፈደ፡ "to spend the forenoon," in the Preterite: when parting, with the Verb ዋለ፡ or አዋለ፡ (*c*) *Noon* and *afternoon*, to sun-set. When meeting, they use ዋለ፡ in the Preterite: when parting before five P.M., አዋለ፡ when after five, the Subjunctive of አስመሸ፡ "to make pass the evening," or Imperative or Subjunctive of መሸ፡ "to pass the evening." (*d*) *Evening* and *night*, from sun-set to the first break of the day. When meeting, the Preterite of መሸ፡ when parting, either the Subjunctive or the Imperative of አደረ፡ "to pass the night," "to rest," or Subjunctive of አሳደረ፡ "to make pass the night," &c. is used.

ይማር፡ "May He (*i.e.* God) be gracious!" and ይፈውስ፡ "May He heal," "restore!" both with Suffixes, is used for addressing sick persons. The former wish also is used when a person sneezes. ገባ፡, in the Preterite, is used when meeting a person who has newly arrived at the place: in the

Subjunctive with Suffixes, when parting with a person who goes to another country. ሰነበተ፡ "to pass the time from one interview to another," is used in the Preterite, when persons meet who have not seen each other for some time. አሰነበተ፡ "to make pass &c., is used at parting, when they do not expect to meet again for a considerable time. Then they add, ያገናኘን፡ "May He bring us together again!" ከረመ፡ "to pass the rainy season," and አስከረመ፡ its transitive, is used in the same manner.

The following Specimens of Conversation will illustrate the preceding remarks. We choose the imaginary meeting of the servant Gabru, with his master Kiddana Maryam, after his return from an errand to a friend, Aito Malku, who lives in a distant part of the country. The meeting is supposed to take place in the morning.

K. M. በደህና፡ ገባህን፡ ገብሩ፡	Hast thou arrived in health (safely &c.), Gabru?
G. እግዚአብሔር፡ ይመስገን። ደህና፡ ሰነበቱን፡ ጌታው።	God be praised! Have you, master, been well all the time since I saw you last?
K. M. እግዚአብሔር፡ ይመስገን፡ ደህና፡ ሰነበትህን፡ አንተ፡	Thank God! Hast thou been all the time well?
G. እግዚአብሔር፡ ይመስገን፡ እርሰዎን፡ ደህና፡ ነው፡	Thanks to God! Are you well?
K. M. እግዚአብሔር፡ ይመስገን። ደህና፡ ነኝ። መንገድህን፡ ቀንቶ ፡ ነበረ፡	Thanks to God! I am well. Hast thou had a good journey?
G. መንገዴ፡ ቀና። ከዚህ፡ ተነሥቼ፡ በሶስት፡ ቀን፡ ደረስሁኝ፡ ከዚያም፡ አንድ፡ ቀን፡ ውሌ፡ ተመለስሁኝ፡ በሁለት፡ ቀንም፡ ተኩል፡ ገባሁኝ፡	I had a good journey. I arrived there in three days after I had started from hence, and staying there one day, I returned, and in two days and a half arrived here.
K. M. ምንድር፡ ይላሉ፡ አይቶ፡ መልኩ።	What does Aito Malku say?
G. ደህናሉን፡ ደህናሉን፡ ደህናሉን፡ ደህና፡ ሰናበቱን፡ እጅጉን፡ ደህና፡ ነዎን፡ ደህና፡ ከረሙን። ወደጅነቴ፡ ሰማይና፡ ምድር፡ ያህል፡ ናት፡ አሉ። እርሰዎም፡ የሰደዱትን፡ ነገር፡ ሰጠኋቸው፡	"Are you well? Are you well? Are you well? Have you been quite well since our last interview? Are you well? Have you passed the rainy season well? My friendship amounts to heaven and earth," he said. — What you sent to him

እጅግም፡ ደስ፡ አሉበት። እግዚአብሔር፡ ይስጠዎ፡ እግዚአብሔር፡ ይስጠዎ፡ እግዚአብሔር፡ ያመስግነዎ፡ አሉ፡	I delivered, and he was very glad of it, and said, "May God give it (reward) you! May God give it you! May God glorify you!" (*i.e.* I am very much obliged to you.)
K. M. ጉዳዬሳ።	But how is (what did he say to) my request?
G. እሺ፡ አደርገዋለሁ፡ አሉ።	He agreed to do it.
K. M. በጎ። አሁንም፡ ምሳህን፡ በልተህ፡ ወደ፡ ታመመች፡ ሴት፡ ወደ፡ ወለተ፡ ገብርኤል፡ ሒድና፡ እግዚአብሔር፡ ይማርሽ፡ እግዚአብሔር፡ ይፈውስሽ፡ ዛሬ፡ ጥቂት፡ አልቀለለሽምን፡ በልልኝ።	Very well. Now eat thy dinner, and go to Walleta Gabriel, a sick woman, and (give her my respects, and tell her that I sympathize with her in her illness) say for me, "May God have mercy on thee, and restore thee! Doest thou not feel a little better to-day?"
G. እሺ። ሔድሁኝ፡	Very well. I go then.
K. M. እሺ። በደህና፡ ያውልህ።	Very well. (Mayest thou spend the middle of the day well!) Good bye!
G. በደህና፡ ያውሉ፦ (ዋሉ፡)	(May you spend the middle of the day well!) Good bye!

TASFU, another servant, enters, announcing a visitor.

Tasfu. አይቶ፡ ወልደ፡ ድንግል፡ አሉ። ሊገቡን።	There is Aito Walda Dengel: Shall he come in?
K. M. እሺ። ይግቡ።	Yes, let him come.

On entering, KIDDANA MARYAM attempts to rise; but AITO WALDA DENGEL hastens to prevent it; saying, ይኑሩ፡ ይኑሩ፡ "Remain remain!" or as usual:

በእግዚአብሔር። በማርያም።	By God! by Mary! (*i.e.* Do not rise.)
W. D. እንዴት፡ አደሩ፡	How have you passed the night?
K. M. እግዚአብሔር፡ ይመስገን። ደህና፡ አደሩን፡	Thank God! Have you passed the night well?
W. D. እግዚአብሔር፡ ይመስገን። ደህና፡ ረፈዱን፡	Thank God! Have you passed the forenoon well?

K. M. እግዚአብሔር፡ ይመስገን፡ እጅጉን፡ ደህና፡ ረፈዱ፡	Thanks to God! Have you passed the forenoon very well?
W. D. እግዚአብሔር፡ ይመስገን። ምሽትዎና፡ ልጆችዎ፡ ሁሉ፡ ደህና፡ ናቸው፡	Thank God! Are your wife and all your children well?
K. M. እግዚአብሔር፡ ይመስገን። ምሽቱ፡ ዛሬ፡ ታማለች።	Thank God! My wife is poorly to-day.
W. D. ኣይ። ሕማማቸው፡ ምንድር፡ ነው፡	Ah! What is her complaint?
K. M. ሆድዋ፡ ያማታል።	She has pain in the bowels.
W. D. ተስፋ።	Tasfu!
T. አቤት።	Sir!
W. D. እግዚአብሔር፡ ይማረዎ፡ እግዚአብሔር፡ ይፈውሰዎ፡ በልልኝ፡ እመቤትህን።	Speak to thy mistress in my behalf; saying, "May God have mercy on you! May God restore you!"
T. አሁን፡ ጥቂት፡ ይቀለኛል፡ ይላሉ።	She says that she feels now a little better.
W. D. እንጊዴህ፡ ያውቁኝ፡ ባልደረባዮንም፡ ይስጡኝ።	Henceforth, know me (as your friend), and give me a Baldaraba* (a man that introduces me to you).
K. M. እሺ። አንተ፡ ተስፋ፡ አይቶ፡ ወልደ፡ ድንግል፡ ቢመጡ፡ ወትሮ፡ አድርሳቸው፡	Very well. Thou, Tasfu, whenever Aito Walda Dengel comes, do thou introduce him.
W. D. ሔድሁኝ።	I go then.
K. M. እሺ። በደህና፡ ያውሎ።	Very well. May He make you spend the middle of the day well *i.e.* Good bye!
W. D. በደህና፡ ያውሎ፡	May He make you spend the &c.
K. M. አሜን፡	Amen!

* See ባልደረባ፡ in the Dictionary.

2. A FEW EXERCISES.

SALVATION.

(See Amharic Spelling Book, p. 20.)

አሁንስ፡ እንዲህ፡ ሲሆን፡ ሰውም፡ ሁሉ፡ እግዚአብሔርን፡ በኃጢአቱ፡ በድሎታልና፡ ከእግዚአብሔር፡ ፍርድ፡ ከዘላለምም፡ ኵነኔ፡ በታች፡ ሲኖር፡ እግዚአብሔር፡ ሌላውን፡ የጸጋውን፡ መንገድ፡ ከፈተልን፡ በታላቅ፡ ምህረቱ፡ የተወደደውን፡ ልጁን፡ በኛ፡ ፈንታ፡ ቤዛ፡ አድርጎ፡ በሰጠው፡ ጊዜ።

Now, as it is thus, all men having by their sins offended God, and fallen under the divine judgment and eternal damnation, God has opened for us another way, a way of Grace, when He in His mercy gave His Beloved Son as a ransom in our stead.

BEST USE OF GEOGRAPHY.

(See Preface to the Amharic Geography.)

ይህችን፡ በጣም፡ ብትማር፡ በቤት፡ ተቀምጠህ፡ ወደ፡ ሩቅ፡ አገር፡ እንደሚሔድ፡ ሰው፡ ትሆናለህ። በቀደምም፡ ስማቸውን፡ እንኳ፡ ያልሰማሀውን፡ አሕዛብ፡ መኖርያቸውን፡ ጠባያቸውንም፡ ስራቸውንም፡ ንብረታቸውንም፡ ከዚህ፡ ታገኛለህ። ሁላቸውም፡ ወንድሞችህ፡ ናቸው፡ ሁላቸውም፡ ታላቆችና፡ ታናሾች፡ ብልሃተኞችና፡ አረዊትም፡ በጎችና፡ ክፎችም፡ ዘመዶችህ፡ ያባትህ፡ ያደም፡ ልጆች። እወቃቸው፡ ተማርባቸውም፡ ስራቸውንም፡ መርመር። የምታገኝባቸውንም፡ በጎ፡ ነገር፡ ጠብቅ፡ ከክፉም፡ ሽሽ። ሁላቸውንም፡ ውደድ፡ ነፍስህን፡ ትወድ፡ ዘንድ፡ እግዚአብሔር፡ እንደሚሻ። ከሁሉም፡ ይልቅ፡ እንዲህ፡ ብለህ፡ ነፍስህን፡

If thou learn this (Geography) perfectly, thou wilt, even whilst remaining at home, become like a man that goes into a distant country: and of nations, whose very name thou didst not hear before, thou wilt find here their residences, their nature, employments, their state and conditions. And all these are thy brethren; all of them, great and little, civilized and barbarians, good and evil, are thy relations, the sons of Adam, thy father. Know them, learn of them; and examine into their works. Whatever thou findest good in them, keep, and flee from evil. Love them all, as God wills that thou shalt love thyself. But above all things, ask thyself, saying,

ጥየቅ። እግዚአብሔር፡ ስለ፡
ምንድር፡ ፈጠረኝ። የእግዚአ
ብሔርም፡ ፈቃድ፡ በኔ፡ ምንድር፡
ነው። እኔም፡ እንዴት፡ እፈጽማ
ለሁ፡ የእግዚአብሔርን፡ ፈቃድ።
ምንድር፡ ነው፡ የእግዚአብሔር፡
ፈቃድ፡ በሕዝቤ፡ በወገኖቼም።
እኛም፡ የሐበሻ፡ ሰዎች፡ እግዚ
አብሔር፡ የሚሻብን፡ እናደርገዋ
ለንን። ባላደረግነውም፡ ምን፡
ይገባናል፡ እንጊዴህ፡ እናደርግ፡
ዘንድ። እንዲሁም፡ ብትጠይቅ፡
መጽሐፍ፡ ቅዱስ፡ በጣም፡ ይመ
ልስልሃል። እርሱንም፡ ስማ፡
ተከተለውም።

"Wherefore has God created me? "What is the will of God with me? "and how do I accomplish the will "of God? What is the will of God "concerning my people and nation? "And we, the people of Abyssinia, "do we perform what God requires "us to do? And if we have not "done it, what is our duty henceforth "to do?" If thou askest in this manner, the Holy Scriptures will satisfactorily answer thee. Hear them, and follow them!

THE END.